LAW REFORM 2015

LAW REFORM 2015

A MANIFESTO FOR CHANGE

EDITED BY **STEPHEN HOCKMAN**
WITH A FOREWORD BY **ED MILIBAND**

P

PROFILE BOOKS

First published in Great Britain in 2014 by
PROFILE BOOKS LTD
3A Exmouth House
Pine Street
London EC1R 0JH
www.profilebooks.com

1 3 5 7 9 10 8 6 4 2

A CIP catalogue record for this book is available from the British Library.

Typeset in Times by MacGuru Ltd
info@macguru.org.uk
Printed and bound in Britain by
Clays, Bungay, Suffolk

ISBN 978 1 78125 401 1
eISBN 978 1 78283 147 1

The paper this book is printed on is certified by the © 1996 Forest Stewardship
Council A.C. (FSC). It is ancient-forest friendly. The printer holds FSC chain of
custody SGS-COC-2061

Contents

The contributors

Naomi Angell is a consultant in Osbornes Family Law Department and head of the firm's adoption team. She is a specialist in child protection, international and domestic adoption, children's cases where there are significant immigration issues, and domestic and international surrogacy. She is co-chair of the Family Law Committee of the Law Society, and a member of the Law Society Children Panel and of the Resolution Accreditation Panel. For ten years Naomi chaired the adoption panel of a national adoption agency and was a member of the Lord Chancellor's Advisory Committee on Family Law. She regularly writes and lectures and is involved with the media and in policy work in relation to children's law issues. She is also a patron of the Coram Children's Legal Centre, which she was instrumental in establishing during the International Year of the Child in 1981.

Catherine Atkinson is a barrister at 9 Gough Square. She enjoys a wide-ranging practice with particular interests in personal injury, employment, fraud and public family cases. She has been a contributing author to books on occupational health, employment law and clinical negligence and has also written articles on a wide range of topics. Catherine is secretary of the Society of Labour Lawyers and Labour's 2015 parliamentary candidate for Erewash.

Vera Baird QC was elected as Northumbria's first Police and Crime Commissioner in 2012. Prior to this role, Vera was Labour MP for Redcar and became a minister in the Labour government in 2006. In

2007 she was appointed Solicitor General, the House of Commons' most senior law officer, integrating policy development within government and particularly involved in criminal justice policy and legislation, especially on gender and equality policies. She was the lead minister with responsibility for taking the Equality Act through Parliament in 2010. With this wealth of experience, Vera continues to be a strong voice for the North East, speaking up for the Northumbria police force, partners and communities at a local and national level.

John Bowers QC practises in employment law, discrimination and human rights at Littleton Chambers. He has written or co-authored 14 books including works on industrial action and whistleblowing. He sits on the council of the University of Kent and was formerly a member of the Standards Board for England.

Barbara Connolly QC was called to the English Bar in 1986 and appointed Queen's Counsel in 2011. She specialises in family law, with particular emphasis on children, vulnerable adults and medico-legal issues. She has a special interest in legal issues affecting families created using surrogacy and assisted reproductive technology, including international cases, and has written a number of articles on these and related matters and has spoken at conferences both in the UK and internationally. Barbara is a member of the Family Law Bar Association and of the International Bar Association and a fellow of the International Academy of Matrimonial Lawyers.

Jonathan Cooper is a member of Doughty Street Chambers. He is a human rights specialist with experience before English and international courts and tribunals. He has carried out human rights training for various UK government departments, including the Foreign and Commonwealth Office (FCO) and the Ministry of Justice (MoJ). He devised and wrote the human rights and counter-terrorism programme and manual for the Organization for Security and Co-operation in Europe (OSCE). Jonathan is one of the general editors of *Halsbury's Rights and Freedoms*, and is the editor of the *European Human Rights Law Review* (Sweet & Maxwell). He has published extensively on human rights. In 2007, Jonathan was awarded an OBE for services to human rights.

Andrew Dismore is the London Assembly member for Barnet and Camden and Labour's 2015 parliamentary candidate for Hendon. From 1997 to 2010, he was the Labour MP for Hendon. He promoted many law reform issues relating to personal injury law and chaired the Joint Select Committee on Human Rights from 2005 to 2010. Andrew has practised as a solicitor specialising in personal injury and industrial relations law. He commenced his career with Thompsons in 1978, becoming a partner in that firm, and moved to Russell Jones & Walker as a partner in 1995 prior to entering Parliament. He holds law degrees from Warwick University and the LSE.

John Hobson QC is a barrister specialising in Planning, Local Government and Environmental Law at Landmark Chambers, London.

Stephen Hockman QC has been in practice at the Bar since 1970 and is a specialist in all forms of regulatory law. He is head of chambers at 6 Pump Court, Temple, and a former chair of the Bar Council. He has been a member of the Labour Party, and of the Society of Labour Lawyers, since his early years in practice. As chair of the society, he has been responsible for drawing together the essays in this volume.

Michael Horton is a barrister who specialises in family law – in particular, financial remedy cases.

Tom Jones is a senior partner at Thompsons Solicitors, holding the brief of Head of Policy and Public Affairs. He works closely with Labour MPs generally and the Trade Union Group of MPs in particular on issues of mutual interest. Tom has led the firm's activities to challenge the insurance industry myths about a compensation culture and is a regular speaker and writer on trade union legal issues.

Rt Hon. Sadiq Khan MP is the Member of Parliament for Tooting, the Shadow Lord Chancellor and Shadow Secretary of State for Justice (with responsibility for political and constitutional reform). He is also

Shadow Minister for London. He previously held ministerial positions in both the Department for Communities and Local Government and the Department for Transport (where he became the first Asian and the first Muslim to attend cabinet). A former chair of the Fabian Society, he has written the award-winning *Fairness not Favours: How to Connect with British Muslims* and edited *Punishment and Reform: How Our Justice System Can Help Cut Crime*. Sadiq was previously a human rights solicitor with Christian Khan and a councillor in the London Borough of Wandsworth for 12 years.

David Lock QC practises from Landmark Chambers, London, where he has a predominantly public law practice involving issues concerning the NHS, social care, the Court of Protection and related public policy matters. He served as Labour MP for Wyre Forest between 1997 and 2001, and was a Minister in the Lord Chancellor's Department. He is a member of the BMA Ethics Committee, a trustee of Brook (the young people's sexual health charity) and a non-executive director of one of the largest NHS hospital trusts in the country.

Rt Hon. Ed Miliband MP was born in 1969. He studied Philosophy, Politics and Economics at Corpus Christi College, Oxford, and later took an MA in Economics at the London School of Economics and spent time as a visiting scholar at the Centre for European Studies of Harvard University in 2002/3. In 1993, while working as a television journalist, he was recruited as a researcher for the Labour Party's shadow Treasury team, working for Harriet Harman MP. He served under Gordon Brown both in Opposition and Government, later becoming chairman of the Treasury's Council of Economic Advisers. He was elected MP for Doncaster North in 2005, serving as Minister for the Third Sector from 2006 and Secretary of State for Energy and Climate Change from October 2008. Since his election as Leader of the Labour Party in September 2010, he has set out his vision of 'One Nation Labour', which emphasises building a society where everybody has a stake, where benefits and burdens are fairly shared, and where we protect the institutions that make us who we are, from our NHS to the United Kingdom.

Gordon Nardell QC is a barrister at Thirty Nine Essex Street Chambers in London, specialising in energy and natural resources law. He currently serves as Leader of the European Circuit of the English Bar. Gordon is a lifelong Labour activist. He writes and blogs regularly on political and economic issues and has served as a councillor in the London Borough of Southwark, where he helped set up community-based energy project Peckham Power. As a parliamentary draftsperson he worked on implementation of key elements of Labour's 1997 programme, including the Human Rights Act 1998, the Competition Act 1998 and the Financial Services and Markets Act 2000. More recently he has advised the Labour front benches in the Commons and Lords on energy legislation.

Andrew Powell was called to the Bar in 2008 and is a specialist family law barrister at 4 Paper Buildings. He was supervised by David Williams QC during part of his pupillage. Andrew has a particular interest in the law relating to the Human Fertilisation and Embryology Act 2008. In 2014 he spent three months as a Pegasus Scholar working at a Los Angeles law firm that specialised in surrogacy and fertility law. Andrew is also a volunteer at the Toynbee Hall Legal Advice Centre in East London.

Sarah Sackman is a barrister specialising in public, planning and environmental law. She holds degrees from Cambridge and Harvard universities. She practises at Francis Taylor Building, has also taught public law at Queen Mary University and is currently a guest lecturer on the LSE Cities programme. Sarah is standing as Labour's parliamentary candidate for Finchley and Golders Green in the 2015 general election.

Richard Scorer is a Principal Lawyer and Head of the Abuse Cases Team at Slater & Gordon lawyers. Rated as a Band 1 'Leader in the Field' of serious injury law by *Chambers Legal Guide*, he has acted in numerous high-profile abuse cases, including representing victims of the Rochdale child sexual exploitation ring, and has dealt with many cases involving abuse in schools, churches and other institutional settings. He has published widely on this area and his book *Betrayed:*

The English Catholic Church and the Sex Abuse Crisis was published by Biteback Books in 2014. Outside work he serves as a Labour councillor in West Yorkshire and was a Labour parliamentary candidate at the 2010 general election.

Roger Smith OBE is a long-time advocate for, and defender of, legal aid. He has been director of JUSTICE and of the Legal Action Group and director of legal education at the Law Society. With Professor Paterson, he wrote *Face to Face Legal Services and their Alternatives: Global Lessons from the Digital Revolution*, published in January 2014. He has written widely on legal services and human rights, edits a bi-monthly newsletter for the International Legal Aid Group, and produces regular columns for the *Law Gazette* and the *New Law Journal*.

Reuben Taylor QC is a barrister specialising in Local Government and Planning law at Landmark Chambers, London.

Simon Taylor is a barrister in EU, public procurement, state aid and competition law practising at Keating Chambers. Having previously been a competition partner in a leading law firm, he has over twenty years' experience in advising companies and public bodies in this field. He is currently working on the joint Society of Labour Lawyers and Labour Finance and Industry Group task force on public procurement. Simon has a 'License spéciale' in EU law from the University of Brussels.

Emily Thornberry MP is Labour's Shadow Attorney General and the Member of Parliament for Islington South and Finsbury. Before entering parliament in 2005 she practised at the Bar for twenty years and was a member of Tooks Court Chambers.

Samuel Townend is a barrister in construction, engineering, energy and related professional negligence law practising at Keating Chambers. Currently vice-chair of the Society of Labour Lawyers and convenor of a panel of legal advisers to the Labour Party, Samuel is a former member of the Bar Council, former councillor of the London

Borough of Lambeth and former Labour parliamentary candidate (for Reigate in 2005, and Bristol North-West in 2010).

David Williams QC is a barrister and mediator based in London. Before coming to the Bar, David worked for the Legal Aid Board as a case-worker where he was chair of the MSF Legal Aid London branch. He resigned in 1989 following a run-in with the LAB management over legal aid administration reforms. He now specialises in international family law and has appeared in the Court of Justice of the European Union and the UK Supreme Court. David is the Labour Party parliamentary candidate for Wycombe and chair of the Family Law Group of the Society of Labour Lawyers.

Foreword

Rt Hon Ed Miliband MP

I am delighted to acknowledge the publication of this book of essays by prominent Labour lawyers.

The present volume is the latest in a distinguished series, starting in 1951 with *The Reform of the Law*, edited by a remarkable academic lawyer, Glanville Williams, and leading eventually to *Law Reform for All* (1996), edited by David Bean.

As in the past, this book shows that lawyers are not necessarily either conservative or dull. They can be progressive, imaginative and committed to social change in the interests of the community as a whole, especially those of its members who are least well off.

The Labour Party does not subscribe to all of the ideas in this book. But this volume represents an immensely valuable contribution to the debate about legal reform, and I welcome the book for that reason.

I congratulate all those involved, and I look forward to working with them to deliver a progressive agenda for the reform of the law.

Introduction

Those on the left in politics have always had an ambivalent relationship with the legal profession. This does not stem from any scepticism as to the value of law as an instrument of social change. Rather it flows from the fact that lawyers are seen as responsible sometimes for frustrating necessary changes by an over-strict interpretation of the law, as well as by the extent to which they have tended to capture and hold on to the reins of political power. The Blair government contained a remarkable number of talented lawyers or ex-lawyers, and succeeded, especially in its transformative policy towards human rights law, in restoring the reputation of the law and lawyers among those of progressive views, but – for various reasons – only temporarily.

I hope that the present volume will demonstrate on a more enduring basis the contribution that lawyers can make, not only to the just and efficacious resolution of legal disputes, but also to the development of legal policy and law reform. Ed Miliband MP, to whom I am most grateful for his Foreword, refers to some of the earlier volumes in this series of publications promoted by the Society of Labour Lawyers, which I have been privileged to chair in 2013 and again this year. The Society was founded in the late 1940s by Gerald Gardiner QC (later Lord Chancellor in the first Wilson government) and is the pre-eminent professional association for lawyers on the left of politics. A glance at the contents page, and at the useful summaries at the end of each chapter, will show just how comprehensive and imaginative the contributors to this volume have been. I hope that our predecessors would regard this as a worthy successor to earlier efforts, but more importantly, I hope that readers today will be impressed and inspired in equal measure.

Much is owed to Stephen Brough, Paul Forty and the Profile team who have steered this book with a steady hand towards its destination, and to the law firm Slater and Gordon for their generous support.

Stephen Hockman QC
August 2014

1

Child Abuse

Richard Scorer

The threat of children being groomed through the internet, the problems of gang-related abuse and child sexual exploitation, and allegations of historic abuse by those with status and power, such as Jimmy Savile, have all attracted huge media attention. As this book goes to press, the media is convulsed with talk of child abuse scandals involving Westminster itself.

Political initiatives and the national debate

Party leaders, however, have struggled to give voice to the ensuing public disquiet. Policy initiatives have tended to come from back-bench MPs – for example, the report of the Home Affairs Select Committee in relation to child sexual exploitation.[1] The former Director of Public Prosecutions (DPP), Sir Keir Starmer is now heading a Labour group undertaking a review of the rights of victims in the criminal justice system, and has talked of a statutory 'victim's law'. Thus far, however, Labour's substantive policy response to the sex abuse scandals has been limited and broad brush. Yvette Cooper has called for a 'single overarching inquiry' into child abuse, and has pledged a new national commissioner for sexual and domestic abuse, while Sadiq Khan has called for the criminal justice system to be 'rebalanced in favour of the victim'.

In the context of shadow cabinet nervousness about spending commitments, Labour's relatively thin gruel to date may reflect a fear that any substantial policy response in this area will inevitably involve significant expenditure; increased numbers of victims coming forward needing more support, and so forth. It may also reflect an unspoken fear that some of the problems identified, like the low rate of conviction in rape cases, might be quite intractable. However, it is clear from the sexual exploitation scandal in Rochdale – where a fundamental review of police and Crown Prosecution Service (CPS) practice between 2008 and 2012 led to criminal convictions in cases which had previously been thought hopeless – that policy reforms in this area can make a significant difference.

The national debate about sexual crimes gives rise to the opportunity to lead and shape progressive change on issues that arouse significant public concern, and which directly affect vulnerable members of society. In this chapter I suggest that policy development and campaigning should focus on three areas – mandatory reporting, improvements in the court process and (underlying these) the promotion of fundamental attitudinal change towards victims.

Mandatory reporting

Media attention over the past two years has focused both on so-called 'celebrity' abusers such as Savile, whose crimes were largely historic, and the much more recent cases of child sexual exploitation by organised gangs. The two categories of case differ in important respects, but a common feature was the failure to act on credible allegations of abuse – in Savile's case, apparently because of his perceived power, and in the child sexual exploitation cases because the crimes were interpreted as 'lifestyle choices' by victims (even though most of them were under the age of consent). In many other cases now coming to light we have seen organisations and institutions failing to report allegations of abuse to statutory authorities (i.e. police and social services), not least because – as in the Catholic Church and many private schools dependent on their reputation for their income – fealty to an institution can outweigh the responsibility to protect children.

In response, many victim groups have campaigned for mandatory reporting, meaning formal legislation that would require certain categories of people to report suspected cases of child abuse to the authorities. The campaign for mandatory reporting has gained wide support and Labour should be at the forefront of arguing for this change.

Legislative and regulatory background

Currently, in England and Wales (and Scotland) there is no formal requirement in law to report child protection concerns to the authorities. There are professional reporting obligations, for example for teachers or carers, which are emphasised through local and national guidance, and various inter-agency protocols. But the failure to report abuse does not constitute a criminal offence. One campaigner, discussing an abuse scandal in 2008 at a Catholic private school in West London, pointed out that:

> *The amazing fact is that in failing to report abuse at the school to the police or social services, [the school] didn't break any laws. It is possible for a headteacher to know for certain that a member of staff has raped a pupil on school premises, and the headteacher has no statutory obligation to report anything to anybody. Any obligation towards the child and its parents exists only as contract law, a school's child protection policy being an implied part of the contract between school and parents.*[2]

Of course a 'contract' between school and parents would exist only in the case of a private school, and would not extend to the state sector. There is no reason why children at state schools should be disadvantaged in comparison with children in the independent sector, but in any event a contractual relationship is insufficient because the obligation most needed is not an obligation to report to parents, but to the authorities who are empowered to intervene to protect the child and prevent further abuse taking place.

Campaigners in the UK have therefore argued for 'Daniel's Law', named after Daniel Pelka, a little boy starved and beaten to death by his mother and stepfather; a serious case review found that Daniel was 'invisible' at times due to delays and failures in sharing information about his plight.[3] Daniel's Law would make it mandatory for child protection concerns to be reported by professionals and organisations working with children, introducing clarity especially in circumstances of conflicting duty, where a teacher or cleric might be torn between child welfare and protection of the institution. Campaigners point out that there are ample precedents internationally for such a law. Most states in the USA, all Canadian jurisdictions bar one and all Australian states have mandatory reporting laws.

In the Republic of Ireland the backlash against clerical abuse inspired a campaign for a constitutional amendment making it mandatory to report any complaint from a child about abuse, thus enshrining children's rights in a state constitution which, traditionally and in conformity with its Catholic origins, placed much more emphasis on privacy and the authority of the family. In Northern Ireland, s. 5(1) of the Criminal Law Act (Northern Ireland) 1967 already provides for a criminal offence of failing to disclose an *arrestable* offence to the police, which, de facto, includes most offences against children. Something similar, campaigners argue, could be brought onto the statute book in the rest of the UK.

Framing the policy

It is not difficult to see how mandatory reporting could have made a difference to child protection in many of the abuse cases that have now come to light. Public opinion surveys also suggest that most voters see mandatory reporting as a 'no brainer'. Front bench politicians from the major parties, however, have tended to shy away from campaigning for mandatory reporting, perhaps reflecting the reservations of some child protection charities, who have expressed the reasonable concern that mandatory reporting might be counter-productive, particularly if police and social services are swamped with inappropriate reports that drain investigative resources from genuine cases. For example, the NSPCC has argued that mandatory reporting laws 'may overwhelm services that are supposed to be targeted at the most at-risk children and families who then receive less attention than is required to prevent neglect or abuse'[4] (although it also acknowledges that this view has been contested).

Others claim that experience from overseas jurisdictions suggests that it does not result in any significant increase in reports of abuse. But the difficulty in weighing evidence from overseas is that mandatory reporting laws come in many different forms; for example, some apply just to professionals, others apply to the whole population. Reporting thresholds also vary: thus in Australia the law in Tasmania requires professionals to report 'all suspicions of risk', but the law in South Australia requires reporting if the professional 'suspects on reasonable grounds' that a child is being abused. The variations in reporting thresholds between different Australian states, together with uncertainties about the laws relating to confidentiality, seem to have led to confusion among professionals, and even more so among the general public, as what exactly professionals are legally obliged to do, and when. However, these problems are not intractable, and there is evidence from overseas that where mandatory reporting laws are clear and consistent they can be effective in raising awareness of abuse and the need to pass information to investigators.

In view of the reasonable concerns that have been expressed and the difficulties involved in formulating a law that will be effective, the best way forward for Labour would be to argue for a mandatory reporting law focusing on institutions – i.e. requiring disclosure to the authorities of actual or suspected abuse in an institutional setting. This would address the most pernicious problem revealed by cases such as Savile, namely the failure to report abuse due to a conflict of interest between the immediate needs and reputation of the institution, and the needs of the child. The reporting obligation would be a mandatory, non-discretionary duty to report imposed upon a designated person within the organisation who would be under a legal duty to refer all allegations of wrongdoing vis-à-vis children to external authorities. The law would apply only to 'regulated activities' as defined in the Safeguarding Vulnerable Groups Act 2006 (i.e. activities and settings where children are looked after other than by their parents, schools, hospitals, children's homes, etc.). This would exclude helplines like Childline or Rape Crisis confidential hotlines from mandatory reporting; obviously to include them in the scope of mandatory reporting would render their work impossible. Provided such a law is accompanied by clarity around reporting thresholds, and around the rules on confidentiality of information, then there is every reason to believe that it could help to prevent some of the appalling abuse in schools, religious organisations and other institutions that has recently come to light.

Court processes

Keir Starmer has argued forcefully that, from the point of view of victims, the criminal justice system is 'hardly fit for purpose'. Highlighting in particular the experience of child victims and witnesses in the sex-grooming trials (in the Rochdale case, some were cross-examined by no fewer than 11 defence barristers) he observes that, 'for many victims, the adversarial journey through our courtrooms is such an ordeal that most vow never to repeat it', and he urges a 'fundamental rethink' including a 'legally enforceable victim's law'.[5] Starmer is right to recommend a fundamental reappraisal, but there are immediate changes, informed by cases like Rochdale, that could quickly improve the experience of victims within the criminal justice system pending a root-and-branch review.

The most obvious of these is the implementation of the 'full-Pigot' provisions for the cross-examination of vulnerable witnesses. The Youth Justice and Criminal Evidence Act 1999 (YJCEA 1999) already provides for a series of special measures which the court can direct in respect of vulnerable and intimidated witnesses. These include screening witnesses from the accused, the removal of wigs and gowns in the courtroom, and giving evidence by video link or in private. The concept of 'special measures' (a somewhat outmoded term as they are now routine) emerged from the Pigot Committee in the late 1980s,[6] which concluded that children were adversely affected by giving evidence in the traditional manner in trials involving serious criminal offences. But the radical solution envisaged by Pigot – taking children out of the formal criminal trial process altogether by videotaping their entire testimony (including cross-examination and re-examination) before trial – was never implemented due to parliamentary and Law Society opposition in the early 1990s.

Failure to implement 'full-Pigot'

At that time the then-Conservative government adopted a diluted 'half-Pigot' approach, with the Criminal Justice Act 1991 providing that a videotaped interview of the child witness would be admissible at trial as evidence-in-chief (subject to the trial judge's discretion) but that the child would still be required to attend trial for cross-examination. That cross-examination, of course, will typically take place many months after the original videotaped interview, so that, as the NSPCC has observed, in some circumstances the 'half-Pigot' regime can actually place the child at even greater disadvantage.

Throughout the 1990s, however, a series of public inquiries into the investigation and prosecution of child abuse in England and Wales strongly endorsed the 'full-Pigot' approach, and in 1998 a government working party developed comprehensive recommendations for children and vulnerable adults appearing in the courts that broadly adopted 'full-Pigot'. These recommendations formed the basis of Part II YJCEA 1999, s. 28 of which provides for video-recorded cross-examination or re-examination of child witnesses.

Section 28, however, is not yet in force. The main reasons for this appear to be political inertia and opposition from the Bar: some defence barristers have argued that the full disclosure which is necessary before cross-examination can take place is typically a very lengthy process that is usually completed only shortly before trial, and therefore to have a separate pre-trial procedure for children would be unfairly disadvantageous to defendants. The sensible counter-argument is that this problem can be addressed by effective case management and fast-tracking of child abuse prosecutions.

In his Toulmin Lecture in March 2013 the Lord Chief Justice, Lord Judge, was clear that there is an urgent need to implement 'full-Pigot', and emphasised that all the objections and obstacles that had been raised to it were 'eminently resolvable'.[7] Once full-Pigot is implemented, he predicted, 'we shall all be astounded what all the fuss was about'. The Ministry of Justice promised in 2012 to examine 'whether the implementation of s. 28 could be made to work in practice'. But although some pilot schemes are now underway, progress has been slow: an inexplicable state of affairs given the media attention on child sexual exploitation cases. In its 2013 report on child sexual exploitation the House of Commons Home Affairs Select Committee rightly commented that:

> *We are at a loss to understand why the Ministry of Justice, fourteen years after the Act was passed, has still failed to implement this measure. If the Lord Chief Justice, Lord Judge, with all his unrivalled experience, can find no reasonable obstacle to the implementation of [full-Pigot] there can be no justifiable argument for continuing to subject highly vulnerable victims to cross-examination in court given the highly publicised risks this carries. [Full-Pigot] represents the will of Parliament and it is for the MoJ to implement this measure in a timely manner.[8]*

The slowness of the coalition government in adopting a sensible Labour measure for the protection of vulnerable witnesses in the face of widespread public concern about child sexual exploitation should be an urgent campaigning issue.

Intermediaries and specialist courts

Drawing on the recent trials, there are also other immediate improvements in special measures that could improve the criminal justice system for vulnerable complainants.

One example would be to extend the use of intermediaries. Vulnerable witnesses under the age of 17 are eligible for the assistance of an intermediary when giving evidence: the intermediary is introduced to them at the start of the investigative process and can assist with any difficulties of communication or understanding whilst giving evidence. But witnesses over 17 years old are only eligible for the assistance of an intermediary if they have a mental disorder or significant impairment of intelligence. In the Rochdale grooming case, because of a failure to take their allegations seriously back in 2008, a number of my clients who were sexually abused and exploited in their early teens did not give evidence in criminal trials until several years later. As a result, they were deprived of the assistance of an intermediary during particularly harrowing and distressing evidence. Extending the use of intermediaries would, I believe, be a valuable and relatively inexpensive step in helping victims of child exploitation through the court process.

A broader change we should also pursue is the introduction of specialist courts for sexual offences. At present, judges, prosecutors and magistrates who hear sex cases are expected to have had special training, but no such stipulation applies to defence counsel, and in acting for victims I have heard too many accounts of inappropriate questioning at trial. For example, *The Times* journalist, Andrew Norfolk, whose reporting of child sexual exploitation has done much to bring this scandal to public attention, recounts hearing a defence barrister at the long child sexual exploitation trial at Stafford Crown Court in 2011 asking of a teenage rape victim, several days into harrowing evidence, whether she had 'repented her sins'.[9] There have been many other examples, and a requirement for specialist courts and specialist training would help to address this problem. It need not involve the creation of new bureaucracies, merely the concentration of existing expertise into specialist hubs with the most experienced judges and counsel (both prosecuting and defending) and the best technology.

Attitudinal change

Underlying all this, as Keir Starmer has pointed out, is an urgent need to secure attitudinal change towards victims throughout the criminal justice system.

This may seem a more nebulous objective but it is fundamental. In Rochdale in 2008, the credibility and reliability of victims of child exploitation was assessed by reference to ill-informed stereotypes about whether the girls concerned (who were often in fear for their lives) reported abuse quickly, whether they returned to their abusers, whether they had previous criminal convictions, and whether their recollections were affected by drugs or alcohol. On that basis, prosecutions were rejected on credibility grounds. It was only thanks to the leadership of individuals like the Chief Crown Prosecutor of the CPS for North West England, Nazir Afzal, and a determination to improve the response to victims of child sexual exploitation in cases that previously had been considered hopeless, that prosecutions were undertaken resulting in numerous criminal convictions. Traditional prejudices about victim behaviour were challenged head-on.

Following public debate about the Rochdale cases in 2012–13, the CPS under Starmer revised its internal guidelines for prosecution of sexual offences, to ensure that prosecutors are not misled by myths about how 'real victims' behave – a change that Starmer saw as part of a fundamental attitudinal shift across the criminal justice system.

As Starmer's successor, Alison Saunders has emphasised, that shift has to be constantly reinforced. The trial process for victims is deeply invasive and personal, and many are still deterred from coming forward. New prejudices can replace old ones. As Saunders says: 'It used to be that if a rape victim wore a short skirt her credibility was undermined. Thankfully we have moved on, but we must be careful not to establish new myths that victims come forward only for financial or other motives.'

The drive to embed and constantly strengthen the recent positive change of attitude towards victims within the CPS and other agencies must be led from the very top. In government from 1997 to 2010, through a mixture of legislation and active promotion of progressive values, Labour secured widespread changes in social attitudes over such issues as racism and gay rights. The challenge for the next Labour government is to ensure a fundamental change in attitudes to victims throughout the criminal justice system.

Summary of principal recommendations

- To introduce a mandatory reporting law requiring disclosure to the authorities of actual or suspected abuse in an institutional setting.
- To implement s. 28 of the YJCEA 1999, which provides for video-recorded cross-examination or re-examination of child witnesses.
- To extend the use of intermediaries to assist vulnerable witnesses in giving evidence.
- To introduce specialist courts for sexual offences.
- To ensure a fundamental change in attitudes to victims throughout the criminal justice system.

2

Civil Legal Aid

Roger Smith

If Labour wins in 2015 it will inherit a truncated civil legal aid scheme, the funding for which will have been slashed by something between a third and a half. The largest single group of casualties will have been women in relationships that are breaking up. However, a range of people with a whole series of 'social welfare' problems will have also lost out. It will be harder to make a judicial review application. The cuts would have been worse but for the Human Rights Act 1998, and it is clear that the coalition government has gone to some trouble to avoid a successful challenge to its proposals.

There are all sorts of things that might be said – that are being said – in lament for the first major cut to civil legal aid schemes since they were begun after the Second World War. Labour spokespeople have said many of them in support of the campaign against the cuts. A certain unreality holds over these since everyone knows, but finds its somewhat inopportune to admit right at this moment, that Labour itself planned cuts of around 10 per cent to the legal aid budget if it had been re-elected at the last election. It is probably true, however, that Labour's pattern of cuts would have been different. Social welfare law might have been protected in favour of cuts to crime. Be that as it may, the next election raises a question for Labour which, in microcosm, is what it faces over the whole political field. OK, you don't like the cuts, and neither do we, but, in the resonant words of the Small Faces from half a century ago ...

'Whatcha gonna do about it?'

To win in 2015, Labour needs a strategy with three key components (in relation to civil legal aid as much as anywhere else). First, in the jargon of these things, there needs to be a meta-narrative. What is Labour's overall story? This is an enormous issue of general political purport and if Labour does not get it right then any detailed policies are a waste of time. And this will be difficult: Labour made mistakes. Like almost everyone else, it did not read the financial bubble right; it famously proclaimed that it had brought an end to boom and bust economics; and it engaged in expensive foreign adventures that history now indicates – and many of us then predicted – we could not afford, which alienated its support base and made things, like terrorism, much worse. We, the public, know this. So, Labour might as well admit it and also proclaim that it was motivated, more than anything else, by a driving and egalitarian desire to improve life for everyone – even, if mistakenly, those in Iraq.

Labour is – deeply, fundamentally and sometimes despite its leadership – a party on the side of those who struggle against the interests of the rich and the powerful, even when they include a sometimes cold and hostile state. And let's hear a bit more about the crippling cost to the welfare state of keeping banks in the style to which they have been accustomed. The funding of legal aid, like our armed services, is being taken to keep afloat a bloated financial sector whose responsibility for its gross failure is fundamentally its own. The meta-narrative is, however, clearly a matter for a wider politics.

Second, closer to legal aid but also with a wider applicability, Labour needs to bring about a particularly difficult combination of arguments – mixing lament for lost services; painful recognition that no magic wand will bring them back, at least in the short term; and a message of hope and inspiration for a better future. This is a tricky argument to pitch to its various audiences – voters, former beneficiaries of services and for those who once drew their employment from state-funded provision. For the latter, the words of another popular song, this time from Bruce Springsteen, drift hauntingly in the air: 'these jobs are going, boys, and they ain't coming back'. Labour cannot credibly argue that it will reinstate the legal aid cuts.

Third, Labour has to advance some notion of a new and inspiring future. For legal aid policy, which, let's face it, will not determine the fate of the next election, this will need to chime in with an overall approach taken by the party. Legal aid, however, gives an opportunity to study the issue in microcosm – in a tiny area of expenditure within a far-off corner of the welfare state but where there might be larger lessons to be learnt.

In the midst of our current adversity there may be some possibilities for a new approach. For most of its life, legal aid has been a source of assistance to the poor but also, importantly, a project of the legal profession. It was devised in its current form by the Law Society; sold to Parliament after the Second World War; and has developed to provide a source of substantial income to both branches of the legal profession. In the early 1970s, law centres were seen off as a challenge to private provider provision. Even now, legal aid provides around 10 per cent of solicitors' total turnover and substantially more than that for the Bar: it has supported the historical structure of the legal profession with its small, widely located high street solicitors' practices and its more concentrated, solo practitioner Bar.

Partly as the result of legal aid cuts but more because of the creation of new forms of practice involving outside capital and providers (the alternative business structures which are a creation of Labour's legal policy when in government), this structure, with which we have become so familiar, is about to be blown apart. Providers using the full resources of the internet, national branding and centralised services, like Co-operative Legal Services, will largely wipe out traditional high street practice as we have known it. Prices will fall for consumers and – unhappily for them – remuneration for providers. This, combined with the consequence of the cuts now being implemented, will cause the decimation of existing providers while simultaneously, as a paradoxically beneficial side effect, giving more chance of changing the pattern of expenditure since the vested interests in current provision have been weakened.

Proclaiming what Labour stands for

So let's take advantage of the unique circumstances of this moment in time to set out what Labour's objective should be for what was civil legal aid. One initial point becomes immediately apparent in any attempt to do this. Civil legal aid represents only a means to an end. It makes no sense to talk about legal aid without saying what it should be for. Why do we want to fund lawyers, paralegals and other forms of assistance? Labour might spend some time proclaiming the fundamental answer. We want legal aid because we want a fair society. We want all to know their rights and responsibilities. We want any disputes to be decided in ways that are determined by their intrinsic and substantive merits. We do not want a society where inequalities of wealth or influence decide how a dispute will be determined between the rich and powerful and the poor and the powerless. We want, we might say, 'equal justice under law'. And, if we put it in that way, we would only be using the language chiselled into the architrave of the Supreme Court of the United States. In its turn, the phrase reaches back to Pericles ('the law secures equal justice to all alike in their private disputes') via various US Supreme Court decisions. This was the aim of the original legal aid scheme, put to Parliament as 'no one will be financially unable to prosecute a just and reasonable claim or defend a legal right'.

So Labour has good historical and contemporary precedent for avowing that the purpose of its legal system, of which civil legal aid is a part, is to provide 'equal justice for all'. It is the 'all' that should give Labour its distinctive position. Labour stands, if for anything, for inclusiveness in access to justice as elsewhere. And a goal of equal justice for all puts the emphasis on the outcome not the process – despite the appearance of the phrase on a court building. That, in turn, makes a further important point. Labour is for an inclusive goal and a comprehensive approach. It would be worth being much clearer about this fundamental objective. In government, Labour allowed its legal aid policy to be swamped by technological detail and a fixation with the objective of compulsory competitive tendering, a policy which, ironically enough, has just been repudiated by the coalition Lord Chancellor as unethical in terms of removal of client choice.

Labour should shout its commitment to equal justice for all from the rooftops, even if it also should not seek to hide the fact that its achievement will be difficult in the context of a struggling economy. Nevertheless, it will do its best and use every lever. This, by itself, would help to change the terms of the debate. But, legal aid policy is, in any event, not just about money.

Legal aid has been seen for far too long as a self-contained ghetto where policies have been isolated from others. If we are to achieve justice for all in modern society and with contemporary budgets, then money alone will not do it. Labour needs to conceive of policy as a unity. So, our first step from specification of the goal should be to the primary means of its attainment – i.e. the laws that are required to meet the goal. Thus, Labour should unequivocally shout its support for the much traduced Human Rights Act and European Convention on Human Rights. Yes, there are difficult issues – such as prisoners' votes – but, frankly, these are resolvable with a degree of good will and a descending from high horses. The Human Rights Act has protected what is left of civil and criminal legal aid. Be in no doubt, the cuts would have been infinitely worse both here and elsewhere without it. The Human Rights Act gives strength and sinew to rights that are deep in the British constitution – to privacy, fair trial and so on – but which are susceptible to a government's domination of Parliament. It is one of the great legacies of the Blair–Brown years, and any successor should proclaim its continuing support for a measure that fundamentally shifts the balance between the individual and the state.

Linked with a commitment to the Human Rights Act should be a commitment to judicial review as a crucial way in which an individual can hold those in power accountable for their decisions and actions. Of course, any minister does not like to be challenged in the courts and one can understand why, when in power, the opportunity to curtail judicial review might seem attractive to any government. However, the coalition has gone too far in seeking to penalise applicants through costs at the application stage and over-tight time limits. These were actions that were motivated by a totally different politics – a desire to exclude not include – than should appeal to Labour. An incoming Labour government should commit itself to their removal. There will be minimal financial consequence: these cuts were ideological, not financial. Labour should unequivocally occupy the ground of demanding the transparency and accountability of power.

Former Treasury Minister, Liam Byrne achieved a period of unfortunate celebrity just after the last election by leaving a note for his successor, David Laws, which read simply, 'Dear Chief Secretary, I'm afraid there is no money. Kind regards – and good luck! Liam.' For politicians, the fate of this note, which was splashed with glee over the *Daily Mail*, may stand as a dreadful warning of the danger of giving in to a sense of humour. For strategists contemplating Labour's position at the next election, it stands as a stark indication of what we all know (and Labour needs to admit): there is no new money. Indeed, it would be surprising if a Labour Lord Chancellor was not under pressure to deliver more savings to fund initiatives seen as more central to Labour's concerns for economic and social equality.

Labour might as well, therefore, openly admit that the likelihood of more funds for legal aid in the next Parliament is unlikely. It could add that, on the other hand, it hopes to impose no more cuts and that the task for Labour's Lord Chancellor – which will be, Heaven knows, difficult enough – will be to live within the budget that it is bequeathed after the two rounds of coalition cuts. That would set a very clear and understandable parameter to policy-making. It would give us some minimal framework and financial stability within which to work.

Addressing the challenge

So, with a broadly defined goal but limited financial means, how should Labour proceed? It needs to manage expectation. There is going to be no simple answer. Civil legal aid has been cut to the bone. General legal advice has been dismantled. Provision has been constructed around the requirements of the Human Rights Act. Remuneration has been reduced. It is difficult to see that further savings can be squeezed out of the civil legal aid system for some time. That being so, there is unlikely to be a rabbit to be plucked out of the hat and promoted as 'the answer' to the problems of civil legal aid. The future is going to be a hard slog, for both ministers and practitioners.

One sensible point of departure would be to look at how other jurisdictions are facing up to the same challenge. We are, after all, not alone. There are plenty of other countries that have a commitment to providing access to justice within similar sorts of justice system but are hit by financial pressures in doing so – most notably the United States, Canada, Australia, the Netherlands and so on. What ideas arise from studying their response? We are used to bestriding the world as the colossus of legal aid and not really taking much notice of what is happening elsewhere. However, we are being rather cut down to a common size. It is time to look outward.

An obvious place to begin would be the United States. This, like us, is a common law country. It has national provision of a kind, funded from a variety of sources including federal grant through the Legal Services Corporation but at lower levels than we are used to. As a result, it has had to be as creative as it can be about how to deliver sources. It has historically favoured salaried services rather than private practitioners, but most schemes use private lawyers to some extent, if only for pro bono assistance. From its range of activity, I would select one element – its approach to the use of technology, an area where I think that it has much to inspire us.

The LSC total budget for the whole of the US (over 330 million people) is less than our civil legal aid budget (for a population of 56 million) even after the current cuts. Perhaps as a result it has really looked to get maximum leverage for its developmental funding. In 1998 it decided that it should invest in innovation in new technology. From 2000 it has done so by way of announcing an annual competition for relatively small grants out of a relatively small overall budget. The result is that since 2000 it has made over 500 awards totalling around $40m (or £26m) in Technology Innovation Grants. The process is approved by Congress and appears very well organised. There is a defined marking scheme and a set of annual priorities. Currently, and for the next five years, these are:[1]

1. Document assembly – automating form creation and standardising the data collected.
2. Expert systems – creating intelligent checklists that guide clients and advocates through the steps needed for processes such as initiating or responding to court actions and dealing with government agencies.
3. Remote services delivery – can each state have an online portal that mitigates the physical barriers to seeking representation?
4. Mobile technologies – what assistance and services can be delivered on smartphones and tablets?

5. Triage – how to further automate the complex processes of matching clients to resources?

So I would begin by finding an eminently findable sum of money, like £500,000, and setting up the Lord Chancellor's Technology Challenge Fund. I would aim the first round at websites giving legal advice and I would open up the challenge for anyone or any institution who wishes to put forward a case for funding a project designed to increase access to justice in civil cases via the web. This would have the enormous merit of introducing a degree of positivity at relatively low cost and inclusiveness in terms of inviting responses from private providers (perhaps such as the Co-op), individual agencies (like some law centres that have good websites) and national lay advice agencies like the CAB service or Shelter. It would also lead up to the second element in a proposed Labour strategy.

Legal advice websites are not the complete answer to providing information to everyone. There is a very real digital divide: in the UK and the US, around a fifth of the population do not use the internet, and this sector will disproportionately include the poor and marginalised. However, the internet has the enormous advantage of being accessible to all – not just the poor – so that it reimposes a universalism of provision.

The second element would follow the Dutch or, in a slightly different way, the Australian experience in New South Wales in terms of remodelling legal aid so that it is seen as a service that is website-led. This involves reconceiving provision around its objective – to provide equal justice for all rather than supporting providers of a particular kind. Physical providers will be needed, but the website and an associated telephone service provides the sharp end that draws in demand and seeks to meet as much of it as it can. Physical provision, by private and other practitioners, then follows (rather than being the first port of call) for those whose needs cannot be met. The Dutch have developed a really interesting rechtwijzer.nl site which is being designed with the intent of taking users through the 'journey' of resolving their problems. New South Wales has produced a website, LawAssist, which is designed to provide assistance and information combined with telephone help. This was very much the idea behind

NHS Direct as devised under the Labour government before the guts were ripped out of it under the coalition government; it was broken up; put out to tender; expenditure cut; and its services dumbed down.

At the moment, there are two general advice websites covering England and Wales, together with a number of specialist ones, such as Shelter's housing website. There are various private practitioner websites, such as some covering road traffic accidents, which give free information and advice in return for the identification of suitable referrals. The ultimate goal would be to build up a comprehensive set of linked websites that would cover the most common areas of law on which people have problems. Like the Dutch site, these could progress from informational 'passive' sites that simply offer information to those that follow a user through the journey of resolving their case.

Testing the Dutch initiative

It is worth taking advantage of the wobbly assistance of google translator and following the Dutch site (http://www.rechtwijzer.nl/) through the assistance that it gives someone dealing with marriage breakup. We can test how the site works with a mythical case. Assume that you are 40 years old, in employment, you want to separate or divorce, and you have two children in their early teens. You are led through the system as follows:

1. The opening screen offers you a choice between saying that things are not going well; or you and your partner have decided to split; or you have already split but a new problem has occurred. Suppose you answer that you have decided to split up and register accordingly. The option on screen is actually phrased that you have decided to split up and need to arrange your affairs, signalling the process to come.
2. You are now prompted to give details on marital status, children, marriage contracts and ownership of any company.
3. The following screen begins to get interesting. You have to rate your level of educational attainment and that of your partner (for this example, assume you are both graduates with paid jobs). You

are then asked two questions. First, 'If you compare yourself with your partner do you have more or less skills to find a good solution?' You answer 'more', obviously, and then you are asked, 'If you compare yourself with your partner do you have more or less people in the area on whom you can rely?' Less, predictably.

4. The next screen leads you to think about the options. For the first time, we encounter a block of text rather than short questions to elicit answers. The text explains that you have choices. In the English google translation there is a lack of balance, with the choice phrased as between mediation and 'messy divorce'. No doubt, the Dutch is slightly more nuanced. You then have to rate on a sliding scale how much you want a messy divorce or a 'consultation separation'. You, of course, want the latter: you enter your assessment of your unreasonable partner who is all for the messiest divorce possible.

5. You are now asked if you have a good understanding of the implications of the divorce for your children, your partner, yourself and in relation to finance. You say yes to all but the last, and you are led on again.

6. You are given the option to indicate if you have other worries. If you indicate that there is 'talk' of violence just to check what is offered, the system leads you out of the mediation stream, taking you to a page explaining victim support and lawyer referral.

7. And so it goes on. Somewhere around this point, your patience with the English translations will break but if you stay with it (which will involve a lot of fiddling around returning to the site) you will be encouraged to mediate, draw up an agreed parenting plan, and will be given access to a financial calculator.

Dutch private practitioners are taking this unit from the recht-wijzer site and incorporating it into their own websites. There is potential here for a state-led revolution in how problems can be resolved, in which the funding comes for the website development and its maintenance more than for individual cases. Assistance of this kind would allow private practitioners to reduce their own costs so that they can price themselves lower in order to meet some demand formerly funded by legal aid.

Gradually, we could move to changing the model of provision. For each area of civil law there is a website accredited by the Lord Chancellor as meeting the best standards. There are annual awards and celebrations to encourage (at minimal cost) development of the best sites (maximising the value of free publicity), and private practice then builds low-cost, fixed-fee services around the website. Publicly funded provision is built around the website as a source of first response – for most people. This could be supported not by a 'telephone gateway' as envisioned by the coalition but by telephone-based assistance where experts actually seek to resolve cases, providing full services rather than simply act as a gateway onward. This, in turn, would be supplemented by physical provision on the ground. In one way, this would be a simple evolution from where we are now: in another, it would represent a fundamental paradigm shift.

As a mark of its commitment to justice, Labour should establish a methodology building on the work of the Legal Services Research Centre that was funded by the Legal Services Commission before abolition by the coalition. We want an access-to-justice index which measures the extent to which citizens recognise and solve their legal problems so that we can see how this improves. This should be published and promoted as an indicator of Labour's commitment to its ideal of equal justice for all.

For all the excitement of technological possibilities, websites and hotlines are not going to compensate for the cuts in face-to-face legal services. Courts are going to encounter increasing numbers of DIY litigants; many people are going to be involved in cases without legal assistance. If we cannot afford to reinstate cuts (and we probably cannot), then what are we actually going to do other than throw our hands up in the air and lament the loss? We are surely going to have to follow the Americans again. Faced with exactly the same situation, they have had to develop self-help centres and court-based websites, many of which use accessible document assembly programmes to help individuals through the process. Many US courts use a package originally funded by the Legal Services Corporation and which combines a visual front-end in which a character takes you on a journey to the courthouse by asking you the various questions required to complete a particular form. We need to take some sort of similar initiatives if only to avoid our courts being choked with cases that take excessive judicial time because of the lack of representation. We need to build on the experience of provision such as the Royal Courts of Justice CAB and provide 'just in time' assistance for the increasing numbers of those going through the courts on their own. We all recognise that this will not be as good as providing full legal aid, but we are going to have to act on the basis that it is better than nothing. We can scale up court-based assistance at relatively low cost and again we can use the potential of the web.

Conclusion

Civil legal aid and assistance is on the floor. After 60 years of expansion, it has been cut off at the knees. The legal advice scheme, introduced by a Conservative government in the early 1970s to cover any issue of English law has been cut back into a complicated forest of entitlements and exclusions. It has become impossible to explain simply who is entitled to legal advice or legal aid. In these circumstances, and with no realistic chance of additional funding of any size, there is no one great big idea that can be proclaimed as the answer.

Small sums of money might be squeezed out of criminal legal aid, particularly if it is possible to bring together all the players in the system. Very small sums might be releasable within the civil budget to finance the very modest innovations suggested above. However, the grim reality is that those facing the delivery of civil legal aid services face years of hard slog on minimal provision, and there is no point in hiding that. Let us, at the very least, seek to avoid making things even worse by not recognising the limitations of the current potential. In a place that is not of our own choosing, this chapter suggests what is admittedly a very cautious way forward, and the main points are summarised below. So, let's end with Coldplay: 'No one said it was easy. No one ever said it would be this hard'. But, hard it will undoubtedly be.

Summary of principal recommendations
- Greater clarity and more ambition for a Labour government's objectives for what was civil legal aid.
- A lead role for government in exploring the potential of new technology.
- A reorientation of legal aid into some form of unified and logical system that would merit the name of a community legal service (something that escaped the Labour government).

3

Constitutional Rights

Rt Hon Sadiq Khan MP

In 2015, the same year as the next general election, Magna Carta will be 800 years old, while in 2013 the European Convention on Human Rights marked the sixtieth anniversary of its coming into force. Both are, in their own way, crucial milestones in the creation, development and evolution of constitutional rights both in the United Kingdom and across the rest of the world. Both too are rich reminders of our gift to the world of constitutional protection for citizens' rights. Many nations – most notably the United States – still look to Magna Carta as the original convention protecting citizens' rights, while the European Convention on Human Rights affords protection to some 800 million people in countries from the Atlantic to the Pacific. The UK's influence spreads far and wide.

But at the same time as we celebrate these important historical occasions, our rights in the UK are being eroded. Constitutional checks and balances that allow the people of this country to hold to account those in government are being slowly chipped away, and a Labour government will face the challenge of piecing back together constitutional rights that have been threatened, weakened or removed on the Conservative–Liberal Democrat coalition government's watch. Systematic or otherwise, under the coalition there has been a piecemeal dismantling of citizens' rights to hold those in positions of authority to account.

If Labour is to reconstruct these constitutional rights, a much better case must be made as to why they are central to the lives of each and every one of us, why our democracy is strengthened by them, and why politicians should not be fearful of the checks and balances they entail.

Recent history

Another important anniversary that took place recently was the twenty-fifth birthday of Charter 88. The group, calling for constitutional and electoral reform, developed from the groundswell of opposition to what were seen as growing problems with the UK constitution during the 1980s. Charter 88 came out of the social and economic changes at that time that were seen as making our country's traditional political structures redundant, coupled with a fear that an 'elective dictatorship' as foretold by Lord Hailsham in 1976 was becoming a reality.[1] Deference for our elected representatives was on the wane, with the public no longer happy to restrict their contribution to democracy to just voting while leaving the politicians to run governments until the next election came round. They demanded more of those in power, and on a continuing basis. Key issues included that:

- That Northern Irish, Scottish and Welsh citizens increasingly viewed Westminster as a government distant to their interests and needs.
- Cases involving domestic abuses of human rights took years to resolve via the European Court of Human Rights in Strasbourg, with no domestic remedy in our own courts on offer.
- There was no adequate mechanism for scrutinising public spending through a legal right to access information.
- The country's most senior judges at the time – the Law Lords – still sat in the legislature's second chamber, raising concerns about inadequate separation of powers between legislators and those charged with upholding the law of the land.

Charter 88 sought to reflect these concerns by calling for a thriving democracy through active citizen participation. The aim was to put in place a system with appropriate checks and balances so that governments and organs of the state abide by the rule of law, just as citizens must. Moreover, citizens would be given the tools to hold to account governments so that they did indeed abide by the rule of law. The Charter's specific demands included devolution for Wales, Scotland and Northern Ireland, a Bill of Rights, freedom of information legislation, an independent and reformed judiciary, a democratic second chamber and proportional representation.

As a movement, the Charter formed the latest chapter in a long, rich tradition of British reform initiatives on human rights and civil liberties – from Magna Carta, through the Bill of Rights, the Habeas Corpus Act 1679, the Great Reform Acts, the Chartists and the Universal Declaration of Human Rights, to the European Convention on Human Rights signed in 1950. As citizens accumulated more rights, and associated responsibilities, less power was concentrated in the hands of governments and the ruling classes, all with the intention of preventing arbitrary abuses of power.

Labour's track record

The enthusiasm of those involved with Charter 88 proved infectious to many in and around politics during the 1990s. John Smith was an early and enthusiastic supporter of the Charter. He was one of a growing number who agreed that Whitehall needed reining in, that unfettered power leads to bad decision making by public authorities and that democracy extends much further than the right to vote.

Labour's manifestos from 1992 onwards reflected the aims of the Charter. A central theme was the dramatic widening of political participation and devolution of power away from the centre – in short, the greater empowerment of citizens. There is no doubt that these vibrant and exciting proposals for political and constitutional reform helped propel the Labour Party into government after 18 years in the wilderness. The mix of commitments on civil liberties and constitutional reform contributed to Labour's fresh, modern outlook, as being fit and prepared to take on the challenges of twenty-first century Britain.

The constitutional changes the Labour government made were arguably its most radical achievements. Vernon Bogdanor, Research Professor at the Institute for Contemporary British History at King's College London, refers to this period as 'comparable to that of the years of the Great Reform Act of 1832 or the Parliament Act of 1911.'[2] Contrary to the accusations levelled at Labour by many people over these years, a central theme was the devolution of power. Cardiff, Edinburgh and Belfast were given their own elected assemblies and governments, and a London-wide authority returned to the capital after a gap of 14 years. Judicial independence was bolstered through the creation of a Supreme Court, and individual citizens were given additional powers under the Human Rights Act 1998 and the Freedom of Information Act 2000.

This has, however, not always been easy territory for Labour. Traditionally it has found it difficult to reconcile individual rights with collective spirit. Labour has seen a strong state as the means through which economic vested interests can be tackled and wealth redistributed, and that the state can develop vested interests that lead it to abuse its power wasn't always fully realised.

Those attracted by Charter 88 understood that strengthening the rights of citizens and bolstering constitutional checks and balances should be absolutely central to Labour policy, and, indeed, the Labour government's track record was impressive. It devolved power away from Westminster, passed the Human Rights Act, established a Supreme Court (under the Constitutional Reform Act 2005), and it empowered citizens to have access to information about how central and local government operates. All this amounted to a substantial shift of democratic structures and systems in favour of alternatives less dominated by the executive and the legislature. By 2010 the chances of Lord Hailsham's elective dictatorship becoming a reality had significantly diminished.

But it wasn't all rosy on Labour's watch and, particularly after 9/11, the government faced difficult choices. A government must prize liberty, but it must also fight crime, anti-social behaviour, terrorism and unfair treatment by commercial interests. The test is always how to strike the right balance. Unfortunately, on some important issues – for example, the right to detain terrorism suspects for 90 days before they are charged and on ID cards – the government got the balance wrong, paying too little attention to the rights of citizens.

The truth of the matter is that security and liberty are not, despite what some might argue, mutually exclusive. In fact, both are equally important. Lord Neuberger, the Supreme Court President, hit the nail on the head when he said:

> *The historic justification, and primary duty, of any civilised government is to ensure the defence of the realm from foreign threats and the rule of law at home – i.e. to ensure its citizens are free from both foreign and domestic threats. The state has a duty to protect the rights and freedoms of all its citizens including, but not only, their security.*[3]

These are words a new Labour government should bear in mind.

Constitutional rights under the coalition

With the advent of the coalition, the agenda has changed. By the end of Labour's time in office, the party that gave the country the Human Rights Act, freedom of information, devolution, separation of powers and a Supreme Court was criticised in some quarters for being too statist, too controlling and too casual with the rights of citizens. The Conservatives and Liberal Democrats capitalised on this, and the coalition came to power promising to 'restore the rights and freedoms of individuals in the face of encroaching state power', and, indeed, Labour has supported some of the changes they have brought in, including:

- reducing pre-charge detention in terrorism cases from 28 days to 14
- scrapping ID cards and
- reforming the Regulation of Investigatory Powers Act (RIPA) 2000 to increase the safeguards that prevent councils abusing the parts of the legislation on the use of surveillance and monitoring techniques.

On other fronts, however, the rights of citizens have been under attack:

- Legal aid has been cut back dramatically, with most social welfare law stripped from the scope of what is eligible.

- Restrictions on 'no win no fee' (also known as 'conditional fee') arrangements, closing down this important route by which many people obtained access to the legal system.
- Judicial review has been curtailed, and there are proposals to weaken further this important tool.
- Public information has become more difficult to access because of tighter rules on freedom of information requests, and increasing amounts of public money are handed over to private companies that are beyond the scope of the law.
- The role of secret courts has been extended into civil cases without adequate judicial checks and balances on their use.
- Fees have been introduced for employment tribunals and equality impact assessments have been abolished, making for a worrying erosion of workplace rights.
- Legislation has been introduced to restrict third-party campaign expenditure, which will muzzle charities and campaign groups and restrict their ability to contribute to our democratic processes.

The prevailing orthodoxy among Conservatives is one of governments being free to take decisions without fear of being held to account – even, on some occasions, free to ignore the rule of law. Judges applying the laws of the land are lambasted for making up policy and exceeding their responsibility. The irony is that historically the Conservative Party has been naturally mistrustful of the power of the state, and should firmly be on the side of mechanisms to rein in that power. Instead, they appear relaxed about seeing important checks and balances on abuse of state power removed.

Mixed in with this desire for central control is some fervent anti-Europeanism and a belief that wrong-headed, unelected European judges in Strasbourg want to impose their version of human rights on the UK. But let's be clear, implementation of increasing calls on Conservative benches to tear up the Human Rights Act 1998 and to withdraw from the European Court of Human Rights would be a disastrous step backwards, increasing the power of the state to trample on individuals' rights. If the UK does withdraw from the court, it would send a clear signal to states with far more dubious human rights records that we no longer had confidence in the international human

rights framework, placing the UK on a par with Belarus as one of
the European nations not signed up to the European Convention on
Human Rights. It would also send out a worrying message about the
UK's belief in the rule of law.

The Conservatives' solution is a nebulous 'British Bill of Rights'
to replace the Human Rights Act 1998, but it has never been clear
which rights in that Act would be ditched or if any additional rights
might be included. The clear impression given is that the Conservatives do not believe in rights for all but only in certain rights for
certain types of people. This impression was reinforced in the appen-
dix to a Commission on a Bill of Rights report in which a paper by
Conservative lawyer Martin Howe QC proposes a hierarchical Bill of
Rights in which only certain citizens are eligible for all rights – which
does not bode well for the vulnerable, the marginalised or foreigners.[4]
This is a far cry from the universality of human rights as envisaged by
those who drafted the European Convention or the UN Declaration.
The party of David Maxwell Fyfe and Winston Churchill – architects
of the European Convention on Human Rights – would not recognise
the insular, narrow-horizon Conservative Party of today.

The next general election

The battle lines for the next general election are being drawn. On
the one side are the Conservatives who see democracy as nothing
more than elections. Their obsession is with the size of the state, not
necessarily the power of the state, and their desire is to be free to do
as they please once in government, unfettered by citizens' concerns
about the rule of law. Their aim is the preservation of existing elites
and the protection of powerful blocs. Uncomfortably in the middle are
the Liberal Democrats, who have been discredited by their readiness
to acquiesce to dominant Conservative views on constitutional rights.

Firmly on the other side is Labour, with a belief in the importance of a healthy civic society, constitutional checks and balances,
and citizens empowered to seek recourse when things go wrong. That
Labour is on the side of the individual citizen sits squarely within
Ed Miliband's wider narrative of taking on powerful elites, whether
that be bankers and their bonuses, Rupert Murdoch and irresponsible

journalism, train companies and exorbitant price hikes or utility companies and the stifling cost of energy. When James Purnell (cabinet member from 2007 to 2009) said Labour had been 'too hands off with the market and too hands on with the state' he was dead right. Lessons have been learned from the mistakes made while Labour was in government and from those made by the coalition, and Labour should emphasise this in the lead up to the next general election.

Labour's aim should be to turn passive citizens into active citizens in order to refocus the economy on responsible capitalism. The party must show that it sympathises with individuals' fear and resentment about their helplessness in the face of powerful vested interests. Individual voters need to trust in the political system to hold to account bankers, corporate giants, media conglomerates and, yes, politicians. Core to this is enshrining and defending the public's basic rights, clarifying precisely what citizens can expect from the public sector and, in addition, their recourse to challenge unresponsive public agencies. This is part of active democracy – not some unnecessary hindrance or obstructive bureaucracy.

In practice, this means no retreat from the Human Rights Act and the European Court of Human Rights. We want to reform these institutions; the Conservatives want us to withdraw from them altogether. It is the elderly, the disabled, the poor, and the victims of crime and homelessness who benefit from our human rights laws. From the elderly woman who now has the right to grow old in dignity, to the rape victim who no longer has to face the ordeal of being cross-examined by the accused. Vital protections too for the children of women fleeing domestic violence who no longer need to be taken into care, for individuals suffering discrimination on grounds of sexual orientation and for others seeking to protect journalistic sources. Without these safeguards, it is the marginalised, the vulnerable and the excluded who will suffer.

Running through all of what we offer is a confidence and belief in the power of people to play a role in our democracy. We will heed the comments of author Timothy Garton Ash, famed for his work on the blossoming freedom movements in 1980s communist Eastern Europe, who said, 'one measure of how democratic a political system is, is precisely the degree of ... pressure from below on the people in power.'[5] This should be our yardstick of success.

Summary of principal recommendations

- To ensure further devolution of power from Westminster, particularly in England, to help address the growing sense of disempowerment.
- To restore judicial review to its rightful place as a key constitutional tool. This is because we believe it is right that the failures of the West Coast Mainline franchising, or the shabby cancelling of the Building Schools for the Future programme should be scrutinised via judicial review.
- To extend freedom of information to cover the delivery of public services by private companies, because we believe citizens should know what G4S, Serco, Capita, A4E and others are doing with our money when delivering multi-million pound contracts.

4

Employment Law

Catherine Atkinson, John Bowers QC and Tom Jones

This chapter addresses the key issues we think an incoming Labour government will need to tackle. It is tempting to focus simply on a root and branch reversal of the policies of the Conservative–Liberal Democrat coalition, but we seek to go beyond that and suggest radical changes to areas that are causing concern.

Scope of employment: Worker status

Our employment law has been built upon a definition of contracts of employment that does not fit the reality of work in the twenty-first century. British employment law is derived from the nineteenth and early twentieth century law of master and servant. Employment protections divide working people between employees and the self-employed, with the latter working under a contract for services (as distinct from an employment contract) and generally considered to be outside the protections of employment law.

The rights not to be unfairly dismissed, to reasonable notice before dismissal, to maternity and paternity leave and to redundancy payments only apply to 'employees'. Other protections apply to all workers – e.g. under the National Minimum Wage Act 1998 and the Part-Time Workers (Prevention of Less Favourable Treatment) Regulations 2000. Some further definitions complicate the position in that rights under Part 5 of the Equality Act 2010 extend to 'employment', but that concept is defined to include not only those who work under a contract of employment but also those who contract personally to do work.

In relation to the Employment Rights Act 1996 (ERA) an employee means 'an individual who has entered into or works under ... a contract of employment'.[1] The ERA[2] defines a 'worker' as an individual who has:

> entered into or works under ... a contract of employment or;
> any other contract whether express or implied, ... whereby the
> individual undertakes to do or perform personally any work
> or services for another party to the contract whose status is
> not by virtue of the contract that of a client or customer of any
> profession or business undertaking carried on by the individual.

Modern work relationships

Over the past thirty or so years there has been a movement to part-time, temporary and casual work, and agency work – so-called 'precarious employment'. There is a whole spectrum of workers, but far from acknowledging the spectrum our system generally lumps all non-employees together as being self-employed. This aggregates into one category of 'self-employment' all sorts of arrangements, including freelancer IT technicians, construction workers, office temps, financial consultants and part-time cleaners.

The contractual basis of our employment law as between an employer and employee does not provide easy solutions to triangular or even quadrilateral employment relationships, with agency workers or umbrella companies offering to a client individuals who have obtained work (typically via an agency) on a fixed term contract of employment through which their skills are provided to the client of the agency. Umbrella companies, for fees, provide administrative, tax and other support. (We use 'umbrella company' to mean an entity solely or mainly set up to provide a particular staff member or small group of staff members.)

The functions of hirer, remunerator, manager and user may be shared between different employing entities so that no one bilateral relationship can give a complete picture as to who acts as 'the employer'. There is a reluctance to accept or construct multilateral employment with more than one employing entity, even in situations where the employment functions are genuinely distributed between more than one distinct organisation.

Tax avoidance

There are differences that should be recognised between those who voluntarily work through companies and those seeking low-skilled work who have no real choice as to their employment status. However, both have implications not only in relation to avoiding employer responsibility but also relating to taxation.

Several attempts have been made by Labour governments before to deal with false self-employment. Legislation on intermediaries sought to crack down on personal service companies but, since its introduction, there appears to have been a significant rise in the use of umbrella companies. Umbrella companies act as employers to agency contractors who work under a fixed term contract assignment, usually through a recruitment agency. The umbrella company will usually issue invoices to the recruitment agency or client and will pay the contractor, usually through PAYE. However, the contractor will be able to claim tax reliefs (in the form of travel and subsistence) to reduce taxable income.

Sham standard form contracts

Some companies seeking to class their workers as self-employed use standard form contracts that deliberately include clauses inconsistent with an employee–employer relationship – for example, a 'substitution' clause, allowing the 'self-employed' person to designate a substitute at their discretion, or a 'no mutuality' clause stipulating that the employer is not obligated to offer work and the 'self-employed' person is not obligated to accept work. The courts have gone some way to try and deal with sham contracts.

The Supreme Court in *Autoclenz Ltd v Belcher and Others*[3] acknowledged that a critical difference between contracts of employment and other commercial contracts was often the unequal bargaining power between the parties in circumstances where some organisations offering work were in a position to dictate written terms which the other party has to accept.

The question is how should our employment law combat collusion and exploitation while enabling flexible working patterns to flourish?

Redefining employee and worker: The concept of 'personal employment contracts'

We agree with Dr Freedland of Oxford University, who in his important work in this area suggests redefining our employment law around his concept of 'personal employment contracts'. These comprise 'contracts for employment or work to be carried out normally in person and not in the conduct of an independent business or professional practice'.[4] Those working under 'personal employment contracts' Dr Freedland terms 'workers', and the other party to the contract he terms 'employing entity or employing party' rather than 'employer'. This category of worker would include all dependent and semi-dependent workers.

Rebuttable presumptions

We believe that we should go further than the 'purposive' approach adopted in the *Autoclenz* case to the interpretation of contracts, and create a presumption of employee or worker status that can only be rebutted by clear evidence to the contrary. Creating a rebuttable presumption in favour of the application of worker/employment rights would underscore the need to mitigate unequal bargaining power between many employers and workers and should better ensure that employment protections are enjoyed by those they are designed to protect.

Joint and several liability

Rather than the legal requirement of finding the 'agency' to be the employer as asserted in a written contract, even where that agency is neither the manager nor the user, the concept of 'employing entities' far more accurately reflects the reality of working relationships in the twenty-first century.

Unfair contract terms

Compared with consumers, those working under standard form contracts have little protection. To protect consumers from unfair standard form contracts we have the Unfair Contract Terms Act 1977 (UCTA) and the European Directive on Unfair Terms in Consumer Contracts.[5] Section 3 of UCTA confers on judges the power to invalidate unfair and unreasonable contractual terms. It applies to either contracts where one party is a 'consumer' or where the contract is made on the other party's 'written standard terms of business'.

The Law Commission in 2005 proposed draft legislation that provided for separate treatment of standard form contracts of employment.[6] The proposed legislation provided much weaker protection to employees than is enjoyed by consumers. It related only to terms which 'exclude or restrict liability for breach of contract' and did not declare many kinds of terms to be presumptively unfair. Furthermore, it was drafted so as to be restricted to 'employment contracts'. However, it provides a statutory framework that could be used to enact legislation to deal with unfair contract terms in standard form contracts, especially where these purport to exclude implied terms and conditions that workers would reasonably expect to rely upon.

– Unfair contract terms in contracts for work

Between 1959 and 2006 New South Wales courts could undertake a 'review of contracts and arrangements' under which work is performed on the grounds of 'unfairness'.[7] The courts had a broad discretion to make orders in relation to contracts or arrangements that were 'unfair, harsh or unconscionable', 'against the public interest' or designed to avoid the remuneration, terms and conditions that workers would have enjoyed as a consequence of statutory or industrial instrument entitlement.[8] The Industrial Relations Commission[9] was able to order complete rescission, variation of terms and payment of any money considered just in the circumstances of the case.[10] Extending the concept of unfair contract terms to employees and workers and providing a jurisdiction to intervene and remedy the use of unfair contract terms in the employment context would prevent abuses while enabling flexible but fair work practices.

Regulating hours and methods of work

In this section we consider the regulation of unsatisfactory practices relating to work methods.

Interns

There is growing concern about the poor treatment of interns, who are usually people at the start of their careers and open to exploitation.[11] This is a major problem. In 2010 the Institute for Public Policy Research estimated that there were 100,000 people on unpaid internships in the UK. Most are doing actual work, contributing clear value to the employing organisation, but they are not being paid. They do this work in the hope either that the experience will increase their chances of gaining paid work elsewhere in the future, or that the organisation in question will subsequently employ them under a contract of employment.

This can be simple exploitation of vulnerable persons, and in most cases is already unlawful under national minimum wage legislation if the work they do can be properly identified and quantified. However, the understandable desire to improve rather than hinder one's future employment prospects acts as a significant restraint on individuals challenging a failure to pay the minimum wage.

In many sectors (for instance, law, finance and charities) an unpaid internship, probably in a central London office, is becoming a standard career entry pathway. The silent majority who cannot afford independently to finance such work (having already borne the cost of university and possibly professional education) are effectively excluded from access to this gateway to employment. This is a clear restriction on social mobility and equality of opportunity, and a deeply regressive development.

An internship is not the same as a work experience or a work-shadowing placement, and the two should be distinguished in legislation.

Nor should there be much risk of confusion between unpaid interns and volunteers. Helping out twice a week with the scout troop or at the Age Concern shop is not the same as working 14-hour days doing data entry at a national newspaper. Most of the time, there is scant risk of confusion of the two, but in areas where lines are blurred, legislation should err on the side of the right of individuals to be paid for their work.

It is an underlying precept of employment law that individuals may not waive their fundamental rights. The most fundamental right of all is to be paid for one's work, but this principle is flouted by the 'unpaid internship'.

Interns who do regular work contributing value should be paid at least a minimum wage for it. A future Labour government should define what an internship is, and what it is not. Unpaid internships should be outlawed from the workplace save in exceptional cases. Such legislation must also make clear the legal responsibility for the hosting organisation for the health and safety of the intern, and that limits are placed on the use of internships to guard against misuse by employers.

Zero hours contracts

The legal exterior of a zero hours contract (ZHC) is typically bland: the employer is not obliged to offer the worker any work, and the worker is not obliged to accept any work that may be offered.

For the employer, the model worker is reborn: flexible, able to sustain themselves when not in work, and capable of being disposed of at will. For the worker, the ZHC represents a modern-day early morning line up, once prevalent in the docks (then known as recruitment on the coals) and agriculture, but now managed by the written word, the phone and the internet. The employee is unquestionably subordinate to the employer in every sense. Under a ZHC an employee is permanently 'on call' and with that comes insecurity and everything that goes with it – stress, social dislocation and alienation.

The number of workers on ZHCs is not officially quantified. Research by Unite and the Resolution Foundation has indicated that up to 5 million workers may be employed in this way and that ZHCs are increasingly prevalent in all areas of the economic landscape.[12]

One employer – Cineworld – is reported to have 80 per cent of its 3,600 workers on ZHCs.

ZHCs are a symptom not of success but of economic failure, creating fear and uncertainty in the lives of disempowered workers who have no option but to accept the position; the alternative being no prospect of any income because an individual who refuses the 'offer' of work on a ZHC puts at risk their benefits.

The acceleration in the prevalence of ZHCs in the public and third sectors reflects current budgetary pressures on public authorities and the relentless drive to limit the price of the services that they commission. This in turn creates downward pressure on the terms and conditions of workers in firms providing services to public authorities. The major growth of ZHCs in, for instance, the social care sector, is a direct consequence of this. However, it should be noted that ZHCs are not limited to unskilled low-paid sectors, with their use also rising in clinical areas of the NHS, such as psychiatry and even cardiology.

The argument put forward by some employers that the ZHC has the benefit of allowing the worker to have the flexibility of second jobs is spurious. While some students or retired people may welcome the flexibility to decline work and the opportunity to have a second job, for most people, most of the time, a ZHC is an unsatisfactory and unacceptable way to live, with wide weekly/monthly variations in income making financial planning impossible. The freedom to supplement one's meagre income with a second job should not be considered a benefit, nor should the 'liberty' to decline work that may not be offered.

Workers on ZHCs have the statutory rights to paid holiday and the national minimum wage. However, whether the worker benefits from any additional employment rights is dependent on whether they have the status of an employee or a worker. The legal tests for employment will generally exclude the worker contracted on genuinely zero hours from having the status of an employee. Rights that are attached to status as an employee provide for basic fairness and grant employees redress where those rights are breached – for example, the right to claim unfair dismissal. Those rights are a valuable asset as well as being vital to day-to-day exigencies such as getting a mortgage or tenancy, paying the bills and reducing reliance on the benefits system.

In the majority of cases, by using a ZHC the employer avoids those rights and obligations, stripping away workplace rights and leaving the worker with the employment status of the self-employed, even though this reflects neither that individual's wish nor the underlying reality.

Alexander Ehmann of the Institute of Directors summed up the situation perfectly while attempting to defend ZHCs in August 2013: 'It is ostensibly a buyers' market at the moment, with the unemployment levels that exist; and those businesses [using ZHCs] don't feel the same pressures, I'd imagine, of losing high turnovers of staff. They will do again, and they will need to change their practices, I suspect.'[13] It would be wrong to simply wait for the pendulum to swing back. The current high levels of unemployment are enabling unscrupulous employers to increase the rate of exploitation of workers at the lower end of the labour market.

We recommend that ZHCs should be outlawed because they fail to offer any real protection to the worker, whose individual position within the economy vis-à-vis his or her employer is so weak as to render notions of choice and 'a fair bargain' meaningless.

– Legal options

As an alternative to prohibition, there are legislative steps that could be readily implemented to regulate ZHCs. Section 23 of the Employment Relations Act 1999 could be used to confer existing statutory rights, modified to fit the circumstances, on individuals of a specified description (workers on ZHCs) against an employer – for example, entitling the ZHC worker to particulars of employment (e.g. on pay, hours and holidays) after 26 weeks.

We recommend an amendment to the definition of employee within the Employment Rights Act 1996 to provide a statutory presumption that any individual engaged on a ZHC is an employee, and not self-employed.

Regulation 15 of the National Minimum Wage Regulations defines 'time work' as not just time when a worker is working but also 'time when a worker is available at or near a place of work for the purpose of doing time work and is required to be available for work', except where the worker lives near their place of work and can be at home.

There is a similar definition in paragraph 17 of the Agricultural Wages Order.

Consequently, regulation 15 and paragraph 17 should be modified to include in the definition of 'work' time when the worker is required to be available for work and is prohibited by the contract from working for another employer ('exclusivity'). This would have the effect of bringing periods of exclusivity of work into the national minimum wage calculation. The consequent increase in the cost of exclusivity would have the effect of limiting those periods when the worker is required to be 'on call' and thus enable them to manage their time and take other work at other periods.

Section 1 of the Employment Rights Act 1996, which requires employers to provide employment particulars, including 'any conditions relating to hours of work (including any terms relating to normal working hours)' should require employers to state for each employee a minimum number of work hours (say 16 a week) and a maximum number of hours when the individual is required to be available for work. Limits could be set over a reasonable 'reference period' (probably 12-week cycles as for other rights).

Exclusivity clauses, which require workers to be available for work and prohibit them from working for another employer at that time, should be banned outright, or alternatively should be interpreted as restrictive covenants restraining the worker from engaging in their trade. Exclusivity clauses should be strictly interpreted against the employer and be deemed unenforceable if they are unreasonable and not justified.

Other mechanisms to achieve similar results, but which fall short of banning ZHCs, could include:

- Legally enforceable collective agreements or wages councils to apply the 'living wage' (discussed in the next section) across sectors, including provisions defining 'work' in the way described above.
- Provisions that treat ZHCs as an opt-out or derogation from employment rights which can only be agreed following independent advice (similar to a settlement agreement) from a recognised trade union or a legal adviser.
- Provisions that treat ZHCs as a derogation or opt-out which can

only be agreed under a collective agreement with a recognised trade union.

- A restriction on the proportion of workers employed by an employer who are on ZHCs and/or a restriction on the number or proportion of a workers' hours which are 'zero hours'. The number and proportion would be published in company accounts.
- The proportion of workers on ZHCs should be no more than reasonably needed to cover genuine fluctuations which cannot be anticipated (for instance, not just known holiday periods).
- Where no work is provided for a period of three weeks the worker should be entitled to request a severance payment of the hourly rate multiplied by the number of weeks worked since the start of the engagement. This would not serve to replace any redundancy payment due.
- A requirement that public and third sector organisations commissioning procedures include a stipulation that bidders do not utilise ZHCs.

Overarching any or all of these changes there should be an 'Employment Inspectorate' to survey and enforce employment rights, reducing the cost to the public purse of the tribunal system and, adequately resourced, providing a more effective method of enforcement. In accordance with the principle that the polluter pays, an Employment Inspectorate could be part-funded by a small increase in employer national insurance contributions, with fines to be levied by the Inspectorate providing an additional funding stream. Businesses which were not subject to a fine or had less than the average adverse number of tribunal claims within a defined period might be eligible for a tax rebate, providing for the first time a tax incentive for good employer behaviour.

Living wage

A living wage for all those working in Whitehall departments was a Labour manifesto pledge in the 2010 election. Building on this was a central pillar of Ed Miliband's Labour leadership campaign, and he has promised that it will feature prominently in Labour's 2015 manifesto.

Labour councils are gradually adopting the living wage for their employees and directly contracted staff, and even Boris Johnson has announced his support. 'Living wage local councils' are likely to number at least 30, including some of the biggest local authorities, by the next election. The next phase is to extend the living wage into the private sector, and some private sector firms have already signed up to it. The Labour front bench is currently exploring the possibilities of Living Wage Zones and other tax reliefs as incentives to encourage private sector employers to pay the living wage, and we strongly support this.

A voluntary and incentive-based approach will inevitably be partial and provide less than full coverage. A voluntary strategy leaves those employers paying the living wage exposed to being undercut by those who do not. Legislation to make a living wage an obligation for all except micro-businesses would ensure a level playing field and mitigate some of the worst aspects of the cost of living crisis.

In our view the right approach is therefore for legislation to be passed, or the existing minimum wage legislation to be amended, to require the payment of the living wage.

Tribunal reform

There are several issues in relation to employment tribunals that the next Labour government should address.

Representation

It is vital for employees to have a level playing field in employment tribunals. This is the key to increasing the effectiveness of the tribunals, and there is much research indicating that those bringing or defending cases without effective representation are placed at a disadvantage. The Donovan Commission recommended in 1968 that tribunals should be 'easily accessible, informal, speedy and inexpensive'.[14] Although employment tribunals were intended to be informal in this way, the increasing range and complexity of the law which they apply has rendered it difficult for an employee to conduct a case without some form of representation (including law centre or advice centre representatives). Trade union officers used to often act as representatives in tribunals, but this is rare today.

Often there is an imbalance of representation, with the respondent having a battery of high-powered legal representation while the claimant represents him or herself. This may be seen to be inevitable given the amount of money at stake in some cases. Some of the multiple equal pay cases for example have resulted in awards of hundreds of millions of pounds. Tribunals were originally intended to be much less formal than the courts.

It is also true that some have seen employment tribunals as a revenue source and that unscrupulous advisers need to be controlled further in the interests of protecting those they represent. For example, with some 'no win no fee' representation (particularly common in equal pay claims), the 'small print' may say that in the event of a change of solicitors (even for reasons of dissatisfaction with the service provided) up to £1,000 becomes payable, and this may be after very little work has been carried out.

There is an existing regulatory framework under the Compensation (Regulated Claims Management Services) Order 2006,[15] which gives power to the regulator to authorise persons providing claims management services. There is, however, concern that this has not been sufficiently robust to curb regular abuses that affect some of the most vulnerable. There is a case for provision of public funding for bodies such as the Bar Pro Bono Unit and law centres.

Fees

The central question is whether fees will interfere with claimants' abilities to pursue their cases. It is too early to say definitively how the introduction of fees in October 2013 will affect the functioning of tribunals, but the high level of those fees is likely to militate against claimants pursuing properly brought allegations. The present indications are that the number of claims has considerably reduced. The original purpose of the employment tribunal was that it should be an easier mechanism for enforcing claims than that provided by the courts. Part of the government's reasoning for introducing fees, as expressed in their consultation document, was so that claimants should think through putting in a claim, but, bearing in mind the stress and costs likely to be involved, it is ludicrous to suggest that claimants do not do think through claims in the absence of fees.

It is grossly unfair that only claimants have to pay such fees. The new system is not an attempt merely to reduce *weak* claims (as the coalition government asserts) but all claims. A major problem is that employees have to pay these fees up front.

As Baroness Drake said in the House of Lords debates on the Employment Tribunals and Employment Appeal Tribunal Fees Order 2013:[16]

> ... *[the claimants'] motive is not always compensation. They can often feel frustrated and humiliated at the way they have been treated, and it becomes important to have a public record that they were badly treated ... They may bring a case for unfair dismissal because they know that unless they can win that claim they cannot get a decent reference or a comparable job.*

The fees here are higher than those in the Supreme Court, which is a preposterous position.

Moving discrimination claims from county courts to employment tribunals?

At present, employment tribunals have jurisdiction only over employment disputes (although this is broadly defined), and all discrimination claims brought relating to goods, facilities, services, housing and education go to the county court. The county court is not an ideal venue for such claims, and indeed only some are designated to conduct discrimination hearings, which means that litigants and witnesses have to travel further than they would need to for most employment tribunals.

Although the county court judge sits with assessors for such claims, it is not always easy to find such assessors. While county court judges have training in diversity, they would not deal with such claims as regularly as employment tribunal judges and they are not as familiar with such concepts as indirect discrimination and justification. Hardly a week goes by without a tribunal dealing with a discrimination claim, whereas for a county court judge, even at a designated county court, it would be likely to be less than one a year. Furthermore, the differentiation between county court and employment tribunal leads to costly jurisdictional debates that could be avoided.

We consider that there is an overwhelming case for allocating all discrimination disputes to employment tribunals, with the possible exception of housing cases where the county court has considerable experience.

The enforcement of judgments

Ministry of Justice figures show that 40 per cent of tribunal awards in England and Wales are not paid within 18 months of the hearing and fewer than 50 per cent are paid in full.[17] The 2013 study into *Payment of Tribunal Awards*,[18] carried out for the government by an independent research company prior to the introduction of the new employment tribunal rules of procedure, interviewed over 1,000 successful claimants in England, Wales and Scotland between May and June 2013 to examine whether awards were paid, the reasons for non-payment and the effect of enforcement action. The findings reveal that only 49 per cent of claimants had been paid their tribunal award in full; 16 per cent had been paid part of their award; and 35 per cent had received nothing at all. The most common reason for non-payment was that the employer had become insolvent, but many claimants whose employers were citing this reason believed that the company they had worked for was now trading again under a different name. Another common reason for non-payment was the employer simply refusing to pay. Of those claimants who had pursued enforcement action to recover their award, only around half were successful in receiving either all or some of it.

In many insolvency cases there is no realistic chance of a successful claimant getting any money at all. Furthermore, in order to enforce an employment tribunal order, it is at present necessary to register it in the county court, an extra procedure not required for other civil law matters. Because of this, and because few employment solicitors have experience of county court enforcement mechanisms, the responsibility for enforcement should be taken away from claimants and handled by a public enforcement office for tribunal awards using HMRC to collect. HMRC has proved effective in enforcing minimum wage regulations.

Range of reasonable responses test

There has been a whole series of cases over many years that interpret the general terms of the unfair dismissal provisions as requiring tribunals to operate a 'band of reasonable responses' test. This is similar to the stand-off approach traditionally adopted by the courts in challenges to public authorities in judicial review proceedings whereby intervention is on the basis that the authority acted as no reasonable authority could act. The band of reasonable responses test has no real place in private sector disputes. It unbalances matters in favour of the employer. This may be seen most clearly in the judgment of Browne Wilkinson J in *Iceland Frozen Foods v Jones* [1992] IRLR 439:

> *(2) in applying the section the Industrial Tribunal must consider the reasonableness of the employer's conduct not simply whether they (the members of the Industrial Tribunal) considered that the dismissal to be fair; (3) in judging the reasonableness of the employer's conduct the Industrial Tribunal must not substitute its decision as to what was the right course to adopt for that of the employer; (4) in many (though not all) cases there is a band of reasonable responses to the employee's conduct within which one employer might reasonably take one view, another quite reasonably take another; (5) the function of the Industrial Tribunal, as an industrial jury, is to determine whether in the particular circumstances of each case the decision to dismiss the employee fell within the band of reasonable responses which a reasonable employer might have adopted.*

There is a particular problem now that all unfair dismissals are heard by a judge alone (following the employment tribunal rule changes in 2013) so that claimants will not have someone with experience of the workplace on the panel. It is now necessary to redraft

s. 98(4) Employment Rights Act 1996 and eliminate the focus on the reasonableness of the employer's actions. There should only be a straightforward consideration of whether dismissal was fair or unfair as considered by an employment tribunal, retaining a reference to equity and substantial merits of the case so that it is what the tribunal considers reasonable.

Reinstatement

Reinstatement was originally intended to be the primary remedy for unfair dismissal. It was a simple equation; the unfair loss of a job should be redressed by regaining that job; compensation was viewed as merely a secondary remedy. The number of employees who are now being reinstated is tiny. In the period from April 2011 to April 2012 there were only 5 re-engagement orders out of 5,100 successful unfair dismissal claims. It is true that the last thing that many employees want is to go back to the employer who dismissed them (and often who made them angry and distressed). However, there is resistance by tribunals to make orders that are often based on old fashioned notions of whether trust and confidence could be maintained on a return to work. Some of this is a hangover from the doctrine about not specifically enforcing contracts of employment because it is a personal relationship; but in the complex modern workplace that is usually a quaint notion. Furthermore, even if reinstatement is ordered by a tribunal it is frequently ignored by the employer because the only sanction on the employer is a financial deterrent, which they may prefer to pay.

One aspect of the current scene that militates against reinstatement orders being made is the length of time between dismissals and cases being heard. Twelve to fifteen months is not an uncommon gap and the delays may be increased due to reductions in funding. Such delays should be reduced by an appropriate allocation of resources to the tribunal system, which has been significantly cut back during the term of the Conservative–Liberal Democrat coalition.

It is difficult to judge how it will be possible to get back to reinstatement as the primary remedy, but we believe that there are two possible ways forward:

1. To generalise the interim relief power, which at present is only available in trade union and whistleblower dismissals; it requires the employee to seek such a remedy within 7 days of the dismissal. A preliminary hearing before the tribunal would then be held at which the tribunal decides whether to continue the existing contract, thus preserving the status quo until the final hearing.
2. The civil courts could be given the power to specifically enforce the contract of employment.

Withdrawal of lay members

The Enterprise and Regulatory Reform Act 2013 prohibits lay members from sitting on the Employment Appeal Tribunal (EAT) unless a judge orders otherwise. This removes the characteristic that since 1975 has distinguished the EAT from its unsuccessful predecessor, the National Industrial Relations Court, which was introduced by the Heath government's Industrial Relations Act 1971. Although the issues on appeal can only raise points of law, the value of the lay members was the knowledge of both sides of industry that they brought to their role, and that they often brought experience of having sat on the tribunals. Given the relatively low cost of bringing them back, lay members should be reinstated because of the confidence that they can build up in the system as a whole.

Summary of principal recommendations

- Ways should be sought to ensure employment law combats collusion and exploitation while enabling flexible working patterns to flourish, including adopting 'personal employment contracts' and creating a rebuttable presumption in favour of the application of worker/employment rights.
- Extending the concept of unfair contract terms to employees and workers.
- A future Labour government should define what an internship is, and unpaid internships should be outlawed from the workplace.
- Zero hours contracts should be outlawed save in exceptional circumstances.
- Legislation should be passed to require the payment of the 'living wage'.
- Discrimination disputes should be allocated to employment tribunals rather than county courts.
- Responsibility for enforcement of employment tribunal awards should be taken away from claimants and handled by a public enforcement office, using HMRC to collect.

5

Energy Law and Policy

Gordon Nardell QC

It is bad news for government when opposition dominates the news agenda. It's even worse news when opposition dominates the policy agenda. Ed Miliband's bold intervention on energy prices at the 2013 Party Conference – his condemnation of the 'broken energy market' and the surprise announcement of a 20-month retail price freeze – precisely judged the public mood.

It is easy to underestimate the significance of this policy initiative. For sure, it firmly staked out the cost-of-living territory as ground dominated by Labour in this key pre-election period; but, just as importantly, it signalled the return of state intervention as a defining feature of Labour's economic policy. This was the real reason why Labour's opponents were so badly caught out.

Does energy have to be left to the markets?

On the day of the announcement, Centrica responded with extraordinary hyperbole, decrying the new policy as 'unworkable' and that it would result in the lights going out. Other members of the 'Big Six' UK energy suppliers swiftly followed suit, warning among other things that the 'political risk' created by Labour would scare off investment.

Coalition ministers duly lined up to echo these complaints. But, in an embarrassing *volte face*, the hyperbole soon gave way to a steady flow of announcements from the Big Six that they would introduce their own long-term price freezes. The coalition was finally forced to act: months after the event, Energy Secretary Ed Davey announced a reference of the sector to the Competition and Markets Authority (CMA) for a full inquiry into competition in power supply and generation. The coalition had no choice but to admit, at least tacitly, that this is a fundamentally dysfunctional market, while simultaneously attempting to kick the issue into the long grass. The CMA reference is unlikely to be completed before the 2015 election.

The confusion among Labour's opponents in the wake of Ed Miliband's 2013 speech reflects their utter disbelief that a seemingly permanent political consensus dating from the Thatcher era – that markets know best and government should stay on the sidelines – had suddenly been shattered. Having scored a major political success on this issue, Labour has a unique opportunity to radically reshape energy policy, leaving the Tories and Lib Dems defending a discredited system. To be sure, the policy package announced at the 2013 Party Conference goes well beyond the eye-catching prize freeze. It also pledges to 'reset' the broken market with measures including separation of the generation and supply arms of electricity companies, replacement of the Office of Gas and Electricity Markets (Ofgem) with a new, tougher regulator operating in the interests of consumers, and the introduction of genuine competition to the sector. But should this be the limit of Labour's ambitions?

A new model for the energy sector

There is a great deal of evidence for the proposition that the problem in the energy sector is not just a 'broken market', or one rigged against the consumer: the problem *is* the market. This is quite simply not a sector in which the model of a competitive market can ever work in the interests of consumers; nor, for that matter, can it effectively meet the other key goals of energy policy – decarbonisation and security of supply. This chapter examines why the competition model does not and cannot work in the energy sector, and considers two possible alternatives:

• a publicly owned, integrated system of generation and supply; and

- a decentralised, cooperative model in which consumers become their own producers.

It describes the legal framework within which these models could operate, and the reforms necessary at EU level to bring about the change.

Just how uncompetitive the current UK energy supply framework is has been well documented, not least in Labour's own Energy Green Paper, *Powering Britain,* published in November 2013.[1] Average consumer prices for 'dual fuel' tariffs rose 24 per cent between 2009 and 2013, outstripping the rise in wholesale coal and gas prices over the same period. The retail profits of the present Big Six and their predecessors rose from £223m in 1989 when electricity was privatised (three years after gas) to £1.1bn in 2012.

In a functioning, competitive market, rising profit levels of this kind should attract a host of new entrants. But a defining feature of the retail energy sector is the persistent dominance of the Big Six. One of the greatest ironies of the 1980s privatisation programme is that despite the accompanying rhetoric of eliminating 'monopolies', the policy actually diminished the number of major players. Pre-privatisation, consumers were supplied via fourteen separate organisations: the twelve regional electricity companies, the Central Electricity Generation Board (which also operated the transmission network) and British Gas. Now, to all intents and purposes, there are six, controlling about 96 per cent of the retail market. Even the largest supplier outside the Big Six – First Utility – has a market share of less than 1 per cent.

The point is that privatisation was incapable of achieving liberalisation. Privatisation consisted of the transfer of the asset base of the publicly owned companies to new owners, the most valuable asset being the customer list. None of the private players who acquired the supply side of the industry had to invest a penny in marketing their 'product' to potential 'buyers' because they enjoyed a captive consumer base from day one. The right of consumers to switch has made almost no difference because, of the 40 per cent of households who have switched since privatisation, nearly all have simply moved between Big Six companies. It is the complex monopoly position of the Big Six, not Labour's reform proposals, that removes any incentive for serious investment.

Underpinning the empirical evidence of lack of competition is the conceptual clash between the idea of a competitive market and the physical reality of energy supply. Gas and electricity reach each home and business via a single supply pipe and mains connection. The gas molecules and electrons that reach the consumer are identical regardless of who sends the bill. Indeed, the physical distribution networks and connections are owned and operated separately from the company with whom the consumer contracts. That raises an interesting question about exactly what, in the perverse world of retail gas and electricity, a 'supplier' really is. The companies that hold supply licences under the Electricity Act 1989 do not in any meaningful sense 'supply', still less produce, anything: they are simply administrative operations buying and selling an intangible commodity produced and delivered by someone else, and taking a profit on the 'turn' between wholesale and retail prices. They add not an iota of value anywhere in the supply chain.

If profiting in this way is so simple, why isn't everyone doing it? Why is the retail market so resistant to new entrants? A key reason for the entrenched position of the Big Six is their combination of retail and generation businesses. As Ofgem admitted in 2013, there is no objective 'wholesale price' for electricity because the majority of generation capacity belongs to the Big Six themselves, who account for transfers between their wholesale and retail arms in a wholly opaque way rather than participating in an open market. It is simply impossible for new retail entrants to replicate this: they face the full risk of volatile market rates, while the Big Six hedge their own generation against their supply.

Worse, the difficulties faced at the retail end are replicated, higher up the supply chain, by independent generators seeking a sufficiently predictable wholesale offtake for their production. Uncertainty in wholesale demand and price has a disproportionate impact on generators of electricity from renewable sources because the capital costs of new capacity are higher than for fossil-fired plant. So, once more, it is the dominance of the Big Six that undermines new investment and hampers achievement of decarbonisation objectives. There is a similar complex monopoly situation in upstream gas, with most UK exploration and production in the hands of the former British Gas, now morphed into a series of group companies under the Centrica umbrella (including, of course, one of the biggest electricity and gas retailers).

So far, the policy response has been to devise patches for specific pinch-points in the system. For example, the coalition government's Energy Act 2013 introduces 'contracts for difference' (CfDs) – broadly supported by Labour – that seek to create price certainty for generators and so make investment less risky. Labour's Green Paper proposals to ring-fence supply and generation, and reintroduce trading pool arrangements, would aid that process by improving price transparency and making it harder for the Big Six to squeeze the competition by their vertical integration of production and retail supply. Much can be said for and against these various measures. One major disadvantage of CfDs, for example, is that the bill for underwriting wholesale trades is ultimately borne by the consumer. But the more important point is this: the very fact that increasingly elaborate measures are necessary in order to address the problems of the market model must surely tell us something about whether that is the right model in the first place?

As observed earlier, competition in supply can be no more than a fiction when there is in practice a natural, physical monopoly of power delivery to individual premises. And given that 'supply' is ultimately a speculative trade at the customer's expense, would it not make more sense to cut out this wasteful middleman operation entirely and accept, rather than outlaw, vertical integration of production with delivery to the consumer? In other words, why not abandon the pretence of a competitive market entirely and establish a vertically integrated energy network tasked with the explicit aim of delivering those elusive triple goals of affordability, security and decarbonisation – in place of the primary aim of turning a profit for shareholders?

Public ownership works

It is instructive to see what happens when public entities are made players in other service sectors privatised under the previous Tory government. The obvious example is rail. In 2005 the InterCity East Coast (ICEC) franchise was awarded to Sea Containers subsidiary GNER, with a promise of returning a £1.3bn premium to government over the seven-year life of the franchise. A year later the franchise ended prematurely when Sea Containers filed for Chapter 11 bankruptcy protection in the United States. But the government carried on paying GNER to operate the line until 2007 when a new franchise was awarded to National Express. National Express also promised to return a substantial premium to the Department for Transport, but its strategy for meeting that commitment was to introduce significant cuts to staffing levels and services – an approach shown in July 2009 to have failed ignominiously when National Express defaulted on the franchise. The Department for Transport bowed to the inevitable, returning the service to the public sector by appointing Directly Operated Railways (DOR) to operate the line.

Under DOR's tenure, the ICEC route has been a resounding success. ICEC carries more passengers per mile than any other service in the UK, and is among the best performers in Europe by that measure. A survey by Passenger Focus in Autumn 2013 gave ICEC the highest overall customer satisfaction ranking among high-speed/long-distance operators, at 91 per cent (3 per cent higher than the average for those operators).[2] Revenue has grown rapidly, and DOR has returned to the Department for Transport £620m – more than National Express paid during its tenure, and some £227m more than Virgin has paid on its West Coast franchise since 2009. Public subsidy accounted for just 1.2 per cent of ICEC's total income in 2011–12, compared with an average of 32.1 per cent of the income of the private operators running the other franchises. The fact is that public ownership works – although of course the facts haven't deterred the coalition from allowing dogma to dominate common sense by attempting to reprivatise the ICEC franchise (a decision under challenge in judicial review proceedings at the time of writing).

Replacing the retail and power purchase end of the energy supply system with one or more bodies resembling DOR would be immensely popular. Upstream, it would strengthen the opportunities for independent green generators to enter the sector. Without super-profits leaching away to shareholders in the Big Six, investment-friendly pricing for renewable generation would involve far less of a burden on consumers.

A decentralised, cooperative model

An alternative approach – potentially an attractive one given renewed political interest in cooperatives in other areas such as land development – is to mutualise the retail sector, and couple that with a move towards decentralised generation in which mutual schemes dominate new green power projects.

A number of community-based mutual schemes have attempted to replace commercial suppliers by linking consumers together to create economies of scale. These schemes have generally raised local awareness about energy issues, but so far have gained little traction against the commercial market players. However, it is on the generation side of the equation that community-owned schemes have the greatest potential to transform the sector, and especially in accelerating decarbonisation. A key reason for the growing opposition to onshore wind projects is the problem of globalised benefits versus localised impacts: the power is sold into the grid rather than directly benefiting the community who face the visual, and sometimes other, impacts of the turbines. The idea of the community owning its own power source is a popular one elsewhere in northern Europe and is one of the main factors in the success – and public acceptance – of onshore wind in Denmark. Owning an interest in your own power source also means you are likely to use energy more wisely, so this approach increases public buy-in to demand-side carbon reduction measures. Generating locally for supply locally also reduces the need for new long-distance grid capacity.

So perhaps the most effective – and attractive – overall system would be a combination of the public and mutual models, spinning the already vertically integrated Big Six into a new public power network, and giving it a statutory duty to promote decentralised, locally owned and locally connected renewable schemes as the preferred source of new generating capacity wherever possible.

Building a legal framework to accommodate these models

Devising a domestic legal framework for either of these approaches is not difficult. A new Energy Act could be on the statute book within the first parliamentary session of a Labour government elected in 2015. There would be a wind-down of the big operators' supply and generation licences as the new system is established. Meanwhile some of these ideas – especially promotion of green decentralised energy projects – could be kick-started under existing legislation.

The greater challenge lies in compatibility with EU law. The direction of travel in recent years, culminating in the EU's 'Third Energy Package' (three regulations and two directives adopted in 2009), has been unmistakeably towards the 'small state': phasing out the public sector as a player in favour of a liberalised market subject to independent regulation.

But EU policy is no more than a reflection of trends in member state politics. The UK is by no means the only European country in which the public mood has swung against the abusive behaviour of privatised utilities. Again taking rail as an example, the EU regime favours liberalisation but has arrived at a compromise, reflected in Regulation 1370/2007 on public passenger transport services by rail and road.[3] This established a bespoke set of procurement rules under which states may, if they wish, appoint public sector entities to operate services. Article 5(2) provides:

> *Unless prohibited by national law, any competent local authority, whether or not it is an individual authority or a group of authorities providing integrated public passenger transport services, may decide to provide public passenger transport services itself or to award public service contracts directly to a legally distinct entity over which the competent local authority, or in the case of a group of authorities at least one competent local authority, exercises control similar to that exercised over its own departments.*

The quid pro quo – found in Art. 5(2)(b) – is that such an appointed operator may 'not take part in competitive tenders concerning the provision of public passenger transport services organised outside the territory of the competent local authority'. The same rules apply to national competent authorities. The result is that a state can run its rail services publicly so long as it does not distort competition at EU level by causing its national operator to undercut commercial players in franchising competitions elsewhere.

In the wake of the global financial crisis, the sort of free market fundamentalism that produced the Third Energy Package holds noticeably less sway in the EU institutions and among member states. The response to the euro crisis has precipitated something much more akin to a solidarity model of trade and finance within the EU. There is every reason to suppose that an incoming Labour government led by Ed Miliband will be able to negotiate a consensus for the energy sector around a position similar to the Rail Transport Regulation. Significantly, the Court of Justice has accepted that the Treaties contain no prohibition on states reserving defined activities in the energy sector to publicly owned undertakings. In *Staat Nederlanden v Essent NV*,[4] the court accepted that Art. 345 of the Treaty on the Functioning of the European Union (TFEU) does not prevent a member state from prohibiting transfers of shares in the public sector distribution system operators to private sector entities. There could be no fundamental Treaty objection to legislation permitting member states to reserve retail supply to a public sector entity; to insist that any non-public sector entity undertaking that activity be structured with mutual ownership and control; or to structure the power purchase element of the system in a way that gives preference to mutually owned generators, so long as the usual rules about non-discrimination and state aid are observed.

Having found the courage to step away from the bleak consensus of leaving everything to the market, Labour's energy policy must now take a further radical stride.

Summary of principal recommendations

- To replace the private complex monopoly of the Big Six with a publicly owned, integrated system of generation and supply.
- To promote decentralised, cooperative green energy projects in which consumers become their own local producers, which the public sector supplier would have a duty to prefer as the source of new capacity.
- To start urgent negotiations at EU level to permit member states to appoint public sector operators within their own territory in place of private licensees.

6

Equalities Law and Tackling Inequality

Sarah Sackman[1]

'No society can surely be flourishing and happy of which the far greater part of the members are poor and miserable.'

Adam Smith, *Wealth of Nations, Book I*

Back in 2011 the rallying cry of the Occupy movement, 'We are the 99 per cent', catapulted inequality to the forefront of our public consciousness. As the protestors camped outside St Paul's Cathedral, they responded to a stark social truth that Britain is a more unequal country than it has been in a generation.

From the late nineteenth century until the 1970s British society became less unequal. Thanks to the development of welfare systems, progressive taxation and the provision of social services, our democracy appeared to have shed the extremes of wealth and poverty. However, over the past thirty years the greatest extremes of inequality have resurfaced. A recent report by Oxfam revealed that the country's five richest families today own more wealth than the poorest 20 per cent of the population.[2] Britain is now more unequal – in incomes, wealth, health, education and life chances – than at any time since the 1920s. It is no exaggeration to say that our life chances are primarily determined by who our parents are and that intergenerational mobility has become significantly harder. Without a change of direction, children in Britain today have little expectation of improving on the social condition to which they were born. The rich will stay rich and the poor will stay poor.

The problem is that the more unequal our society becomes the harder it is to imagine extreme inequality as anything other than inevitable. As the British historian, Tony Judt has written, reductions in inequality are self-confirming: the more equal we get the more equal we believe it is possible to be.[3] The opposite is also true. The past thirty years have convinced us that extreme inequality is a natural condition of our economy about which we can do little. However, while the scale of the inequality is staggering, its existence is neither inevitable nor immutable, but is the product of political choices.

In recent times inequality has been exacerbated by the coalition's policies. Ed Miliband has warned of the unequal effects of the current government's policies: 'A recovery for the few is not an accident of this government's economic policy – this is its economic policy'. If Labour forms the next government it should not shy away from talking about inequality and the damage that extremes of inequality cause to our society.

The concept of an equal economic recovery

In this chapter I look at the patterns of inequality that have emerged in the past four decades and examine Labour's record on inequality in government. Despite Labour's progressive achievements and success in lifting millions of children and pensioners out of poverty, it was unable to reverse decades of growing inequality since the late 1970s. Inequality stabilised under New Labour but did not decline. Attention was focused on improving outcomes for those at the bottom but tackling inequality per se was not a priority. More should have been done.

Any future Labour government, with a commitment to social justice at its core, needs to adopt a new first order goal of economic policy: ensuring that income and wealth inequality is reduced and that the material well-being of low-to-middle income households rises as part of an equal recovery. Reducing inequality should be placed alongside traditional policy goals of poverty reduction, high employment and sustained growth in GDP. The notion of an equal recovery recognises that the costs of the recovery should not be borne solely by those who gained least in the period before the crisis, but should be shared in a progressive manner so that those in the strongest position to bear the costs do so.

Accepting this aim would have real implications across a range of policy areas. In this chapter I focus on the particular role that law can play in achieving an equal recovery, arguing that there are no simple legal levers capable of alleviating extreme socio-economic inequality. Indeed, there are inherent dangers in asking judges to make distributional choices which are properly for elected representatives to make. However, there are certain limited ways in which the law can help to frame the decision-making process so as to require decision makers to put inequality reduction at the forefront of their thinking. In particular, I examine the ways in which a Labour government might strengthen the Public Sector Equality Duty (PSED) to include socio-economic inequalities, which would embed a broader 'equalities culture', by requiring decision makers to explain and justify to the public the effect that their decisions will have on the objective of reducing inequality. In forcing decision makers and the public alike to confront the distributional impacts of policy decisions and to ask themselves whether we really are 'all in this together', we may produce a more progressive set of political choices.

Even with a robust legal framework, Labour will need to make bold political choices to tackle inequality and create a balanced, high-wage, high-skill economy with markets that work to ensure the proceeds of growth are shared. The law alone will not reduce socio-economic inequality. From linking the minimum wage to average earnings, to tackling market failures by freezing energy prices and reforming the industry; from addressing the failure of banks to lend competitively to small business, to stabilising private rents; from introducing a 50p rate of income tax on top earners and capping bonuses, to investing in vocational skills to equip our young people for future success, we will need to ensure that Labour's policies deliver a recovery that benefits the many and not just the few.

Just as Disraeli in the nineteenth century comprehended the dangers and unfairness of 'two nations between whom there is no intercourse and no sympathy, who are as ignorant of each other's habits, thoughts and feelings as if they were dwellers in different zones ... and not governed by the same laws',[4] Labour should place the reduction of inequality at the heart of the recovery and of policy making. An equal recovery would begin to realise the promise of One Nation Labour.

Putting inequality at the heart of the agenda

Extremities of wealth and poverty are not just harmful for the poor but harm us all. Inequality has been shown to be damaging to our economy, to our health and to our politics. In their influential book, *The Spirit Level: Why More Equal Societies Almost Always Do Better*, Richard Wilkinson and Kate Pickett showed how economic inequality and the health of society are inextricably linked.[5] Public health, obesity, the erosion of community cohesion, violence and mental health are all demonstrably worse in more unequal countries and act as a drain on the economy. Inequality is therefore not only unappealing in itself but corresponds to social problems that we cannot address unless we understand their underlying cause. Inequality erodes trust between citizens and undermines our sense of a commonality and a shared society across economic divides. As the divide between the super rich and the rest grows, it becomes harder to create a set of policies capable of appealing to different sections of society and makes it impossible to create the cohesive society we would like to see.

The combined effects of the financial crisis in 2007–08, the UK's most severe post-war recession and the coalition's austerity policies have prompted a public debate about tackling this increasingly extreme social and economic phenomenon: is inequality harmful, what levels of inequality are acceptable and how can we take action to reduce inequality? It is part of wider global discussion: even in the United States an economics textbook by the left-wing French academic Thomas Piketty on the causes of inequality has become a bestseller.[6]

The debate is about more than just poverty; it is a particular response to the trend over the past thirty years that has seen the stagnation of real wages and the erosion of living standards of those on middle incomes, while the rich have continued to grow richer. There has been a decoupling of overall growth and the benefits of growth, which no longer seem to accrue to those on low and middle incomes. Addressing the causes and effects of this increasing inequality may well be the biggest challenge for government in the coming decades and it is one that Labour must place centre stage in its policy making.

Labour's record in government

It is easy to forget the radicalism and scale of previous Labour administrations' achievements. In 1997 the Blair government instituted an ambitious programme that was bold in tackling poverty, investing in public services and maintaining economic growth. Changes were far-reaching. Household income was improved including through tax credits, pension credits, increasing employment and the introduction of the national minimum wage.

Labour invested heavily in early years intervention and young people, establishing Sure Start, investing in child care, raising schools standards, and introducing the Education Maintenance Allowance and the Aim Higher programme to get more disadvantaged young people to universities. The scourge of unemployment was tackled through successful New Deals and rights at work were strengthened. Under Labour, the employment rate hit a record high since records began in 1971. Lone parent employment in particular soared by 15 per cent during the Labour years.

Public services saw huge programmes of modernisation and expansion, especially in the NHS, which achieved record patient satisfaction rates. Regeneration and neighbourhood programmes brought major investment to disadvantaged communities and began to return public housing stock to decent standards following years of underinvestment and neglect. Action was taken on street homelessness, combating the scandal of families growing up in bed and breakfast accommodation.

The provision of a robust safety net for those at the bottom proved resilient even when the financial crisis hit. The Future Jobs Fund helped protect young people from long-term unemployment, while Jobcentre Plus geared up its rapid response services to keep more people in work. Meanwhile, Gordon Brown's decisive action in bailing out the banks and the fiscal stimulus provided by Alistair Darling's Budget ensured that people kept their homes and their jobs, and could pay their bills.

And all this activity was placed within a framework of equal political rights, with the government providing the legal architecture to protect those rights through the Human Rights Act 1998, and the Equality Acts 2006 and 2010. Labour also established the Equality and Human Rights Commission with responsibility for the promotion and enforcement of equalities legislation and created the post of a minister in government with specific responsibility for equality.

Yet, whereas successive Labour governments under Blair and Brown focused with considerable success on improving the situation of the poorest groups in society, economic inequality persisted throughout Labour's tenure. Poverty reduction utilising the revenues of sustained economic growth was the dominant political goal, but reducing inequality per se was not. As Peter Mandelson famously quipped, New Labour was 'intensely relaxed about people becoming filthy rich' so long as they paid their taxes.[7]

Despite all of Labour's achievements, the large growth in inequality that had occurred between the late 1970s and early 1990s was not reversed between 1997 and 2010, although Labour's redistributive policies aimed at improving outcomes for poor households did have the effect of stabilising inequality. The Institute of Fiscal Studies has shown that without Labour's policies – which increased benefits for poorer pensioners and tax credits for low-income families with children – inequality would have risen substantially. Moreover, in a whole range of areas such as schools attainment, health outcomes, employment status and social participation, inequalities between different groups fell. However, we must recognise that Labour did not do enough to tackle inequality when in power.

The problem was not lack of attention to improving incomes and outcomes at the bottom, but a wrongly held belief that a rising tide would lift all boats at equal rates. Instead, even under conditions of sustained economic growth and high employment, two concerning long-term trends in the structure of the UK economy emerged. First, a pattern that had begun in the 1980s of the stagnation of real wages for people on low-to-middle incomes continued. This suggested a fundamental decoupling of GDP growth from the benefits that accrue to ordinary working people; a trend that has been observed not just in Britain but in other advanced economies including the US, Germany and Canada.[8]

Secondly, there was a shift in the nature of economic inequality. Leading up to the start of Labour's period in government, rising inequality manifested itself as a 'fanning out' across the entire earnings distribution, with the top moving away from the middle and the middle moving away from the bottom. From the late 1990s, however, while income inequality in the bottom half of incomes began to flatten out and even fall, in part as a result of the national minimum wage, inequality within the top half of the distribution soared.[9] There was a bonanza in executive pay and a detachment of the top 1–2 per cent from the rest of the population. While real wages for the vast majority of people stood still, the top 1 per cent saw their incomes and returns on capital grow enormously, out of all proportion to the rest of the economy.

Labour's period in power demonstrated two key lessons about inequality. First, that unless inequality reduction is a stand-alone policy goal, anti-poverty policies aimed at the worst off will not necessarily address inequality. Secondly, that formal, civil equality is far easier to achieve than tackling socio-economic equality. While Labour made real legislative strides in tackling inequality between groups based on racial, gender, LGBT (lesbian, gay, bisexual and transgender) or disability discrimination, that often masked the stark differences between the haves and have-nots within those groups.

Labour understood that there was more to do. In 2008 Harriet Harman, then Minister for Women and Equality, established the National Equality Panel and commissioned a team at the London School of Economics to report on the relationships between inequalities of wealth and income, and people's characteristics and personal circumstances such as gender, age, ethnicity and geography. The panel's first report in 2010 pointed to the scale of inequality in Britain and urged action to reduce it.[10]

When the global financial crash hit, many within the Labour Party saw it as both a watershed and an opportunity to refocus public policy on the goal of reducing inequality and boosting equality of opportunity. The excessive behaviours that led to the crisis had met with public revulsion, and it was hoped this change in attitudes would galvanise broad support for greater egalitarianism and policies designed to address socio-economic inequality.

The impact of coalition policies on inequality

Instead, the coalition government forged ahead with an austerity agenda that has hit the poorest and the most vulnerable hardest. While introducing tax cuts for high earners, the government has presided over rising prices and a crisis in the cost of living for those on median incomes.

Despite being told that 'We're all in this together', cuts to benefits and tax credits have hit women three times as hard as men, while disabled people have suffered nine times the impact of benefits cuts compared with those who are not disabled. Young people have experienced cuts to financial support. Job losses in the public sector have hit those disproportionately likely to work in that sector – women, disabled people and those from black and minority ethnic backgrounds. Since these people were also more likely to reach senior positions in the public sector than in the private sector, progression opportunities have also become more unequal.

Cuts to public services have been felt most acutely by those who rely most on them – women, the young, the old, the sick, the disabled and their carers. Voluntary and community groups servicing the needs of particular groups – such as LGBT people, black and minority ethnic communities, those fleeing domestic violence and those with learning disabilities – have lost funding, and many have closed, leaving some of the most vulnerable in our society without access to advice, advocacy and support.

Against this backdrop what has been happening to poverty, inequality and incomes? The Chancellor of the Exchequer is proud of saying that income inequality has fallen. In the immediate wake of the global financial crisis that was true because everyone became poorer, except that the rich (who had gained most in the previous decade) lost most. However, top incomes are rising again, while real wages for low-to-middle income earners have been falling further behind inflation for at least the past five years.[11] This suggests a further gradual increase in overall inequality. Office for National Statistics (ONS) figures indicate that the relative poverty figure, which showed a modest fall in the first two years of the coalition, is projected to rise sharply over the rest of the decade. Meanwhile, absolute poverty is rising for the first time in a generation.

For those on middle incomes, as well as for those at the bottom of the income distribution, the position is getting tougher. Ed Miliband has characterised pressure on the 'squeezed middle' as the stand-out effect of the coalition's austerity programme. Tough austerity policies have exacerbated the long-term erosion of living standards, which explains why the hesitant economic recovery has done nothing to improve most people's sense of economic security or confidence in the future. In addition, the government's divisive rhetoric of 'skivers and scroungers' and denigrating equalities legislation as 'red tape' is designed to divert attention from the inequality debate and make people less willing to countenance the sorts of measures that would produce a more equal recovery.

The law's role in enabling an equal recovery

Labour needs to change the terms of the debate and to start by simply talking about inequality. There is a lack of public awareness of the sheer scale of the differences between the high paid and low paid, the wealthy and the asset poor. As the National Equality Panel has reported, most people are unaware both of their own position in the income distribution and the true scale of the differences between high and low paid.[12] It is this lack of awareness that leads to acceptance of the status quo and constrains the sorts of policy choices that are capable of addressing inequality.

Labour should be explicit in establishing the reduction of inequality as a national target. It should advocate an equalities-based approach across all policy areas demanding that policy-makers consider what effect their policy will have – whether in the sphere of transport, environmental regulation, health, education or fiscal policy – in tackling inequality. The law can play a role in this. Through extending the scope of equalities legislation and the public sector equality duty (PSED), and by providing a means of enforcing equalities obligations with a properly supported legal aid system, the law can provide a framework to compel decision makers and citizens alike to confront inequality.

The law can help to provide the procedural framework in which elected representatives and civil servants can make the sorts of policy choices that would start to address an equal recovery. The legal structures requiring decision makers to consider and justify the distributional impacts of their decisions can perform an important democratic function in helping the public understand the equality impacts of the decisions being taken on their behalf. If we understand extreme inequality as the product of a series of thousands of political choices, then exposing those choices to scrutiny and compelling decision makers to explain that certain groups will be left worse off than others as a result of their decisions, will help the public to decide and influence the sort of outcomes they would like to see.

The Equalities Acts 2006 and 2010 were landmark pieces of legislation. These Acts brought together previous anti-discrimination laws – including the Equal Pay Act 1970, the Sex Discrimination Act 1975, the Race Relations Act 1975 and the Disability Discrimination Act 1995 – and provided comparable protections against discrimination across all equality strands. This meant that the same protections would apply to protected groups defined by age; disability; gender; proposed, commenced or completed gender reassignment; race; religion or belief; and sexual orientation. The focus on groups with protected characteristics has been valuable in highlighting and addressing discrimination on the basis of those characteristics. These groups being more likely to be economically disadvantaged so having regard to their protected characteristics can act as a proxy for socio-economic differences.

However, as the 2010 National Equality Panel report showed,[13] despite the gross inequalities that exist between different groups with protected characteristics, the biggest gaps exist not *between* groups but *within* them. Whilst the difference, say, in salaries of professional women and professional men has narrowed, the gap between the salaries of professional women and low-paid women remains staggeringly wide. This reflects the reality that it may be easier to tackle discrimination between different protected social groups than it is to address underlying economic inequalities within those groups. It remains the case that our main equalities laws, which extend over several hundred pages, make no mention of socio-economic inequality.

Labour's approach to inequality should therefore not be framed around the traditional protected characteristics alone. Four suggestions are made here as to how the law could help to tackle inequality. First, there is provision in the Equality Act 2010 for targeting socio-economic inequality in its own right. The problem is that the current government has not brought s. 1 of the Equality Act 2010 into force. The section states that a public body, when making decisions of a strategic nature, must have due regard to the desirability of exercising them in a way that is designed to reduce the inequalities of outcome that result from socio-economic disadvantage. A legal requirement that takes account of the normative objective of reducing inequalities based not solely on protected characteristics but on general socio-economic inequalities is something that Labour should embrace if it wins power. Bringing s. 1 into force would strengthen Labour's commitment to reducing inequality as a first order political goal by enshrining it in law.

Secondly, the public sector equality duty should be strengthened as another important tool in addressing inequality. The PSED means that public bodies have to consider all individuals, and particularly those with protected characteristics, when carrying out their daily work in shaping policy, delivering services and in relation to their own employees. The PSED requires public authorities to have 'due regard' to the need to eliminate discrimination on the grounds of age, disability, sex, sexual orientation, religion or race, to advance equality of opportunity and to foster good relations between different groups when carrying out their activities.

In practice, having 'due regard' means consciously thinking about the three aims of the equality duty as part of the process of decision making. This may require evidence gathering, often by way of an equality impact assessment, about the way in which different groups are affected differently by a public body's actions. Having due regard to the need to advance equality of opportunity involves considering the need to remove or minimise disadvantages suffered by people due to their protected characteristics, and therefore modifying decisions or practices to meet the needs of people with protected characteristics.

This in turn can cause the public authority to modify its decisions or practices to meet the needs of people with protected characteristics to participate in public life or in other activities where their participation is low.

While David Cameron has publicly stated that he regards the PSED as a tick-box duty and ordered a review of the duty in 2013 as part of the government's Red Tape Challenge, Labour should commit to defending the duty which it introduced during its time in government. The PSED has proven especially relevant in the context of public spending cuts, which tend to have a disproportionate impact on protected groups. Public authorities can ultimately take decisions notwithstanding their impact on vulnerable groups. However, the PSED provides a rigorous procedure that requires authorities to take account of the equality impacts of their decisions and to justify those decisions.

The judicial review challenges since 2010 relating to breaches of equalities legislation illustrate the breadth of the PSED. Challenges to the government's austerity programme have touched on a range of policy areas from cuts to school buildings programmes and community care budgets to reduced funding for voluntary and charitable organisations.[14]

Legal challenges to the cuts have met with mixed success, reinforcing the view of the PSED as a procedural duty and the fact that substantive funding decisions are ultimately for politicians. A high-profile claim by the Fawcett Society against the government's failure to undertake a proper equality impact assessment (EIA) in respect of the 2010 Budget's impact on women is a case in point. While the legal claim was ultimately unsuccessful, it shone a harsh light on the particular impact of public sector cuts on women. The claim thus demonstrated the utility of equalities legislation in requiring decision makers at the very least to justify the impacts of their decisions on protected groups that might otherwise be obscured.[15]

As well as protecting the PSED, there is a strong argument for extending the requirements of the PSED to private bodies, particularly where they perform a public function. At present the scope of the PSED is confined to those public bodies named in Schedule 19 of the Equality Act 2010. However, why should the large number of private contractors that now deliver public services, from care homes to prisons, not be subject to the same duty to promote equality within their organisations?

The operation of the duty might also be improved by requiring decision makers to have regard to the cumulative impact of different decisions on disadvantaged groups and by emphasising the continuing nature of the duty. A limitation of the PSED is that, in practice, organisations tend to examine the equality impacts of a decision at a single moment in time, before the decision has been taken. This means that the duty does not necessarily take account of the sum of lots of different decisions over time on disadvantaged groups. While a decision to cut one service may be tolerable, in combination with other welfare and service cuts the cumulative impact of the decisions can be devastating.

The case for cumulative impact assessments of the socio-economic effects of government decisions is strong. The law could be more explicit in requiring public bodies to monitor the equality impacts of their policy choices once they have taken effect. That would make the PSED a responsive rather than simply a predictive duty.

More research is needed on how the PSED is working in practice in order to ensure its effectiveness at embedding an 'equalities culture' across different areas of government. Yet, in my experience, the consideration of equalities duties can lead decision makers to mitigate or avoid unequal impacts altogether. Therefore, while the PSED, as with public law generally, is primarily concerned with due process, it has the ability to influence outcomes by integrating the consideration of equalities impacts into everyday public decision making.

Thirdly, equal access to justice is an important means of enforcing equalities obligations and empowering disadvantaged groups in the decision-making process. Having recourse to legal aid to bring public law challenges allows the poor to enforce the operation of the PSED and to ensure that due regard has been had to the distributional impacts of decisions.

Fourthly, each major policy introduced should be considered for its equality impact. As with the Treasury's Green Book[16] in the sphere of sustainability, the government should be required to examine and justify the distributional impacts of budgets. A Labour administration will need to revitalise the equalities infrastructure and institutions, such as the Equality and Human Rights Commission, the Equality and Diversity Forum and the National Equality Panel, which can hold up a mirror to our society and monitor where there is a greater need for more action. These bodies must have the resources and capacity to do their jobs. Similarly, the importance of retaining a senior minister with responsibility for equality, able to work across government, cannot be overstated.

Policies for an equal recovery

However, law alone will not build an equal recovery. It is not possible simply to legislate for greater socio-economic equality. Law can structure the decision-making process, concentrate the minds of those in charge on tackling inequality and enforce any decisions that are taken to achieve such an ends. Yet it is wrong to think that legal tinkering can produce transformational outcomes on inequality. Within the legal and institutional framework advocated here, Labour will need to make policy choices that go to the root of tackling inequalities in pay, the labour market and wealth.

A person's origins may shape their life chances from cradle to grave, resulting in stark differences at every stage of life including educational attainment and life expectancy. Policy interventions aimed at equalising life chances are therefore needed to tackle inequality at each stage of the life cycle. This is not just about opportunities at the very top and very bottom of society, but supporting those in the middle.

Even before the publication of Labour's election manifesto, the Party has started to unveil an ambitious policy programme and a number of market reforms that proactively address the erosion in the standards of living engulfing millions of middle-income families. It is not possible to review all of those proposed policies here, but the following discussion touches upon a few of the important areas in which Labour's priorities would be different from those of the governing coalition in explicitly tackling inequality and bringing about a more equal recovery.

Beginning with children and young people, Labour would underscore the importance of early years intervention, as was done with the establishment of Sure Start, to ensure inequalities do not widen before school entry. Labour would extend free childcare for 3–4 year olds to

25 hours per week, helping children from all backgrounds to flourish and enabling more parents, especially mothers, to work. There must be investment in young people, recognising academic and technical education as a key driver of social mobility. Preparing the next generation for skilled jobs will deliver decent wages and economic growth.

Priority should be given to those areas where there is a chronic shortage of primary school places for disadvantaged pupils, and emphasis given to improving the educational attainment of low-income children by encouraging them to stay on after sixteen. Cutting university tuition fees and introducing the technical baccalaureate will ensure that our young people receive the best chance to develop the skills they need to succeed in the workplace, and that Britain has the skills to compete in a global market. Labour would introduce a compulsory jobs guarantee to tackle youth unemployment and help to avoid the longer-term damaging effects from early unemployment.

Labour would also take action on low pay and the prevalence of in-work poverty. The Party's announcement of a review of the national minimum wage and the possibility of raising it further in certain industry sectors is welcome. The national minimum wage has proven successful at tackling the worst excesses of low pay without causing any significant negative effect on employment. Increasing the minimum wage and working with public and private sector employers to roll out a living wage would be powerful in reducing labour market inequality. The living wage, which is calculated according to the basic costs of living in the UK, goes further than the minimum wage to re-establish the link between prices and wages. A differentiated increase in the minimum wage for different sectors and within different geographical areas, particularly London, would help address income inequality, while £50,000 fines for businesses who flout the law would create a strong climate for minimum wage enforcement.

Public awareness of inequality needs to be enhanced by measures that increase the transparency of relative rewards for people across public and private organisations. This is not just a matter of publicising salaries and bonuses for those at the very top, but opening up the salaries of people from across the spectrum of an organisation. When in power, Labour legislated for mandatory pay audits to expose pay inequalities within organisations, yet there has been little sign of progress under the coalition's voluntary approach. At a time when FTSE bosses take-home pay is on average 139 times more than the wages of their average workers,[17] it is proper that disparate pay scales should be exposed in order to bring about change. If voluntary measures are ineffective, Labour should legislate to require organisations to publish their pay ratios not just in relation to gender but across the board.

More must be done to address continuing inequality in the labour market – women, the young, the old, the disabled and those from certain black and minority ethnic groups all experience significant labour market disadvantage. Government labour market programmes must be run in a way that overtly recognises and addresses structural disadvantage for groups with protected characteristics. The coalition government's Work Programme has been an abject failure. Its 'black box' approach was supposed to deliver tailor-made, individualised support, but instead it leaves the long-term unemployed, especially those who are disabled, without support. Contrast this with Labour's New Deals, which recognised the specific needs and experiences of lone parents or disabled people in the workplace.

The best way to achieve such labour market reforms will be to devolve responsibility to local partnerships, led by local authorities and with a key role for employers. Labour's proposal for regional investment banks should enable jobs to be created in areas of greatest economic disadvantage. Again, by devolving budgets and empowering local partners, Labour must be clear that the creation of good quality jobs for those on lower or middle incomes is the priority.

Labour should also champion flexible working. Part-time work is preferred by many, especially women, who often also have caring responsibilities. However, part-time work accounts for much of the gender pay gap. Lower levels of hourly pay for part-time work reflect the low value accorded to it and the failure to organise the way we work – such as training and promotion – around social realities. Few senior jobs are advertised part-time or flexibly: a recent study published by the Joseph Rowntree Foundation suggested it was rare for jobs on a full-time equivalent salary of £20,000 or more to be advertised on a flexible basis. Starting in the public sector, Labour should ensure it becomes the norm for all jobs, including senior roles, to be advertised flexibly. There should be an opening up of part-time opportunities beyond routine and low-paid occupations, and also of career progression for part-time workers. That would not only help those with caring responsibilities, it would also help disabled workers, and it would bear down on wage inequality. Moreover, plans for the extension of free and affordable child care will help women in particular to thrive in the workplace.

Incentivising employers to weight training investment towards the lowest-paid workers, and to spread employee benefits packages to junior staff, would also help to boost incomes and enhance future progression. These ideas can be taken forward through local economic partnerships and City Deals. Labour wants to decentralise power and give greater powers to cities and metropolitan regions to exert greater control over labour market policy through Local Works Programmes. Labour local authorities are already showing the way as living wage employers, through procurement policies or by encouraging apprenticeships, and we can learn from and build on their successes.

Finally, while no one should expect cash transfer policies on the scale of previous Labour governments, there is still scope for progressive redistributive fiscal policies. Labour has announced that it would reintroduce a 50 per cent tax rate on top earners. That measure while introducing a basic tax rate of 10p at the bottom, shows Labour's determination to use progressive tax measures to help reduce inequalities and achieve a more equal recovery.

Conclusion

Many argue that inequalities of a socio-economic nature are inevitable and maybe even functional in creating incentives for growth in a modern economy. However, comparisons with other countries undermine arguments about the inevitability of the profound extent of inequality in Britain. The dramatic (though as yet incomplete) success in narrowing the gender pay gap over the last generation shows that such deep inequalities are neither inevitable nor immutable. They are the product of collective political and economic choices that can change over time.

The fundamental problem with inequality is that it suppresses the ability of individuals to develop and reach their full potential and so impoverishes our society. As R.H. Tawney put it in 1964: 'Individual differences which are the source of social energy, are more likely to ripen and find expression if social inequalities are, as far as practicable, diminished.' [18]

For too long, as the economy grew, we comforted ourselves that unequal outcomes might be palatable so long as everyone had an equal opportunity to get on in life. However, where huge disparities in wealth, income and access to political power blight our society it is doubtful that such equality of opportunity exists. This is why the Labour Party must be ambitious about working towards an equal recovery, which would boost prosperity and be good for both society and democracy. Placing the reduction of inequality at the heart of the legal and political agenda is a bolder, more visionary project than mere deficit reduction, and we must take it on.

Summary of principal recommendations

- To establish the reduction of inequality as a national target and to advocate an equalities-based approach across all policy areas.
- To bring s. 1 of the Equality Act 2010 into force.
- To strengthen the public sector equality duty as an important tool in addressing inequality.
- To provide adequate support to equalities institutions such as the Equalities and Human Rights Commission.
- To develop and pursue policies that go to the root of inequalities in pay, the labour market and wealth. For example by increasing the minimum wage; expanding the provision of a living wage; prohibiting unfair zero hours contracts; introducing a compulsory job guarantee for under 25s; and extending free child care for 3–4 year olds to 25 hours a week.

7

Family Law

*Naomi Angell, Barbara Connolly QC, Michael
Horton, Andrew Powell and David Williams QC*

With family law having developed piecemeal over the past 150 years, there is a case for codifying all aspects of it into a single statute – a 'Family Code'. This would make the law far more accessible to all those who need to have reference to it. We recognise that the considerable body of family law and the crossovers into other areas – such as the provisions on parentage and licensing in the Human Fertilisation and Embryology Authority – pose some practical difficulties and that complete codification might not be achievable. Nonetheless, significant areas could still be drawn together while leaving others outside the Family Code.

Children: Private and public law matters

There has been considerable focus on the framework provided by statute and the approach of family courts to children whose parents have separated or who are at risk of harm from their parents.

Very significant changes have been introduced in the way in which care proceedings are dealt with in the family courts, and further changes have been introduced in the Children and Families Act 2014, which passed into law on 13 March 2014. Until these bed in, it would be premature in our view to consider further changes.

The Children and Families Act also contains arrangements

for children after their parents have separated. However, these are limited in their ambit and we believe that there are other matters that would benefit children and parents more and which can and should be considered.

Private law: Parental responsibility

It remains an unusual anomaly that the Children Act 1989 distinguishes between the position of the child of an unmarried father as compared with the child of a married father. All children's mothers (using the phrase in the sense of biological mother) acquire legal parental responsibility for them, which cannot be removed by a court except in the case of adoption. Children's fathers acquire legal parental responsibility automatically if they are married to the mother, and only lose it in the event of adoption. In contrast, the child of an unmarried father only acquires parental responsibility if with the mother's consent he is registered on the birth certificate or a parental responsibility agreement is made, or if a court application is made and the court orders that he should have parental responsibility. In addition, the unmarried father's parental responsibility can be removed by court order.[1]

While such a distinction might once have seemed to be justified (when marriage was the norm perhaps, or when the difference between the role of the mother and father was more marked), social and family norms have changed significantly in recent years. Many couples choose not to marry and to have families, while many prospective fathers who are not in a permanent relationship have a keen interest in the welfare of their unborn child. Equally, assumptions that the mother of an unborn child will have the child's interests more at heart, or will be better placed to care for the child than the father, are no longer valid in many instances.

There is therefore a case for erasing the distinction (which is, of course, discriminatory) and to place married and unmarried mothers and fathers on an identical legal footing in respect of the acquisition and loss of parental responsibility. Such a change is justified for the following reasons:

1. To end this discriminatory anomaly.
2. To reflect changes in the roles of fathers.
3. To encourage further progress in the acceptance of parental responsibilities by unmarried fathers.

The change could be achieved simply by amendments to the Children Act 1989 (ss. 2 and 4) that would delete distinctions between married and unmarried parents. On welfare grounds there would seem to be a case for extending the power of the court to remove parental responsibility not just from unmarried fathers but from all parents. This is the case in many other countries where parental responsibility can either be removed or suspended. The alternative would be removal of the provisions by which parental responsibility can be withdrawn from unmarried fathers.

Support for separating parents and their children

Many of the problems faced by the children of separating parents arise from delay and lack of understanding of the consequences for children of separation.

Ensuring intervention occurs early, and that it provides comprehensive access to the resources separating families require, would address many of the issues that arise for children. In some European countries where a couple separate, the child welfare department automatically initiates a process to assist the parents in resolving issues. Putting in place a network of family centres (perhaps on the Australian model) providing a range of services – from information and assistance with drawing up parenting plans, to mediation counselling, and legal advice and support – could be the answer. Centres might learn of separation by way of school referrals, provision of information to children via schools, through to GP and other professional referrals. An obligation to make a referral on the basis that a child of separating parents was a child in need would trigger automatic referrals. Such a programme would be resource-intensive and might be piloted to ascertain whether the anticipated benefits in fact accrued.

Marriage, divorce, cohabitation and financial provision

Nearly one in two children is now born to unmarried parents. Divorce rates stay high and marriage rates are at an all-time low. While people increasingly opt to live together outside marriage, the law provides no modern framework for the resolution of their property disputes. Meanwhile, the family justice system and the Child Maintenance Service are not seen as promoting justice for anyone other than the very rich. What should be the response of an incoming Labour government to these issues?

Cohabitation

On cohabitation law reform, the Law Commission's 2007 report, *Cohabitation: The Financial Consequences of Relationship Breakdown*,[2] remains on the shelf. The Scottish Parliament introduced legislation in 2006 for unmarried couples to be able to make limited property claims against each other, but against the backdrop of a much less 'generous' law of financial provision on divorce. If individuals want more control over their life, and reject marriage because of the risk of a messy divorce, the answer is not going to be a law that imposes obligations on them regardless, simply because they happen to live together. Just as nuptial agreements are now given more emphasis by the divorce court, unmarried couples should be able to reach agreement as to their property and financial arrangements.

While some scoff at the notion of public information programmes, the reality is that many unmarried couples remain ignorant of their rights and still believe that there is such a thing as 'common law marriage'. More needs to be done to ensure that people buying a property in joint names are aware of their rights and agree what their shares should be. A person moving into a property owned in the sole name of their partner at the date of purchase should be asked to do more than simply agree their claims come behind those of the mortgage provider.

We therefore suggest:

- The creation of an opt-in system for registered relationships (civil associates/civil consorts!), similar to the French '*pacte civile*', to allow unmarried couples to acquire greater legal recognition of their relationship, while it being in no way equivalent to marriage or civil partnership.

- Greater legal information for those who remain outside the opt-in system.
- A strengthening of Schedule 1 to the Children Act 1989 to allow the court to make provision for child care costs, and where the court is satisfied that child support under the statutory scheme is unfair or inadequate, provision for outright property transfer to the child's carer.

Marriage

Such an opt-in system would have to be clearly distinguishable from both marriage and civil partnership. The extension of civil partnership to different-sex couples is both unnecessary and misguided: if a heterosexual couple wish to have a civil ceremony that gives them the status of 'civil partnership' they can get married in a register office. Civil partnership was a temporary institution that should be abolished once same-sex marriage has gained acceptance.

While this is not the place to argue for the disestablishment of the Church of England, we consider there should be a wholesale review of the legal process for becoming married or entering into a civil partnership. Options include:

- Allowing some religious content in a register office ceremony.
- Preventing any religious ceremony from creating marital status so that only a civil ceremony could create a legally recognised marriage.
- Making it easier for religious organisations to undertake ceremonies that create legally recognised marriages.

Many British Muslim women are dismayed to discover that although they have undergone a valid Muslim marriage, they are not married in the eyes of English law. In addition, while few will wish to see Vegas-style marriage parlours, there is a case for some deregulation of approved premises under the Marriage Act 1949: why, for instance, cannot individuals get married outdoors? With marriage rates so low, why should the law make it hard to get married?

Divorce

The orthodox wisdom is that advocating divorce reform wins no votes – merely opprobrium from certain sections of the media. Yet recent and proposed changes in family law will mean that our 'fault-based' divorce law is nothing but smoke and mirrors.

From April 2014, divorce petitions will have to be lodged online. They are to be scrutinised by justices' clerks, the lowest rank of the judiciary to sit in the family courts. There will no longer be any requirement for the parties to lodge a statement of arrangements for the children, nor will the court have any duty to scrutinise these arrangements. The 'special procedure' for divorce cases to be dealt with on paper has long since become the norm. In short, divorce will have the outward appearance of being 'fault-based', whereas the reality is that marriage is effectively determinable by notice, and divorce is an administrative process. There must be a better way.

Financial provision

Although we see some merit in legislating to allow individuals to reach binding agreements without having to seek the court's approval, and to enable greater weight to be given to pre-nuptial agreements, we consider that it would be wrong to engage in piecemeal reform of the legislation governing financial provision on divorce.

One of the strengths of the existing system is that a person who might have been reluctantly persuaded that they are to be divorced can at least know that a court can look at their individual case and find a fair solution, untrammelled by mathematical formulae and rigid rules. On child support, we would favour simplification of the current system together with a provision allowing individuals to opt in to the court system and to stay opted in. We would also favour allowing individuals to be able to reach legally binding agreements for child maintenance that could be enforceable in the same way as an official calculation made by the Child Maintenance Service. The agreement should be capable of variation on specified grounds on application to the court or tribunal.

Adoption
Domestic adoption

With the very far-reaching changes over the past two years in the law and practice relating to care proceedings and adoption, it is necessary that there should be careful monitoring of the effect of all these reforms to ensure that the rights of children, birth parents, their wider family members, as well as prospective adopters, foster parents and adopters are properly protected.

The effective and fair working of these crucial areas of family policy requires a balance to be maintained that recognises the fundamental rights of both the parents and the children and also the need to ensure that there is an adequate number and breadth of adoptive and foster families if children are not able to be cared for within their birth families and where permanent care outside their family is the best option for them.

Many of the reforms are welcome in their objective to speed up the care and adoption process in the obvious best interests of the children concerned. However, there are concerns that changes such as the drive to complete care proceedings within 26 weeks, the reduction in the number of experts and reduced court scrutiny of care plans before final decisions are made may result in an erosion of the maintenance of this important balance. Avoidance of unnecessary delay is crucial, but adoption outside the family is such a far-reaching outcome for a child that the equally important right for a child to be brought up within their birth family if possible must not be compromised by the reforms. With sufficient time to evaluate the effects of the many reforms, changes, or at least fine tuning, may prove necessary.

One issue of crucial importance to the government's drive to increase and speed up adoption placements is that of adoption support. Adoption breakdown is the very worst outcome for a child adopted from care. These children will already have suffered much loss and trauma, and all efforts must be made to ensure support and underpinning of their adoption placements. Currently, adopters have a right to an assessment by their local authority of their need for adoption support but there is no corresponding duty on local authorities to provide the support assessed as being needed. Introducing this duty would increase the number of families prepared to adopt children from care with complex needs and would also reduce the expense for local authorities and society, and the trauma for the adoptive families and their children of adoption breakdown.

Intercountry adoptions

There are now relatively few 'classic' intercountry adoptions (i.e. an adoption from abroad by a family habitually resident in this country), as highlighted by the most recent Department for Education statistics. However, the data hide the fact that there are many other adoptions with an international element that are not covered by the government statistics. These include 'ex pats' adopting a child from the country where they are living and working, or from a third country, who then want to settle back in the UK or to obtain recognition of their foreign adoption and British nationality for their child. The statistics also do not include kinship adoptions. This might occur while the adopting family is living abroad but planning to resettle in the UK. It might also arise when a child from abroad has come into their care in this country and the family here have no legal status in relation to the child, such being necessary if the child is to live permanently with them including resolving the child's immigration status.

Placing children for adoption domestically is regarded understandably as the priority of adoption practitioners in this country. However there are and will remain adoptions with a foreign element of children who though not living here have an equal right to family life, and also adopting families who have a right to expect that the law will assist them rather than place unduly technical legal obstacles in the way of their plans to give permanence to a child in need abroad.

Changes needed to law and practice in this area of adoption include:

- **Removal of immigration anomalies.** Where a foreign adoption order is not recognised in this country, and families re-adopt the child in this country in order to obtain recognition of their foreign adoption order, the child automatically becomes a British citizen under s. 1(5) of the British Nationality Act 1981 if at least one of the adopters is a British national. There are situations where a special guardianship order (SGO) would be a more appropriate order for a child than an adoption order – for instance in kinship cases where an adoption order would skew family relationships. An SGO does not bring with it the same automatic grant of British nationality and risks the child having to leave the UK once they leave full-time education as their right to remain will have expired. Consequently, adoption orders are sought in cases where they are not the most appropriate order, purely for immigration reasons. Section 55 of the Adoption and Children Act 2002 requires that the child's welfare should be paramount in decisions made in respect of them but this does not appear to be carried through in practice when the UK Border Agency is considering leave to remain, leading to British citizenship for a child from abroad for whom an SGO is the best order. This issue needs to be addressed to better meet the needs of each individual child.

- **Conferring parental responsibility prior to completion of adoption.** Where a foreign adoption order is not recognised in this country (as in the previous bullet point) and it is necessary for the family to re-adopt here in order to obtain recognition of the foreign adoption and British nationality for their foreign adopted child, the child has no legal parent in this country until the English adoption order is made. This is because there is no one in this country who will have parental responsibility for the child until an adoption order is made or unless the family applies in advance of the adoption order for a residence order. The latter in reality rarely occurs as it involves yet more litigation for a family that has quite properly and legally completed an adoption abroad and then has to embark on litigation in this country to obtain an English adoption order. The period involved is normally at least one year, when neither the adopters nor anyone else in this country or in the child's country of origin will have parental responsibility to enable them to make crucial decisions on matters such as medical treatment or education for the child. A simple change of the law to grant automatic parental responsibility to the adopters on their giving notice of intention to adopt the child in the English courts (which they must do within 14 days of the child's arrival in this country) to their local authority, would resolve this not inconsiderable problem.

- **School admissions and foreign adoptions.** The recent adoption law reforms introduced changes to the Schools Admission Code to give priority in schools admissions to children adopted domestically from the care system. This reform is welcome but was unfortunately not extended to children adopted from abroad. This is despite these children's significant vulnerability, equal if not greater to that of domestically adopted children. The numbers of these children are not large, but an extension of the benefits of the changes to the School Admissions Code to include them would be immeasurable.

Adoption of children from care by families living abroad

The care community in this country is becoming increasingly diverse with many of the extended families of children in care living abroad. Local authorities have a duty to consider and investigate family placements, whether they are in this country or abroad, where birth parents are considered unlikely to be able to care for their children. Investigation and pursuit of adoptive placements abroad by local authorities are an increasing reality. However, although they may be the best placement for a child they are often not pursued because of the complexities and the length of the legal processes involved.

Many but not all of these placements will involve compliance with Hague Convention requirements. In all cases, cooperation between the authorities in this country and those of the country where it is planned the child should live permanently, will be needed. There are limits to the influence that this country can have on the procedures of other countries, but our own procedures are slow, cumbrous and need streamlining if adoption abroad is to be a continuing viable option for children in care in this country, particularly with the drive to complete care proceedings within 26 weeks.

Assisted reproduction and surrogacy

Society rightly recognises and acknowledges the importance of family life and through it the need to nurture future generations. Sadly, for significant numbers the path to parenthood is not straightforward or easy. Indeed, without the assistance of scientific progress in modern techniques of assisted reproduction (including egg, sperm and/or embryo donation and/or resort to surrogacy), for some it would not be achievable.

While recognising that parenthood should be seen as a privilege and not an automatic right, the reality is that today we have the knowledge and the means to enable adults to become parents to their own genetic children through assisted reproduction and surrogacy. Where assistance is not readily available, in this internet age help is often at hand, whether at home or overseas. Just as the nature of the modern family has changed as a result of relationship breakdown and complex extended families, so too in some cases has the form of the modern family, so that in addition to the majority of families headed by two heterosexual parents, there are families headed by same-sex parents and single parents, and children who may have no genetic connection to their 'family of origin' (as in the case of embryo donation).

The law in this area is extremely complex. There is the Human Fertilisation and Embryology Act 1990, which was significantly amended in relation to parenthood as a result of assisted reproduction and surrogacy by the Human Fertilisation and Embryology Act (HFEA) 2008, and the Surrogacy Arrangements Act (SAA) 1985, as amended. Subject to statutory conditions, HFEA 2008 now recognises married, unmarried, heterosexual and same-sex couples as the legal parents of a child born to a woman of that couple as a result of fertility treatment using donor gametes. Only in the case of surrogacy and parental orders is it a condition that either the woman or her partner is genetically connected to the child. In some, but not all circumstances, it is crucial that the treatment took place at a UK-licensed clinic.

Surrogacy arrangements are not enforceable under English law,[3] nor are commercial surrogacy arrangements permissible, although they are both permissible and enforceable in some other jurisdictions.

Under English law the woman who gives birth to a child will for all purposes be treated in law as the mother of that child, irrespective of whether or not she is also a genetic parent and wherever in the world the child was 'conceived'.[4] Thus, it is possible for a single woman to become a legal parent of a child to whom she gives birth following embryo donation that takes place at an overseas clinic, even though she is not a genetic parent, is past child-bearing age and, but for the fertility treatment she obtained overseas (which may not have been available to her in the UK), would not have been able to give birth.

Single genetic parents

Following surrogacy, provided that one of them is genetically connected to a child born as a result (and subject to certain other conditions) a couple – whether heterosexual, same-sex, married or unmarried – may apply for a parental order[5] in respect of that child within six months of birth (but not within the first six weeks). The effect of the parental order is that thereafter the child is treated in law as their child. However, where a single woman enters into a successful surrogacy arrangement abroad (where this may be permissible) using her own eggs and donor sperm, she will not be able to apply for a parental order in the UK (transferring legal parenthood to herself) in respect of any child born as a result. Yet she would be the genetic mother of that child and the intended parent, and it is possible that under the law of the state in which the surrogacy arrangement was entered into, she is the child's only legal parent. Thus the child is left stateless and a legal orphan. While this situation may arise in some circumstances where a couple enter into a surrogacy arrangement abroad,[6] this will be remedied by the grant of a parental order in favour of the intended parents.

The only remedy for the single intended parent is to apply to adopt the child. Albeit that this is not identical to a parental order, it is now possible for a single person to adopt a child.[7] Where the surrogacy is overseas, adoption may not be straightforward and indeed may fall foul of overseas adoption regulations. Given that a single woman (indeed a single man) may adopt or foster a child, and in the case of the example above may be the only legal parent of a child to whom she is not genetically connected, albeit to whom she did give birth, it is anomalous and discriminatory that the genetic and intended mother of a child born through surrogacy should not be able to apply for a parental order in respect of that child.

Similar, although not identical considerations apply to single men who may enter into surrogacy arrangements using their sperm (whether or not using donor egg – which would be available overseas only – or the more traditional route of artificial insemination). Unlike the intended single mother, in many cases the intended father would also be the legal father,[8] albeit he would share parental responsibility with the surrogate mother. In the absence of a parental order, the only route by which he would become the child's sole parent is via adoption.

We would recommend that the law is changed to allow for parental orders to be granted in respect of single applicants, provided that the applicant is genetically connected to the child.

Survivor of two intended parents

Where one of two intended parents dies after the issue of an application for a parental order, but before its grant, it is nevertheless possible for a parental order to be granted in respect of both the surviving and deceased intended parents.[9] However, were death to occur prior to issuing the application, as the law now stands there could be no parental order even where both are also genetic parents to the child. Again the only remedy for the surviving intended parent would be application for a single parent adoption, with the same potential difficulties if the surrogacy took place overseas. But there would be no legal relationship between the child and the deceased parent, with whom the child may have lived, albeit briefly. This may have far-reaching repercussions, not least in respect of inheritance, but also does not reflect the reality that the couple were to have jointly parented the child.

We would recommend that in these circumstances the surviving intended parent should be able to apply for a 'joint' parental order where there is proof that the deceased intended to be parent to the child, or alternatively should be entitled to apply for a parental order as a single parent.

In response to potential objections on the basis that children should have two parents, we would say:

1. Sadly, although happily rarely, a child may be born after the death of a parent (usually the father), but nevertheless that parent will be recognised in law as the child's parent.
2. A single woman may conceive using artificial insemination, which if through a UK licensed clinic means that the donor will not be treated as the father[10] and therefore the child has only one parent.
3. The law already recognises adoption by a single parent.

Surrogacy arrangements: Criminal offences and obtaining legal advice

Under ss. 2 and 3 of the Surrogacy Arrangements Act (SAA) 1985 it is illegal for an individual to act on a commercial basis in the UK:

1. To initiate or take part in any negotiations with a view to the making of a surrogacy arrangement.
2. To offer to agree to negotiate the making of a surrogacy arrangement.
3. To compile any information with a view to its use in the making, or negotiating the making of, commercial surrogacy arrangements, or to advertise/publish in the UK.

As drafted, this would appear to catch acts done in the UK pursuant to a commercial surrogacy arrangement made overseas, where it may be lawful. Contravention of s. 2 is a criminal offence, liable to fine or imprisonment. Although the Act provides that surrogacy arrangements are unenforceable (whether commercial or altruistic), neither the intended parents nor surrogates will be guilty of criminal offences.

The clear aim is to prevent individuals and agencies profiting from the 'surrogacy trade'. However, the effect of this may be to prohibit lawyers in this jurisdiction from advising individuals who seek to enter into surrogacy arrangements as to the consequences of surrogacy arrangements made overseas and the orders that are available. At the very least, this creates the impression that legal advice may not be available when it is, provided that it does not contravene ss. 2 and 3. Intended parents contemplating overseas surrogacy agreements need to consider legal and immigration issues that may be obstacles to the child's entry into the UK and to obtaining the necessary court orders to regularise the family relationship. What has resonated quite clearly from the judgments of the High Court is the importance of parents obtaining legal advice, in advance, and securing parental orders as soon as possible after the child is born (the time limit is six months post birth). The concern here is the misinformation widely available on the internet that sometimes seeks to discourage intended parents from obtaining independent legal advice on the effects of English law and/or parental orders. This is undesirable.

We believe that the statute should be clear and that legal advice to intended parents should be permissible, irrespective of whether or not they are contemplating entering into a commercial surrogacy agreement overseas. At a time when the High Court is sending out a very clear message on the need for intended parents to be aware of legal consequences in advance, and that parental orders are the most appropriate legal mechanism to secure parental rights, it is crucial that intended parents are afforded the opportunity to get proper legal advice.

– Time for a new review of law and practice

The socio-legal landscape has changed radically since the Warnock Committee Report in the 1980s.[11] Some 15 years on, at the invitation of the then Labour government in June 1997, the Brazier Report[12] sought to review the current law and practice concerning surrogacy. We think the time has come again for a similar review. We outline below a number of suggested areas that we believe need to be reviewed. The list is not intended to be exhaustive.

There has been a significant increase in the number of people applying for parental orders, boosted by the expansion of those falling under the new criteria. However, closer scrutiny of not only surrogacy practice but also the increase in the use of assisted reproductive technologies (ART) suggests the need for an up to date review. There is a strong case that there should be regulation of surrogacy arrangements with a view to protecting the interests of all parties concerned in an arrangement. This was a minority view shared by the Warnock Committee and was considered in the Brazier Report.

There has been an enormous change in attitude since Warnock and Brazier, such that babies born through ART (including using donor gametes and embryos) and surrogacy are openly acknowledged and generally more acceptable than in 1984 when the Warnock Report was published. While we do not advocate a change in the law to permit commercial surrogacy, it must be acknowledged that in reality, where a couple seek surrogacy abroad, then in the best interests of the child concerned the English courts should sanction parental orders despite the fact that commercial payments have been made to surrogate and overseas agencies. In part this is due to the fact that the court cannot consider surrogacy arrangements/parental orders in advance (as is the case in some other jurisdictions). By the time it comes to determine whether or not a parental order should be made, it is likely that the child will have lived with the intended parents for many months, and indeed may no longer be resident in their country of birth. The effect is that, provided they go overseas, couples are able to circumvent SAA and commercial surrogacy is therefore a reality, but without the careful regulation and scrutiny that govern fertility clinics in the UK.

Further, neither Warnock nor Brazier could have contemplated the impact of the internet in this area. For many it is a useful 'tool', but there may be considerable risks where commissioning parents identify a surrogate 'online', without any vetting or oversight by any agency. The case of *CW v NT and another* [2011] EWHC 33 aptly demonstrated the difficulties that can arise in such 'DIY' scenarios where, following the briefest of introductions via email, pregnancy swiftly follows insemination at the initial meeting but the surrogate later reneges on the arrangement, leading to lengthy proceedings in the High Court to determine the child's future. By their nature such arrangements lack any form of basic screening as to the suitability of any of the parties involved from psychological and health perspectives. Formal regulation of surrogacy arrangements in our jurisdiction may prevent many such cases. At the very least, consideration needs to be given as to how introduction websites might be monitored to protect vulnerable users.

The HFEA 2008 requires the respondents to a parental order application (that is, the surrogate and her husband if married) to have freely and unconditionally agreed to the making of an order.[13] Consent is ineffective if it is given less than six weeks after the birth.[14] This can be particularly problematic in some overseas situations where, say, following birth the surrogate or an estranged husband of the surrogate cannot be found, and/or there are immigration issues that cause delay. Currently there is no discretion in the court to extend the six-month period in which application for a parental order should be made. While there is power to override the consent provision in appropriate circumstances, inevitably this leads to delay and expense that might be avoided.

The Hague Conference on Private International Law is currently undertaking research on the 'private international law issues surrounding the status of children, including issues arising from international surrogacy arrangements'. In April 2014 the Council of the Hague Conference considered the report of the Permanent Bureau and agreed that work should continue on the feasibility of a new international treaty in respect of surrogacy, akin to the Hague Convention on Child Abduction or the Intercountry Adoption Convention. The increasing numbers of surrogacy arrangements that include a commercial and international element raise the risks of possible reproductive tourism that need to be considered at a global level. It is clear to us that there is an urgent and overwhelming need for cross-border cooperation in this area. This needs to consider not only legal issues including jurisdiction and conflict of laws, but wider international public interest matters such as medical and ethical issues concerning minimum standards of best clinical practice; potential financial exploitation of surrogates and intended parents; possible human trafficking and/or 'baby farming'; and the exploitation of donors.

We do not doubt that it may be difficult to reach international consensus on the way forward, given that even within Europe there is huge variance between the legal approach of the individual states towards surrogacy and ART. Nevertheless, we believe that these are growing issues that cannot be ignored and there is a strong case for them to be considered within a full review of the area and in the context of other international developments.

Summary of principal recommendations

- To place married and unmarried mothers and fathers on an identical legal footing in respect of the acquisition and loss of parental responsibility.
- To alleviate some of the problems faced by the children of separating parents by ensuring intervention occurs early and that such intervention provides comprehensive access to the resources separating families require.
- To relax or clarify some of the legal requirements to contract a valid marriage.
- To codify family law.
- To amend the Children Act 1989 to provide a wider range of orders that the court can make where the parents are unmarried, including property transfers.
- To introduce a duty on local authorities to provide support following an assessment by that local authority of adopters' need for adoption support.
- To remove various anomalies relating to adoptions from abroad.
- To change the law relating to assisted reproduction and surrogacy to allow for parental orders to be granted in respect of single applicants, provided that the applicant is genetically connected to the child.
- To set up a new, comprehensive review of the current law and practice concerning surrogacy.

8

Serious Fraud and White Collar Crime

Emily Thornberry MP

In 2007–08 a corporate culture of reckless risk taking brought the economy of the Western world to its knees. Yet almost no senior bankers have faced legal sanctions for their role in bringing the crisis about.[1] In 2012 it emerged that our major banks had been rigging the London interbank lending rate for years. This was not the work of one rogue employee; it seems to have been endemic with open boasting about it and bottles of Bolly. This is nothing less than institutional, sector-wide contempt for the law. The European Commission is investigating whether similar practices have been taking place on the oil markets over the past decade.[2]

As these scandals broke, the public demanded action. Instead of action they got the unedifying spectacle of the Serious Fraud Office and the Financial Services Authority squabbling between themselves over who should investigate. Not because they both wanted to take on this high-profile investigation – but because neither of them wanted to take it on. It seemed to be all too difficult and expensive.

Policing the City of London goes to the heart of Labour's agenda to create a new and better economy after the crash, and it is why one of the first things Labour will do if elected is to bring forward an Economic Crime Act to strengthen and consolidate the law.[3] It is clear that we must have an up to date law on corporate criminal liability, robust penalties and confident law enforcement agencies, staffed by the very best people. In the 'One Nation' economy that we want to build, we cannot have an elite that is above the law: a criminal wearing a collar and tie is still a criminal. Furthermore, we should throw the book at companies that allow corporate criminality to thrive. To do that will require major changes to the criminal law, sentencing and the funding structure of the Serious Fraud Office.

Corporate prosecutions

The key to turning the tide on serious economic crime is indicting and prosecuting more companies. Where harm has been caused by a criminal corporate culture rather than a rogue individual, only putting the company in the dock will reflect the true nature of the wrongdoing. Where it has been caused by a rogue individual, the threat of indictment and prosecution of the company that stood behind them will incentivise cooperation and pierce the corporate veil in pursuit of that prosecution. And, as it is unlikely that it will be possible to recoup from an individual defendant the cost of either the harm done or the investigation and prosecution of that harm, the corporation that stands behind them should, with some exceptions, be responsible.

These points are well understood by the US fraud prosecutors whom I met while researching for the Labour policy review on tackling serious fraud and economic crime.[4] In the United States, the law on corporate liability maximises the chances of successful prosecution because it operates on the basis that companies are vicariously liable for the acts of their employees in the course of their employment. The *United States Attorneys' Manual* states that a 'corporation may be held criminally liable for the illegal acts of its directors, officers, employees, and agents. To hold a corporation liable for these actions, the government must establish that the corporate agent's actions (i) were within the scope of his duties and (ii) were intended, at least in part, to benefit the corporation.' This is the doctrine of *respondeat superior*.

This puts US prosecutors in a strong position and it is no surprise that the US Department of Justice (DoJ) has been the driving force behind the most important financial crime investigations, not just in the US but anywhere in the world, and in particular in the United Kingdom. US authorities are in fact tougher with British banks than the British authorities are themselves. For example, the DoJ fined

Barclays $160m (£101m) for Libor-rigging, while the UK Financial Services Authority fined them £60m. The Serious Fraud Office is still investigating. The DoJ fined RBS $150m for Libor-rigging, whereas the FSA fined them £87.5m. Federal prosecutors have also fined HSBC £1.25bn for money laundering and Standard Chartered £227m for evading sanctions on Iran.

These fines were the result of plea bargains, which are an important feature of the US criminal justice system. By making a successful prosecution more likely, vicarious liability also helps prosecutors drive a hard bargain in these plea agreements. Not only that, but it makes companies that are anxious to avoid prosecution more willing to cooperate with prosecutors and less likely to protect the individual employees involved in the crime.

The identification doctrine

In the UK the law is very different. Although it has been an established principle of English law going back to the nineteenth century that companies can be criminally culpable, that culpability is very narrowly drawn. This is because of a legal rule called the 'identification doctrine', also known as the directing mind theory. According to the doctrine, the acts and states of mind of those individuals who are the directing mind and will of the corporation are the acts and states of mind of the corporation itself. The individuals who are the directing mind and will of the organisation can be read as members of the board of directors.

The leading authority on the identification doctrine is the decision of the House of Lords in *Tesco Supermarkets Ltd v Nattrass* [1972] AC 153. After this case, the judiciary took the view that unless statute states that vicarious liability is to apply to a particular offence, the identification doctrine is to apply. Lord Reid stated that a company may be criminally liable only for the acts of 'the board of directors, the managing director and perhaps other superior officers of a company who carry out functions of management and speak and act as the company'.[5]

This is a very high threshold and it's not surprising that the Serious Fraud Office has undertaken no corporate prosecutions in the past two years.[6] The new Director of the SFO, David Green QC, has called for the identification doctrine to be scrapped in favour of US-style vicarious liability.[7] The doctrine has also been heavily criticised over the years, eroding the law's authority and leaving the rules ripe for an overhaul.

Criticism has focused on the doctrine's excessive leniency towards bigger companies with complex and diffuse chains of command. In these companies, directors are highly unlikely to be involved in the day-to-day management of the company. Perversely, this means that companies capable of doing the most harm to the largest number of people are the most insulated from criminal liability.[8] Because the doctrine is so hard to apply to large companies with far-flung units and decentralised health and safety procedures, some legal experts have attacked it as outdated and out of step with the reality of the modern corporate world. According to the criminal law textbook, Smith and Hogan:

> *Only the very senior managers will be likely to fit the description as the directing mind and will of the company. This illustrates one of the major shortcomings of the identification doctrine – that it fails to reflect the reality of the modern day large multinational corporation ... it produces what many regard as an unsatisfactorily narrow scope for criminal liability.*[9]

In recent years, cracks have emerged in the application of the identification doctrine as judges have struggled to reconcile it with the realities of modern corporate structures. None of these judgments have definitively cast it aside, but they have thrown the law into confusion.[10] This has prompted the Law Commission to state that 'it is clear ... that the law in this area suffers from considerable uncertainty.'[11]

Parliament has joined the judiciary in chipping away at the constraints of the identification doctrine. The focus of these efforts initially was corporate manslaughter, where the protection the identification doctrine gives to dangerously mismanaged companies became a source of widespread moral outrage in the aftermath of tragedies such as the sinking of the *Herald of Free Enterprise* in 1987 and the Hillsborough disaster.

These efforts culminated in two important exceptions to the identification doctrine being carved out by the last Labour government. The first of these was the Corporate Manslaughter Act 2007, which introduced a new basis for liability – management failure. The other was the Bribery Act 2010. This too was the result of years of lobbying for reform of the identification doctrine, this time by anti-corruption NGOs calling for the UK to meet its obligation under the 1997 OECD anti-bribery convention.[12] Under the identification doctrine it was very difficult to hold companies criminally to account for bribery overseas. Typically, bribing foreign officials takes place overseas by employees reasonably far down the food chain or even by local 'fixers' not formally employed by the company at all.

Section 7 of the Bribery Act makes a company vicariously liable for attempts to bribe public officials by anyone associated with it. This vicarious liability is, however, subject to the s. 7(2) defence of having 'had in place adequate procedures designed to prevent persons associated with [it] from undertaking such conduct.' The Act recognises that even though individual directors may not have known, or been informed of bribery, the company still benefits from the wrongdoing and therefore has incentives to turn a blind eye. Culpability lies not in a director's knowledge, intent or dishonesty, but in the company's *failure to prevent*.

Corporate manslaughter and bribery are obviously very different crimes. Indeed, the Corporate Manslaughter Act is significantly different from the Bribery Act in that it still keeps the spotlight on senior management. However, what the two Acts have in common is that they focus on the organisation, structure and corporate culture of the defendant company.

The way forward

As argued in Labour's Policy Review, *Tackling Serious Fraud and White Collar Crime*,[13] Parliament could legislate to bring the law up to date and achieve certainty. It is suggested that that the principles that underpin the Bribery Act should be extended to other economic crimes so that where a person associated with a company has committed the offence, the company is culpable if it fails to show that it had adequate procedures in place to prevent that kind of offending. This is the approach adopted in recent years by many European countries, including the Netherlands, Italy and Belgium which are adopting approaches similar to the one advocated here.[14]

Critics of that approach broadly fall into two camps. There are those, particularly in business, who fear that any extension of corporate culpability will add greatly to the risks and red tape that companies face. However, it should be remembered that there was intensive lobbying along these lines before the introduction of the Bribery Act, and so far these fears have proved entirely without foundation. We have yet to see a single corporate prosecution by the Serious Fraud Office under the Bribery Act. But that in turn leads us to the second group of critics who argue that the lack of prosecutions is a sign that the Bribery Act is ineffectual.

The US officials I met dislike the adequate procedures approach because they fear that (a) companies will use boilerplate compliance programmes to create an appearance of adequate procedures, and (b) investigations and prosecutions will get bogged down over quality of the compliance programme rather than cutting through to the underlying criminality.

The experience of the corporate criminality provisions of the Australian Criminal Code (which is similar in some respects to the Bribery Act) could be seen as lending credence to those fears. Despite being the pin-up of advocates of organisational liability, the corporate criminality provisions of the 1995 Code do not appear to have been used since coming fully into force in 2001. The OECD, which once praised Australia for bringing in such 'ambitious and progressive' reforms, expressed 'serious concern' in October 2013 over the lack of prosecutions.

That said, there are promising signs that the Bribery Act, unlike the provisions in the Australian Code, is having an effect. The number of companies voluntarily admitting wrongdoing to the Serious Fraud Office was recently reported as doubling in a year.[15] Twelve companies had confessed to the SFO that they had issues in the year ending 31 March 2012, compared with seven in the two preceding years. According to Barry Vitou, a lawyer at Pinsent Masons, which requested the information via a freedom of information request, 'the harsh penalties associated with the Bribery Act have greatly increased the incentives for corporates to self-report rather than risk being caught out by a hostile SFO investigation.'[16]

This is significant because the primary intention of the Bribery Act was preventative. It was not about dragging companies through the courts but about driving up standards of corporate governance. This is why building on the Bribery Act looks to me like the most sensible approach. However if, after an agreed period of time, enforcement remains inadequate, we should consider the US approach where the question of whether or not a company had adequate procedures changes status from a statutory defence to a factor that (a) influences the prosecutor's discretion over whether to charge and (b) mitigates the severity of the sentence.

Fines

It is not just UK law on corporate liability that is weak by international standards – the fines are too. Fines levied against corporates guilty of criminal offences in the UK are low. The largest fine issued to a company as a result of a bribery prosecution by the Serious Fraud Office is £8.3m,[17] while for fraud it is £2m.[18] Since 2010, British courts have levied only £8.8m in corporate fines for cases brought by the SFO.

Compare this with fines in the United States, where in 2013 HSBC was fined $1.9bn (some 17 per cent of its full-year profit) and Glaxo-SmithKline was fined $3bn for fraud. The US Department of Justice fines for bribery regularly extend into the tens of millions of dollars – even, on occasion, hundreds of millions of dollars. In 2008 the DoJ fined Siemens $450m for corruption and, in the same period of time (between November 2010 and December 2012), extracted $665.8m in fines for bribery alone.

The most notorious example of the discrepancy between the two countries' fining approaches was offered in the BAE Tanzania case. BAE Systems was fined over eight times as much in the United States ($400m, or £250m) as in the United Kingdom (£30m) for bribery and corruption as a result of the same joint investigation. And only £500,000 of the £30m was technically a fine, with the balance comprising a charitable payment to Tanzania.[19]

The discrepancy is accounted for by the very different ways in which fines are calculated. The British fines are not calculated according to any guidelines or formulas (with the exception of the Bribery Act 2010, which introduced an unlimited fine for any company or partnership that is convicted of the s. 7 offence of failure to prevent bribery). The numbers have been essentially plucked out of the air.

In the US, however, the guidelines offer a detailed step-by-step method for calculating the penalty. The first step is to determine the base fine that reflects the seriousness of the offence and the scale of the loss inflicted. Chapter 2 of the guidelines explains how to do this, while Chapter 8 sets out how to apply the fine to corporations. This base fine, which is not a percentage of anything but a prescribed figure, will then be increased according to the company's 'culpability score'. Companies rack up points on this score according to determinations that are made about factors such as the extent of knowledge about the wrongdoing within the company and whether the company has a history of bad behaviour. These factors are listed. Once the culpability score is arrived at, the guidelines specify the minimum and maximum multipliers that can be applied to the base fine, supplying a list of factors to consider when deciding whether to move towards the top or bottom of the range. These include aggravating factors, such as whether the victims were particularly vulnerable, but also mitigating factors as well.

A more robust approach can also be seen in the work of the European Commission's Directorate General for Competition, and fines for breaches of EU cartel law can run into billions of euros. In 2012 the Commission imposed €1.9bn (£1.6bn) in cartel fines,[20] which included a record €1.47bn fine on Phillips and five others for running two cartels over a decade.[21] In 2011, cartel fines levied by the Commission totalled €614m. These offences are civil rather than criminal. It seems anomalous that a UK company could be fined hundreds of millions of pounds for a civil offence, while a presumably far graver criminal act, such as fraud or bribery, would result in a fine a fraction of the size from a UK court.

The Sentencing Council of England and Wales has woken up to the need for a tougher and more structured approach to fining companies. In June 2013, it launched a consultation on new sentencing guidelines for fraud, bribery and money laundering that for the first time set out the approach to be adopted towards sentencing.[22] These represent a huge step forward and draw on the US and EU cartel regime examples. The fine is arrived at by multiplying the harm done by the company by the culpability of the corporate defendant. This is then adjusted up and down according to the particular mitigating and aggravating circumstances of the case. So, let's imagine that a company is convicted of a £1m fraud. Fraudulent practices were encouraged and endemic in that company so it falls into the highest category of culpability (category A). The next step is to multiply the £1m of financial harm done by the company by three, which is the multiplier assigned to companies in culpability category A. If however, that company self-reported and cooperated with prosecutors, the judge can choose to lower the final figure to £2m. If, on the other hand, the company tried to thwart the investigation at every turn, the judge can increase the fine to £4m.

This is welcome and in line with the direction set out in Labour's policy review on fraud. There are, though, one or two areas where I would like to see the Sentencing Council go further. The first concerns how they set the figure for financial harm. In cases of fraud, the harm figure will be the size of gain or intended gain. For bribery, the appropriate figure will normally be the gross profit from the contract obtained, retained or sought as a result of the offending. In cases of money laundering it will be the amount laundered or, alternatively, the likely cost avoided by failing to put in place an effective anti-money laundering programme if this is higher.[23] Only where the gain or intended gain cannot be established will recourse be had to a percentage of turnover, which will be 10 per cent of the relevant revenue (i.e. 10 per cent of the worldwide revenue derived from the product or business area to which the offence relates for the period of the offending).

The percentage of turnover approach is a real deterrent and cannot easily be dismissed as a cost of doing business. Is there any reason why it cannot be adopted even when we do know the size of the gain obtained or intended by the fraud? This is the view advocated by Sir John Thomas, President of the Queen's Bench Division of the High Court, in the *Innospec* case:

*As fines in cases of corruption of foreign government officials
must be effective, proportionate and be dissuasive in the sense
of having a deterrent element, I approach sentencing on the
basis in this case that a fine comparable to that imposed in the
US would have been the starting point, such a fine being quite
separate from and in addition to depriving Innospec Ltd of the
benefits it had obtained through its criminality.*[24]

It would also have been welcome to see the proposed guidelines set out some of the rehabilitative steps that judges could impose to improve corporate governance. With company defendants, as with individuals, the sentence should include elements of both punishment and reform. US sentencing guidelines give the court wide-ranging powers to require that convicted companies implement compliance programmes and carry out community service, and they also set out what is required of an effective compliance programme and how it should be monitored.[25]

Putting more companies in the dock and levying bigger fines on them is in the public interest and, incidentally, will help support the criminal justice system at a time when budgets are being cut by more than 25 per cent. The SFO's budget is in the process of falling from a high of £52m in 2009 to £30m by the end of the current Parliament. The pace and scale of the cuts was always likely to be unsustainable for an agency whose caseload includes concurrent investigations of Barclays, EADS, Rolls Royce and ENRC. And so it proved. In March 2014 the SFO had to ask the Treasury for a £19m emergency bailout just to get to the end of the financial year.[26] The SFO has been lurching from crisis to crisis. It botched the investigation of the Tchenguiz Brothers and accidentally sent 32,000 pages of documents from the BAE Saudi Arabia investigation, which contained details of witnesses' identities, to the wrong place (a cannabis farm).[27]

Conviction rates are also falling steadily. The conviction rate in 2009–10 was 91 per cent, which then fell to 84 per cent in 2010–11 and 70 per cent in 2012–13.[28] Although it has to be acknowledged that the SFO does take on difficult cases, which are more likely to result in volatile conviction rates, the consistency of the slide is troubling, as is the fact that the SFO prosecuted just 20 cases in 2013.

The agency is also having to restore its reputation following a series of scandals surrounding the leadership of its former director who lavished £1m on 'golden goodbyes' to senior staff, without authorisation from the Cabinet Office and Treasury, just before quitting in early 2012.[29] It then emerged that these staff also claimed over £100,000 in travel expenses[30] and almost misled Parliament on how much the SFO was spending on consultants.[31]

The SFO is now under the leadership of David Green QC, who has vowed to bring about change and make the organisation efficient and effective. However, morale and resources are still low, as is the public's patience with the SFO. One way to address this could be to allow the prosecutors to keep more of the assets they confiscate, and perhaps even some of the fines they impose, which would provide necessary funds without demanding more from the taxpayer. It would also hopefully avoid a repetition of the SFO's original decision to decline to investigate Libor-rigging on the grounds of a lack of funds.[32] It is a better solution to the SFO's funding shortage than the government's one of having it go cap in hand to the Treasury for money on a case-by-case basis. The conflict of interest the Treasury might have with the biggest names of UK PLC being investigated for fraud is obvious. There is also no duty for the Treasury to disclose when it has been approached or whether or not it agreed to fund the investigation.[33]

We already have the beginnings of a payment-by-results system, which is far more developed in the US. Under the Home Office Asset Recovery Incentive Scheme, where assets cannot be retraced to their original owners 18 per cent of confiscated criminal proceeds are retained by investigators and prosecutors. Expanding the scheme would be one way of addressing funding shortages in these austere times.

Incentives for whistleblowers?

When I was in the United States meeting federal prosecutors, they all swore by the importance of giving whistleblowers financial incentives. They said that one of the major reasons why their investigations are so much more successful and less protracted than ours is because, in many cases, there is a 'cooperator' who takes the prosecutor by the hand and leads them straight to the crucial evidence.

The incentives that US whistleblowers receive are very generous. The practice began with the Sarbanes-Oxley Act in 2002 and was built on by the Dodd-Frank Act in the wake of the financial crisis, which entitled a whistleblower with a valid tip-off or complaint to a percentage of any resulting fine levied by the Securities and Exchange Commission.[34] The fine can be as much as 30 per cent. It has been reported that the Home Office is now considering adopting this over here to increase the numbers of people coming forward. In 2012–13, no cases investigated by the SFO had been triggered by a whistleblower.[35] In 2013 the agency decided to close its 'whistleblower hotline' after it failed to result in prosecutions.[36]

Furthermore, given the increasingly global nature of business, US legislation provides not just an incentive to blow the whistle, but to do so specifically to the US authorities. It has been suggested that a worker in the UK branch of a multinational bank is now more likely to raise their complaint with the SEC in Washington than with their English employer. This will exacerbate the trend of cases that could and should be being prosecuted here, being prosecuted in the United States instead.[37]

However, David Green, whose agency would be the main beneficiary of increased corporate whistleblowing, has misgivings about the idea. He is concerned that defence lawyers would then find it too easy to attack the credibility of the prosecution witness.[38] English juries may well mistrust evidence driven by a profit motive. Nevertheless, it is clear that not enough whistleblowers are coming forward and it is welcome that the government is beginning to look at proposals to address this.

Conclusion

The SFO gets a lot of 'flak' for its low conviction rates and recurrent bungling. While this is often justified, it is only fair to point out that the odds are stacked against it. English law makes it nigh on impossible to prosecute the companies at the heart of the financial scandals hitting the headlines. The penalties for financial crime are so weak that it sends the message that the government really isn't that bothered about it, which in turn demoralises the SFO even further. It also deprives it of a valuable stream of revenue that it could use to overhaul its depleted resources and forlorn reputation. This is why, looking at what has worked in the UK and what works abroad, Labour has outlined the ideas (summarised below) that would address the major failings of the UK enforcement regime.

Summary of principal recommendations
- To expand vicarious liability.
- To increase corporate fines.
- To allow our prosecutors to keep more of the penalties and proceeds of crime.

9

Human Rights: Reflections on the 1998 Act

Jonathan Cooper OBE

The 1980s was a watershed decade. From the perspective of human rights protection in the United Kingdom it was the decade when the country began the successful shift from a system of government premised principally on civil liberties to one that recognised that the human rights of all within the jurisdiction also needed to be promoted and protected.

This is a bold statement, but it can be justified with reference to, amongst other things, the AIDS crisis which dominated that decade. For those who did not live through it, it is almost impossible to conjure up the fear, hysteria and hatred that surrounded HIV/AIDS and which was aimed at those most vulnerable to it.

I turned 18 in 1980; a young, gay man growing up in a Britain where sexual identity was almost invisible and voiceless. Homophobia did not exist because it was the status quo. Thirteen years earlier there had been a partial decriminalisation of homosexuality in that an absolute defence was created against the criminal law if consensual intimate sexual relations occurred in private between two men, both of whom were over 21. This was meaningless to me: I wasn't counting the years to my 21st birthday. The culture – a combination of hostility towards and denial of homosexuality – had not changed in any meaningful way since the 1950s. Like many other gay kids, I knew my identity. I didn't know what it meant, but I didn't really mind. And then in 1981 the first reports of what came to be known as AIDS began to emerge. I still recall reading about it in the Sunday papers and breaking out in a cold sweat. I was just beginning to get used to this idea of being gay, but now that casual stigma was further intensified by the potential for a shameful and isolated death. I did my best to give up on my sexual identity.

Making the case for human rights

The AIDS crisis touched virtually every aspect of law, yet the law's response was, at best, muted and the reality was that most living through the crisis did not see the law as providing a particularly effective system of protection. The English law tradition of civil liberties was clueless when faced with the onslaught of AIDS. In the absence of an effective human rights regime, the law could play no role in empowering those most affected. People could be detained, they lost their jobs, were made homeless, were deprived of their property, and were excluded from so many areas that society takes for granted. They had their privacy invaded and were subjected to a level of hate speech that fomented violence, forcing many to conceal their status or reject testing altogether. Medical confidentiality could not be guaranteed and healthcare did not seem prioritised. In many instances people died a frightened, lonely death. Discrimination and inequality thrived with impunity. The failure of the legal framework in the 1980s to respond to the HIV/AIDS tsunami is best summed up as a failure to recognise the dignity of those swept up in it.

It is an irony that it was the loss of so many, whose last moments were spent under such wretched circumstances, that led to a recognition that the UK system of government, and its laws in particular, was not working and needed to be recast for the late twentieth century, post-industrial and, arguably, post-modern Britain.

In 1987 I was wholly unqualified for the job, but I was appointed as the AIDS Co-ordinator of the Haemophilia Society. I had a history degree and had worked for indigent people in the United States prior to this. I was about to experience first-hand the failure of the law to assist those living with or directly affected by AIDS. People with haemophilia were infected with HIV through the use of contaminated blood products. The political process granted them an ex gratia payment; the law, apparently, could not compensate them. People with haemophilia faced the same discrimination and hostility as everyone else caught up in the AIDS crisis, but they also experienced their own issues. Kids were excluded from school; women would be encouraged to termi-nate their pregnancies and, in one instance, subjected to sterilisation; already living with a chronic genetic condition, most subsisted on low incomes. Perhaps most importantly, the haemophilia community was caught up in a deferential relationship with their healthcare providers.

In the absence of a rights-based approach to law, it was virtually impossible to formulate legal arguments to remedy the problems that this community and all of those affected by HIV/AIDS were exposed to. Towards the end of the 1980s and at the beginning of the 1990s, cases did begin to emerge – for example, concerning the exposure to doctors with HIV[1] – but these were the exception. The reality was that the law was not there for those whose rights were being violated.

And then, in 1990, very much inspired by Paul Sieghart's work,[2] a group of us within the NGO HIV/AIDS sector decided to draft a Declaration of Rights for people with HIV and AIDS. Prepared by Jonathan Grimshaw and Ceri Hutton, this document drew together the rights in international human rights treaties ratified by the UK and applied them to people with or affected by HIV and AIDS. It proved to be a sea change, but the level of hostility towards the notion that people with AIDS should have rights was extraordinary. I still recall the hate mail Ceri Hutton received after appearing on BBC Radio 4's *The Moral Maze* where she explained that people had rights, includ-ing the right to family life, just like everyone else. Despite all the objective evidence that Ceri put forward, it could not mitigate the hatred.

The need for rights and liberties

The AIDS crisis and my relationship with it represent a microcosm of what was happening across the law in the UK. In all key areas, from policing to protest and privacy to equality, the law was lagging behind.

By 1992 I had been called to the Bar and was starting my pupillage at Doughty Street Chambers. Edward Fitzgerald was my supervisor, and I was immediately immersed in the world of prisoners' rights. Edward had made incremental progress using common law principles and highlighting the arbitrary nature of the executive's control over the sentencing of those detained for life or at Her Majesty's Pleasure. The great common law judges, such as Sir Murray Stuart Smith,[3] were responsive to his arguments, but again, the law – and, in this context, the common law particularly – was constrained.[4] It took recourse to the Strasbourg Court under the jurisdiction of the European Convention on Human Rights (ECHR) to make any significant progress in ensuring that it was only the judges who could control the sentencing process.[5] Despite the creative reticence of the common law, without the help of a rights-based approach, it could not tackle head on this particularly egregious system that had emerged over the centuries, which left politicians, as opposed to expert judges, in charge of the length of a person's detention.

My journey towards an understanding of the limits of the English legal system and its inability to create a rights framework fit for the twenty-first century continued when, in 1994, I was made the most junior counsel in the 'Gays in the Armed Forces' case.[6] I was in Laura Cox QC's team and we were pursuing what are now EU law equal treatment arguments. Peter Duffy, led by David Pannick QC, addressed the core issue: was the blanket ban on gay men and lesbians serving in the armed forces, which demanded their dismissal, repugnant to public law principles? It was a human rights law argument dressed up as administrative law, and through the English courts was doomed to failure (as were, although for different reasons, the Equal Treatment Directive arguments). Even though – eventually – the European Court of Human Rights vindicated the applicants and provided them with their remedy,[7] the human price paid by them as they were buffeted through the English courts should never be underestimated. I then went on to advise a number of others from the lesbian, gay, bisexual and transgender (LGBT) communities who were enquiring as to their rights. In most instances, there were no remedies as a matter of English law.

In 1993 the Labour leader John Smith had accepted the principle that the UK needed far more effective and judicially enforceable human rights protection.[8] He committed Labour to some form of human rights legislation in its first term should it form a government. His reasons for such urgency were that if Labour were only to achieve one term of government, at least it would have left in place a far more effective mechanism to protect human rights from an otherwise overly powerful and unaccountable executive. John Smith's Shadow Home Secretary, Tony Blair, bought into this commitment, as did Tony Blair's junior on the Shadow Home bench team, Jack Straw. This determination was given legal clout through the support of the Shadow Lord Chancellor, Lord Irvine of Lairg, and Labour's pledge to what was to become the Human Rights Act (HRA) was born.

By 1995 it was clear to me that my particular area of interest was human rights law, so when the post of Legal Director of Liberty was advertised, I applied and was offered the position. Working for Liberty put me at the heart of the Westminster human rights debate. In the late 1980s the organisation had committed itself to working towards a Bill of Rights for the UK.[9] This was a period of genuinely exciting human rights activism. Liberty had already hosted its Festival of Rights, Charter 88, chaired by Helena Kennedy, was in full swing, and JUSTICE, led by Anne Owers and chaired by the Conservative titan, Lord Alexander, was steadily highlighting the consequences in the criminal justice system and the prison system in particular of the absence of effective human rights protection.

JUSTICE had always put forward arguments for a human rights regime. Madeleine Colvin and Peter Noorlander were, in due course, to produce their seminal report for JUSTICE on the lack of human rights protection in the UK's surveillance regime, which led directly to the Regulation of Investigatory Powers Act 2000 (RIPA). The Institute for Public Policy Research (IPPR) Human Rights Unit, headed by Sarah Spencer, was doing genuine blue sky and creative thinking, and the Constitution Unit under the wise leadership of Robert Hazel was producing well-thought-through analysis of options for the UK constitution.

Systemic failure to promote and protect rights

By the mid-1990s it was clear that the current arrangement in England and Wales was inadequate to meet the needs of the twenty-first century as far as human rights protection was concerned. Those cornerstones of the British system of government – parliamentary sovereignty, the common law and the rule of law – quite simply could not guarantee the human rights that all within the jurisdiction expected. The Gays in the Armed Forces case had most vividly illustrated this, and to put the issue beyond doubt, *The Three Pillars of Liberty*,[10] written by Francesca Klug, Keir Starmer and Stuart Weir, identified the extent to which the UK system of government could not secure domestically the rights guaranteed by the UK under its international human rights treaty obligations.

On top of that, David Kinley's *Compliance Without Incorporation*[11] identified that, of the UK's violations in Strasbourg to date, two-thirds stemmed from either primary or secondary legislation. Parliamentary sovereignty was, therefore, a cause of human rights violations and not an assurance against them. By the early 1990s the UK, unique at the time for the Council of Europe, had violated all the rights contained in the ECHR with the exception of the prohibition on slavery (although a subsequent violation of this too was found). This startling fact showed that there was something systemically wrong with the UK framework to promote and protect human rights. The victims tended to be the most vulnerable and marginalised as well as 'the worst, the weakest and the vilest amongst us'.[12] They were children, victims of crime (and sexual offences in particular), gay men and lesbians, trans people, migrants, asylum seekers, the Roma and travellers, people with mental illness and prisoners.

The public and administrative law regime that had emerged during the twentieth century and which had established the discipline of judicial review was a welcome development and a credit to the judges and lawyers who crafted it. But that regime, as so startlingly was shown up by the Gays in the Armed Forces case, was limited in the way that it could hold power to account effectively. Judicial review evolved within the world of deference that established power had enjoyed in the UK for centuries. It is no accident, for example, that the judicial review court would only challenge a decision maker who was 'irrational'. And even if attempts were made to identify certain issues as being subject to a more heightened degree of scrutiny than others, the prospects of success in challenging a decision maker were slim to non-existent, unless you could establish that the decision that had been made was so unreasonable that no other decision maker could have come to a similar conclusion. This put the scope of most decisions beyond challenge, despite their impact on human rights, whether they concerned prisoners, access to school, family rights, healthcare rights, privacy rights or free speech. The system of judicial review, in the absence of being underpinned by human rights, in effect cemented in place the system of power in the UK.

Rightly, in my view, the judges were not prepared to dismantle this system. Within the UK's constitutional arrangement it should not be for the judges to dictate a higher degree of scrutiny of the administrative and executive arms of government, or for that matter impose a fully fledged human rights regime, without the sanction of Parliament. Understanding the role of the judiciary in a common law system based on the rule of law is not a precise science; had the courts in the UK opted to create a more effective human rights regime and dictated a higher level scrutiny of decision makers it would have been more likely to foster confusion than clarity. David Pannick's appeal to the House of Lords in the Gays in the Armed Forces case had in effect just one ground: does proportionality apply? In refusing leave the then Law Lords were unambiguous: principles of public and administrative law would not extend beyond *Wednesbury* unreasonableness[13] and any extension of that review to some unfathomable heightened scrutiny in relation to it. In other words, the Court of Appeal had got it right. The Law Lords were making it clear that human rights and the mechanisms which decided how they were to be enforced were to come from Parliament and not the courts.

The road to reform

Once John Smith had committed the Labour Party to creating an effective and enforceable human rights regime for the UK, the process began that was to lead to the Human Rights Act. John Smith's motives were to create more accountable government, but human rights do more than that. They create an inclusive government – a citizenship of equals, saying to all within the jurisdiction that everyone, whoever you are, is recognised as possessing inherent human dignity. By committing

Labour to a human rights-based approach to government and by making those rights enforceable through the courts, John Smith was reaffirming Labour's commitment to the dignity of all. But John Smith's overriding commitment to a more effective and accountable government should not be overlooked. It is all too tempting to focus on the minorities who may benefit from human rights; everyone benefits from a more accountable government, as John Smith will have been aware.

It remains a significant regret that in the late 1990s there wasn't cross-party consensus to work out how to build a human rights framework into the UK's existing systems of government, and the law in particular. The Conservative Party simply wouldn't play ball. John Major's Citizen's Charter (introduced in the early 1990s) was not a constructive contribution to the debate. It was, as Lord Irvine pointed out, 'enervating nonsense'.[14] This lack of engagement is striking when we consider the fact that some of the most eloquent and articulate proponents of improved human rights protection within the UK have been among the Conservative Party's outstanding legal minds. These include Lord Alexander of Weedon QC, Sir Edward Gardner QC, David Maxwell-Fyfe (later as Lord Chancellor, Viscount Kilmuir), Lord Broxbourne (formerly Sir Derek Walker-Smith QC), Sir Nicholas Lyell QC, Dominic Grieve QC and Ken Clarke QC.

It is unfortunate that Labour couldn't bring the Conservatives with them, but while in opposition Labour devoted significant energy to honing their human rights policies. They tapped into all available expertise and delved into many different models of human rights protection. Jack Straw was clear on one point: the courts should not be given the power to strike down primary legislation, thereby displacing the rudiments of parliamentary sovereignty. An impenetrable debate ensued, comparing and contrasting the differences between the Canadian and the New Zealand models. It became turgid and rather meaningless, and alienated a number of people from the process; but thankfully help was at hand in the form of the lucid analysis of Robert Hazel's Constitution Unit. More importantly, Francesca Klug[15] was able to navigate through all of these different options and proposed various suggestions for the incorporation of the ECHR into UK law that would be consistent with the basic principles of the UK system of government.

The model that was conceived between Jack Straw, Lord Irvine and Francesca Klug was sensitive, thoughtful, inspired and in many respects deeply conservative.[16] The rights that would take effect in English law would be drawn from the UK's pre-existing commitment to the ECHR, nothing more and nothing less.[17] The executive and administrative arms of government would be required to adopt a rights-based approach to government. The courts would not be able to dis-apply an Act of Parliament, but in the event that such an Act was incompatible with human rights protection, the courts could make a declaration to that effect. And perhaps the most visionary aspect of the proposal was that, prior to second reading, all new bills would undergo a human rights impact assessment. There was also to be a committee of both Houses of Parliament to ensure that the symbiosis between human rights and democracy became entrenched.

The model is ingenious. It shares human rights protection across all branches of government. Responsibility doesn't rest solely with the courts. The scheme was designed to refresh the basic building blocks of the UK's system of government. It would reinvigorate the common law, give more power to the rule of law and consolidate parliamentary sovereignty. The courts of the UK would be expected to take into account the case law of the European Court of Human Rights, but no more than that. British courts would generate their own jurisprudence. This they have done, and now that case law feeds back into the Strasbourg system. This model of human rights protection would become one of the golden threads running through the UK constitutional arrangement, including subsequent devolution settlements. It has been the HRA which has allowed devolution to work so seamlessly.

The Labour Party did what it could to consult as widely as possible on its plans while in opposition,[18] and when they formed the government after 1997 they bolstered that initial consultation with a government-wide process.[19] Rights were being 'brought home', as the consultation process told us. On reflection, the decision to place the emphasis on this notional repatriation of the ECHR may have been a mistake. On one level the bringing rights home analysis was correct, but something much more profound was also happening, and that should have been celebrated.

True to the commitment of John Smith, Labour prioritised their Human Rights Bill in their first year in government. JUSTICE, recognising this new priority area, advertised for someone to head up their human rights project, which was a new post. It was everything I had always wanted to work on. I applied and was offered the job. The Human Rights Bill was making its way through Parliament and I was able to work on every aspect of it. To take liberties with Wordsworth, 'Bliss was it in that dawn to be alive, but to be working on the Human Rights Bill was very heaven'. Peter Duffy offered his assistance in any way that would be helpful, and we worked with the government on the amendments to put the faith communities' minds at rest[20] and also ensured that freedom of expression was given its proper status within the rights framework.[21]

Labour's scheme was not much altered. The Conservatives, respecting that it was a Labour manifesto commitment, engaged constructively with the process, and the Liberal Democrats were on board. The Liberal Democrats tried to enhance the level of human rights protection, but the government, keeping true to its commitment to bring rights home, would not budge beyond the existing rights contained in the ECHR. The consequences of this had one extraordinary outcome: when the Labour majority did insist on adding ECHR protocols banning the death penalty to the rights that would be protected, Jack Straw, then Home Secretary but also a seasoned campaigner against the death penalty, voted against the motion. The majority ruled the day and the death penalty has been banished since.

The Conservatives gave the Human Rights Bill an unopposed Third Reading. While a commitment to some form of Bill of Rights had not yet become Conservative Party policy, there was genuine cross-party respect for the Bill's scheme as well as its scope. It was also considered to be a model of parliamentary drafting. It is beautifully crafted, and all credit for this goes to Sir Edward Caldwell QC.

There was one feature of the scheme of the Human Rights Bill that was and remains controversial, however, and that is the power to use delegated legislation to amend primary legislation in the event that a Declaration of Incompatibility is made and there are compelling reasons to act expeditiously. This classic Henry VIII clause does offend against treasured democratic values as well as parliamentary sovereignty. In reality, it is not essential to the Act's scheme, although it has been used to good effect in the context of mental health law, yet it allowed detractors of the Bill to garner support and present this new statutory human rights framework as anti British notions of democracy. There is something about the provision that comes across as arrogant, and however well-intended it may have been, it should not have formed part of the HRA. That said, it need not undermine the scheme of the Act as long as it is not used again, outside of the most unimaginable of circumstances.

Impact of the Human Rights Act

The HRA entered into force in October 2000. In the intervening period the government engaged in an extensive human rights training programme, and administrative and executive agencies reviewed their policies and practice. The Judicial Studies Board, under the leadership of Sir Stephen Sedley, undertook a radical training programme in which all judges from magistrates to Law Lords engaged. The police in particular went through a constructive process identifying areas of their practice that were or might be not compliant with the human rights contained in the HRA. The most visible evidence of this was that for the first time the Association of Chief Police Officers (ACPO) released their guidelines on the use of lethal force. Even before the Act entered into force, John Smith's vision of a more accountable state through more effective human rights protection was being realised. My human rights work at JUSTICE intensified. JUSTICE became the human rights trainer of choice for many government departments, including what is now the Ministry of Justice and the Foreign and Commonwealth Office.

The HRA has done and is doing what it was intended to do. Those rights that could not be properly protected under the pre-HRA scheme, from privacy to protest, are now given a clear basis in law. Decisions are now measured against principles of proportionality, thus ensuring a higher quality decision making across the board. No longer can decision makers hide behind the old limits of judicial review. As a consequence, we have all benefited from the HRA. It may feel imperceptible, but whether it's a decision about access to healthcare, immigration status, the rights of those detained or access to education, the HRA has dramatically improved the quality of decision making. The culture of deference, which facilitated complacency, has been replaced by one of accountability.

Children have been the biggest winners.[22] A rights-based approach to children in our society has transformed their lives on every level. The victims of crime and sex offences in particular have also been significant beneficiaries of the HRA.[23] And the other identifiable group whose lives have been altered beyond recognition because of the rights-based culture ushered in with the HRA has been the LGBTI community. Britain would be unrecognisable to my 18-year-old self.

There is another feature of the Act that also deserves some exploration and that is the way the HRA has been used by the courts to bring the common law to life. This process has been rather wonderful to observe as we watch the custodians of our laws develop that synergy between the common law and the Human Rights Act, and, therefore, we have been reminded of those fundamental principles that beat at the heart of the common law itself.[24]

The recent Supreme Court case of *Kennedy v Charity Commission*[25] encapsulates this development.[26] The case concerned whether a journalist could require the Charity Commission to release documents it had relied upon in conducting an inquiry into a charity linked to George Galloway – the Mariam Appeal. There was an absolute ban on the release of such documents under the Freedom of Information Act 2000. The majority in the Supreme Court therefore found that Act to be of no assistance. Similarly they found, based upon the jurisprudence of the Strasbourg Court, that the right of freedom of expression under Art. 10, ECHR could not be extended to provide access to information under these circumstances.

Did common law change the equation? In *Kennedy*, Lord Toulson further developed the common law principle of open justice.[27] In Lord Toulson's view,[28] 'human rights law and public law has developed through our common law over a long period of time', and have been tailored to meet current needs. Indeed, Lord Toulson pointed out 'a baleful and unnecessary tendency' on the part of litigants to overlook the common law. As he rightly stated, 'it was not the purpose of the Human Rights Act that the common law should become an ossuary'. *Kennedy v Charity Commission* embodies a general trend in the Supreme Court's development of common law principles that may complement, but do not depend for their existence on, Convention rights.[29]

The HRA was never intended to replace or circumvent common law or other mechanisms to protect human rights in the UK. Section 11 of the HRA puts this beyond doubt.[30] At the same time as providing for a prescribed rights framework which re-examines and redelineates the relationship between all branches of government, part of the HRA's role is to fill in the gaps left by common law. It does not replace it.

It isn't cracked: The 'mirror principle' in practice

Nor does the case law of the Strasbourg Court take precedence over UK law.[31] The Act's scheme requires it to engage with Strasbourg jurisprudence in determining domestic cases under the HRA. It must take this into account, but no more than this. Lord Bingham sought to clarify what this meant in *R (Ullah) v Special Adjudicator.*[32] He stated: 'The duty of national courts is to keep pace with the Strasbourg jurisprudence as it evolves over time: no more, but certainly no less.'

This 'mirror principle' should not be seen as controversial in the context of the HRA's scheme. Where a Strasbourg case is clear – for example, finding the prohibition of gay men and lesbians serving in the armed forces to be a violation of the ECHR – UK courts should follow that jurisprudence (although they are not obliged to). It is only in this type of exceptional context that it may be appropriate to acknowledge that, 'Strasbourg has spoken, the case is closed'.[33] Under the scheme of the HRA there is no obligation to follow the decisions of the Strasbourg Court, although they must be taken into account. Where a Strasbourg case is not on point, or it can be distinguished, or it requires further elaboration or clarification, or the UK courts do not agree with it, those courts are open not to follow a particular case and engage with a dialogue with the Strasbourg Court.[34] That dialogue is welcome. The scheme of the HRA does not make the Supreme Court subservient to Strasbourg. As Lord Phillips made clear in *Horncastle*, where he had concerns as to whether a decision of the Strasbourg Court sufficiently fully appreciated English law, he 'declined to follow the Strasbourg decision, giving reasons for adopting this course'.[35] At the same time as choosing not to follow Strasbourg case law because they consider it to be in some way flawed, UK courts have also taken the lead in developing the scope of certain rights contained within the ECHR based on the case law of the Strasbourg Court where UK courts have considered that case law to be in a state of evolution.[36] The UK courts are not being stymied by s. 2, nor is UK public policy. There is no need to tinker with this part of the HRA's scheme. Our courts should continue to take account of the Strasbourg case law, but not feel bound by it.

There is also the 'other, less often considered' limb of the *Ullah* principle, as noted by Lord Brown in *Rabone v Pennine Care Trust*,[37] which is as follows: 'It is of course open to member states to provide for rights more generous than those guaranteed by the Convention, but such provision should not be the product of interpretation of the Convention by national courts …'.[38] In other words, courts may develop common law rights that go beyond the Convention, but must do so through domestic law, not by straining the reach of the Convention itself. An example of this is provided in the case of *Al-Rawi v Security Service*,[39] a case concerning the lawfulness of using closed material proceedings in civil claims. Lord Dyson held that 'the lawfulness of a closed material procedure under article 6 and under the common law are distinct questions'.[40] Citing *Ullah*, he went on: 'It is, therefore, open to our courts to provide greater protection through the common law than that which is guaranteed by the Convention'.[41]

Why the hostility towards the HRA?

Pointing out the flaws in the UK system of government's promotion and protection of human rights at the end of the twentieth century is not now controversial. The scheme proposed by the New Labour government to address those failings is sensitive and well thought out. No major political party, including the Conservatives, now questions the need for some form of prescribed rights to sit alongside the common law, parliamentary sovereignty and the rule of law in ensuring the most effective legal framework for the UK. Human rights are here to stay. Why then is there such hostility towards the HRA to the extent that the Conservative Party now has a notional commitment to its repeal? Is it because the rights given effect to by the HRA come from the ECHR and therefore have the word 'European' in them? While this simplistic view may be credible on one level, it does not really make sense for those who are concerned with ensuring the most effective form of good government. There is nothing controversial about the rights contained in the HRA and, as is well known, the ECHR was drafted by David Maxwell-Fyfe who went on to become a Conservative Home Secretary and then Lord Chancellor.

Is it because the New Labour government did not fully engage with the human rights project? There may be a bit more plausibility in this question. With the benefit of hindsight the process that led to the HRA does feel elitist and remote. A handful of MPs were involved, a similar number of peers, a couple of NGOs and one or two newspapers. A mass movement for greater human rights protection this does not make. Tony Blair, as Prime Minister, should have retained control and responsibility for the project and explained what it was and also what it wasn't. John Smith's initial commitment to a Bill of Rights should have been reinforced time and time again.

The hostility of right-wing media to the HRA itself makes no sense (subject to the fact that distorting human rights makes for entertaining copy). All of those newspapers have relied upon the protection of the Strasbourg-interpreted freedom of expression provisions of the ECHR. Common law notions of free speech were meagre before the ECHR nudged it along. And if freedom of expression is the media's golden egg, shouldn't they be careful not to kill the goose? Their scare stories about human rights may end up having unintended consequences.

The HRA had not been in force for a year when 9/11 happened and the world was turned upside down. The UK government's decision to view human rights as a threat under these circumstances rather than a solution was a major error and arguably so undermined their human rights project that it hasn't been able to recover. As successive Labour Home Secretaries opted not to trust the human rights framework, why should anyone else, particularly the Opposition? No leadership was coming from the Prime Minister and, despite valiant attempts by Lord Falconer to promote it, one of the Labour government's flagship enterprises became good sport for media hostile to the government and for the Opposition. But the greatest error of all of this was that the opportunities presented by the HRA were not harnessed to ensure all of our security. Security comes with effective human rights protection. This has been proven time and time again.

A final point to raise is one always put so eloquently by Shami Chakrabarti, Director of Liberty, which is that everyone supports human rights as long as they're their own. It is other people's human rights that some have problems with. This is an age-old dilemma that confronts all human rights-based regimes, but it's one which responsible governments should be able to shoulder.

Is the HRA working?

Metaphors of the Human Rights Act as a troublesome child are tiresome and unhelpful, but Tony Blair, well into his second term, was already asking what we were to do about the HRA. The Prime Minister demanded a review. Lord Falconer's review pointed out that it was working as it should.[42] All the evidence consistently points this out. Gordon Brown, on becoming Prime Minister, ordered another review but presented it more benignly, asking whether we needed improved human rights protection and/or a Bill of Rights for Britain.[43] Again, all the evidence pointed out that the HRA was working.

The coalition government also commissioned a review. It examined the way the ECHR system works in Strasbourg as well as whether we needed a Bill of Rights for the UK. That review was undertaken by independent experts, the overwhelming majority of whom were lawyers. While the quality of the legal minds on that Commission was formidable, in reality none of them had daily experience of dealing with human rights issues in their work. Helena Kennedy is probably the exception to this because of the work she does in terrorist cases and the work she has done as a criminal barrister, but these are exceptional issues in human rights terms. There were no experts on the Bill of Rights Commission with a background in prisoners' rights, the health service, education or immigration. Where were the prison governors, the council leaders, the ombudsmen and women, the human rights professors and the police officers? The majority on the Commission opted to replace the HRA with a Bill of Rights, but this wasn't because of evidence that the HRA was not working. To the contrary, 96 per cent of those that responded to the Commission's consultation process called for the retention of the HRA. The Law Society backs the HRA, as does the Bar Council. Despite this over-whelming support, the reason given by the majority of the Commission for the repeal of the HRA was that, in their view, it had become so unpopular it needed to be reinvented.[44] Helena Kennedy along with Philippe Sands did not agree with the majority. In their view, on any objective analysis, the HRA's scheme and scope is doing exactly what is needed for human rights protection in the UK.

In the next Conservative Party manifesto it is likely there will be a commitment for a British Bill of Rights (BBR) to replace the HRA. The danger is that this exercise may be tinged with xenopho-bia. Its motive, if the reasoning of the Conservative members of the Bill of Rights Commission can be encapsulated, would appear to be Eurosceptic; but more importantly, if the HRA is to be replaced by a BBR, what will the difference be between the two instruments? Will there be fewer rights? It is impossible to see what rights you could take out of the HRA. Will there be more rights? This would seem slightly counter-intuitive, although it may be welcome. It is, however, unlikely. Will the enforcement mechanisms be different? Currently, the test is that all law must be interpreted, so far as it is possible to do so, in a way that is compatible with the human rights contained in the HRA.[45] Will the Tories water down this scheme? This may be likely, but if that is the case, the only real losers will be the majority, if not all, of us whose lives have been imperceptibly enhanced by the HRA and the era of improved decision making it represents. The likes of Abu Qatada will still have the same remedy not to be exposed to torture and its consequences. He would not be affected by a dilution of the scheme.

It is very unlikely that the Conservatives will want a scheme where legislation can be dis-applied by the courts, and so the scheme of the HRA in this respect is likely to be mirrored by that of any Conserva-tive BBR. It is, after all, essentially a conservative scheme. Their Bill of Rights, therefore, has the potential to backfire on the Conservative

Party. Formulating it will be a headache for the Party and the head-lines that they want to avoid will remain, as will the likes of Abu Qatada. But once they have their own BBR they will have no one else to blame.

Margaret Thatcher understood the UK system of democracy. While it is fair to say she did not exactly embrace the Sex Discrimi-nation Act or the Race Relations Act, she maintained them and, by doing so, she was respecting the nature of democratic government. You work with the legacies of the previous regime, particularly in the context of social justice. As there is no evidence that the HRA is not working, Conservatives should be getting on with the government of the UK and respecting the well-thought through human rights legacy of New Labour.

There is, of course, the additional point that must always be made about human rights and other key social developments. Change is embraced, even that which was bitterly opposed. The Conservative Party embodies this principle better than any other, and their now total commitment to the equality of the LGBTI community is, perhaps, the most striking evidence of this. The party which resisted an equal age of consent and which introduced Section 28 is the party that has given us equal marriage.[46] On occasion I have had the opportunity to chal-lenge members of the Conservative Party on which of the Strasbourg decisions from their last period of government (1979 to 1997) they still oppose. The answer is none of them. Those decisions, whether they concerned the rights of children, mental health detainees, privacy rights, use of lethal force, the right to a fair trial and free speech are all now accepted as examples of good practice by the Conservative Party. One MP expressed doubts about *Chahal v UK*,[47] in which Mr Chahal could not be returned to India where he faced a real risk of torture. The prohibition of torture is, of course, a fundamental tenet of the common law, and, interestingly, that Strasbourg decision is based principally on the UN Convention Against Torture, arguably Geof-frey Howe's lasting achievement as a Conservative Foreign Secretary. When pushed the Tory MP conceded that the principles in *Chahal* were correctly formulated.

Conclusion

The Labour Party in its last years in opposition in the 1990s and the early years of the Blair government created a sensitive and well-structured framework to promote and protect human rights in the UK. It provides a coherent basis for all of the UK's jurisdictions to work together, sharing a commitment to the same enforceable fundamental moral standards. In my view, Labour should stand firm with its commitment to the HRA and develop policies whereby it can better promote the benefits of the Act and how it fits into the system of government.

By taking a personal journey, in this chapter I have sought to convey what an exceptional piece of legislation the HRA is. It is subtle and effective. It is also uniquely British. On occasion and in more flippant moments, I have compared it with Sean Connery's James Bond: focused, stylish, powerful and, when necessary, complementary. The Labour Party should be rightly proud of it. It is Labour legislation but it should be cross-party, in much the same way that the ECHR was drafted by a British Conservative, but it belongs to all Europeans. It would be an extraordinary admission if the Conservatives do not believe in the level of accountability that the HRA offers.

I began this chapter by reflecting on the AIDS crisis and the failure of law to address it, although interestingly there was inspired political leadership. We were fortunate that Norman Fowler, for the Conservative government, led the charge. But we should have had more than good luck. The legal framework should also have been in place. It is now, thanks in part to the AIDS crisis and the need to respond to it. Living through the AIDS crisis, I came of age to the mantra 'Silence = Death'. It captured the essential intensity of what was happening. We fought for the human rights of people with AIDS. With those rights came a voice and with that voice incrementally the crisis has been harnessed. We were galvanised by that pithy equation. Now we all have our rights recognised through the HRA, we must all also fight for it and lend it our voices. The HRA gives us accountability, but it also gives us dignity. The Labour movement has always been synonymous with the pursuit of human dignity. Dignity is at Labour's core.

Labour = Dignity. I wear it with pride.

Summary of principal recommendations

- The Labour Party should be rightly proud of the HRA.
- The Party should stand firm with its commitment to the Act.
- The HRA has created a human rights framework that is sensitive and appropriate for the UK system of government.
- Labour should develop policies whereby it can better promote the benefits of the HRA and how it fits into the system of government.

10

NHS and Social Care Law

David Lock QC

The National Health Service remains the envy of the world and is a touchstone issue in British politics. It has been subject to considerable reform by both Labour and Conservative governments since the 1990s.

The present arrangements for the delivery of state-funded health-care services in the UK are of bewildering legal complexity, matched only by the complexity of the management structures of the NHS. The British public has a steadfast commitment to the NHS, and any changes to NHS services have the potential to become politically contentious. However there is a widespread lack of understanding about how the NHS is managed and how it actually functions. In marked contrast, changes to state-provided social care services do not have anything like the political impact of changes to NHS services. Social care services are largely administered by local authorities whose budgets have been radically cut by the present government without any sustained political challenge. However, the successful delivery of health services is dependent on the successful delivery of social care services, and vice versa.

There are however a number of key differences between health and social care services, notably that the NHS is largely free for patients at the point of use,[1] whereas social care services are (and have always been) means tested, with some service users meeting the full costs of their care.

Legal and policy framework

The law relating to the NHS is largely contained within a single consolidated Act, now the National Health Service Act 2006.[2] In contrast,
social care law has been spread across a myriad of different statutes,
including the National Assistance Act 1948 and the Chronically Sick
and Disabled Persons Act 1970, all of which get regularly amended by
new legislation. The Law Commission produced a report criticising
the complexity of adult social care legislation in 2011[3] and proposed
a consolidated Bill. The present government introduced the Care Bill
in May 2013, which became the Care Act 2014 in May 2014 but will
come into effect when an order is made by the Secretary of State.
Once implemented there will be a single Act of Parliament for care
services to complement the National Health Service Act 2006.

It remains to be seen whether a single Care Act will make any significant difference to users of social care services. However, a single
statute should make the job of those advising social care users (who
are very often not lawyers) more straightforward.

The future of the NHS is the subject of academic departments,
policy commissions, endless consultations and vast media comment.
NHS controversies have led to politicians losing their parliamentary
seats,[4] and those who oppose any set of local or national changes
to NHS services can be relied upon to predict the worst and wave
shrouds to support their case. The NHS is, as the former Conservative
Chancellor, Nigel Lawson said, 'the closest thing the English have
to a religion'. A politician therefore meddles with the NHS at his or
her peril.

The Conservative MP Andrew Lansley spent years in opposition
thinking about the NHS and finally got his hands on the ministerial
red boxes when he was appointed Secretary of State for Health in
May 2010. Within a few short weeks he had published his vision
for the future of the NHS in a White Paper called *Equity and Excellence: Liberating the NHS*, which very largely built on the speeches
he had made in opposition.[5] That led to the Health and Social Care
Act 2012, which was one of the most complex Bills ever presented
to Parliament. It eventually got through the parliamentary process
after a tortuous passage (including the famous Spring 2011 'pause'
to facilitate a 'listening exercise'). Despite the complexity of the

2012 Act the vast majority of the changes it introduced to the NHS could have been introduced without legislation. The net result of the political fallout was that Andrew Lansley lost his job as Secretary of State for Health soon after the Bill was passed, even though he said it was the only job in government that he wanted. The new Health Secretary is Jeremy Hunt who is largely carrying on the reforms of his predecessor.

However, political shortcomings in the Lansley vision of a 'Bank of England' type of NHS, largely run by NHS England and free of political control, have become increasingly clear. In June 2014, junior Health Minister Jane Ellison complained that the NHS was largely 'out of control' of ministers, without apparently realising that this was the policy of the former Secretary of State. The 2012 Act provided that ministers remain politically accountable for the NHS,[6] but largely removed their means of control. Ministers were thus left politically accountable for a government service that they had little if any formal means of controlling.

A list of problems

There are a series of problems with the NHS that an incoming Labour government will have to accept. The first is that those who supply the services are trusted far more than those who manage the service. It is thus a sector where 'provider interests' have far more weight than almost anywhere else, apart perhaps from the military. The BMA, the Royal Colleges and the staff trade unions all have tremendous policy influence, and are not afraid to use their voices to object to change that will adversely affect their members. The strapline of the BMA is 'Standing up for Doctors', but it is highly effective in presenting the interests of doctors as being coterminous with the interests of the patients, and thus gaining public support for its positions. Having said that, the professionalism and commitment of the doctors, nurses and NHS managers is a resource that any Secretary of State underestimates at his or her peril.

Second, after the Health and Social Care Act 2012 is implemented, the legal and management structures within the NHS are wholly unclear to the public as well as to most of those working within the system. Lord Darzi, a hugely respected surgeon and former Labour Health Minister commented in a House of Lords debate as follows concerning the Lansley reforms:

> *We now have health and wellbeing boards, clinical*
> *commissioning groups, clinical senates, local healthwatches, the*
> *NHS commissioning board, a quality regulator and an economic*
> *regulator ... At the end of the day, who is responsible for making*
> *sure that the NHS saves more lives this year than last? Who is*
> *accountable for how its budget is spent? Who will inspire NHS*
> *staff to lead the difficult changes?*[7]

Working out who is really responsible for performance in the NHS has never been straightforward and is perhaps even more difficult today than ever before.

The third problem is that many of the complaints made about the marketisation impacts of the 2012 Act failed to appreciate how far a Labour government had already taken the NHS down that path. Lansley was anxious to present his reforms as being a radical departure from Labour policy, while Labour politicians, free from office, were free to complain about privatisation of the NHS by stealth. Simon Stephens, a former Health adviser to Tony Blair and now the Chief Executive of NHS England saw things differently in July 2010 when he said, 'what makes the coalition's proposal so radical is not that they tear up that earlier plan [the NHS plans of the Labour government]. It is that they move decisively towards fulfilling it'.[8] Labour complained about the competition aspects included in Part 3 of the 2012 Act but, unless fundamental changes are made to the structure of the NHS, most of the legal obligations that brought the EU procurement and competition regimes into the NHS were already present. EU competition and procurement law was already having an impact on the NHS before the coalition government took office because of decisions made to create legal separation between commissioners and providers. The duties of transparency, equal treatment and non-discrimination in Part 1 of the Public Contract Regulations 2006 applied to the placing of NHS contracts long before 2010, and thus a disappointed contractor already had the right to sue an NHS commissioner for breach of procurement law duties. Part 3 of the 2012 Act increased the focus on procurement and competition for NHS bodies but, given the structures set up by the Labour government, it probably made little practical difference to legal obligations in this area.

Fourth, the NHS that an incoming Labour government will manage needs to serve an ageing population where demand for NHS services will substantially increase each year by maybe 4 per cent. The Royal College of Physicians reported recently[9] that:

> *The number of general and acute beds has decreased by a third in the past 25 years, yet during the past 10 years there has been a 37 per cent increase in emergency hospital admissions and a 65 per cent increase in secondary care episodes for those over 75 in the same period (compared with a 31 per cent increase for those aged 15–59).*

A 2012 parliamentary select committee report[10] also noted the need to change services and reported:

> *The National Health Service will have to transform to deal with very large increases in demand for and costs of health and social care. Overall, the quality of healthcare for older people is not good enough now, and older people should be concerned about the quality of care that they may receive in the near future. England has an inappropriate model of health and social care to cope with a changing pattern of ill health from an ageing population. Further fundamental reform to the NHS in the next few years would be undesirable, but radical changes to the way that health and social care is delivered are needed to provide appropriate care for the population overall and particularly for older people, and to address future demand.*

It is unclear whether the present government has a coherent plan to manage this increase in activity and equally unclear how an incoming Labour government would do so.

A fifth problem is that, as medical science develops, the treatments doctors can offer that may benefit patients increase each year.

The pharmaceutical industry is a great British success story but each development of new drugs creates a demand for funding for a defined cohort of patients from an already cash limited budget. With every new wonder drug the need increases for robust systems within the NHS to decide what treatments do and do not deliver both clinically effective and cost-effective treatment. An interesting observation on this issue emerged in an NHS rationing legal case where the chief executive of the local primary care trust (PCT) explained the problem as follows:

> *Doctors have a duty of care to their patients and thus press*
> *for the best possible care for each and every patient they are*
> *treating. The treating consultants are generally not concerned*
> *with issues of overall cost effectiveness. Their role is to press for*
> *the best treatment for their patient. Where such treatment is not*
> *routinely commissioned by a PCT, the consultant is not able to*
> *provide the treatment as part of NHS care unless an exception*
> *is made for the patient. The role of the consultant in such cases*
> *is to write letters and reports to seek to persuade the PCT to*
> *fund the treatment for patients ... This means that we need*
> *to consider carefully the costs of different treatments and the*
> *benefits that a treatment delivers before we plan to commission*
> *it. For the PCT, the decision to commission a particular kind of*
> *treatment is not just a question of whether a medical treatment*
> *is clinically effective: if a treatment is not clinically effective we*
> *would not commission it. However, if a treatment is clinically*
> *effective, the PCT needs to judge whether the treatment is a cost*
> *effective use of the limited resources available to it. As the PCT*
> *has a fully committed and limited budget, the duty to break even*
> *means that if we commission additional services we need to pay*
> *for this by disinvestment from other services ... PCTs can only*
> *spend money from taxpayers once.*[11]

NHS policy makers often underestimate the problems caused by the entirely legitimate differences between the perspectives of treating doctors and those of NHS commissioners. These two groups are using the same resources but, as the above quotation explains, they approach the issues of resource allocation in very different ways.

The way forward for NHS policy under Labour

Against this background one political reality is crystal clear – there are no votes in changing the 'wiring' of the NHS.[12] A major reform of the NHS structures is politically undeliverable and should be firmly rejected by an incoming Labour government. Andy Burnham, as Shadow Secretary of State for Health, may have promised to repeal the Health and Social Care Act 2012, but in reality this promise cannot extend further than repealing parts of Chapters 1 and 2 of Part 3 of the Act (concerning the role of Monitor and Competition). However, even that would leave a vacuum which, given the constraints of EU law operating in this field and the Public Contracts Regulations 2006, could not be left unfilled. The last thing that the NHS needs is another major structural reorganisation, and the public and the professions would not stand for it.

However, an incoming Labour Secretary of State may be obliged to recognise that the commissioner/provider divide in the NHS has been largely ineffective and, to date, has been a huge waste of public money. The division between those parts of the NHS that commissioned healthcare and those parts that delivered it was originally devised by former Secretary of State for Health, Ken Clarke, in his 1989 White Paper *Working for Patients* (and at that time called the purchaser/provider divide) in order to introduce some market mechanisms into a state monolith. But there is little evidence that commissioners (as the purchasers are now called) have acted like effective private sector purchasers and so 'market' mechanisms rarely if ever deliver the intended results.

The Health Select Committee came close to recommending the abolition of commissioning in its report of March 2010.[13] The committee concluded that commissioners tended to be 'passive' and added that they failed to justify their own existence. It said: 'Weaknesses [in commissioning performance] are due in large part to PCTs' lack of skills, notably poor analysis of data, lack of clinical knowledge and the poor quality of much PCT management. The situation has been made worse by the constant re-organisations and high turnover of staff.'[14]

There was no evidence that GPs, trained to deliver services to individual patients, would be any better at commissioning population-based medicine than PCTs. Commissioning has been further undermined because a large number of staff with knowledge of NHS commissioning have left the NHS in recent years as part of the £20bn 'Nicholson Challenge'[15] and, as a result, the support structures for the new Clinical Commissioning Groups (CCGs) have been left with fewer experienced staff. However, a King's Fund report published in July 2013[16] was not wholly pessimistic. It observed:

> *Despite the early timing of our fieldwork, we found some evidence that CCGs were already having an impact on members' clinical practice ... The most commonly cited effect of CCGs was that peer-to-peer dialogue had heightened GPs' awareness of their referral and prescribing patterns and how they compare with those of others. In most sites, at least some practices or localities reported that this had led to their succeeding in reducing their referral rates or prescribing costs. Others, however, reported that their clinical practice remained entirely unaffected so far.[17]*

Making commissioning work for the benefit of patients and the taxpayers is perhaps the most serious challenge in answering the Lord Darzi question about who is really responsible in the NHS. The right answer is the commissioners should be responsible and have all the tools and levers to use to make change happen. But if ditching commissioning is off the agenda for an incoming Labour government (because it would involve a major change to the NHS 'wiring'), the only alternative for a Labour Secretary of State for Health is to invest in NHS staff and support structures to make commissioning work as effectively as possible. That means reversing the present 'clinicians good, managers bad' rhetoric and recognising that something as complex as the NHS cannot work effectively without high-quality and effective managers in both commissioning and providing organisations.

Tools available to a Labour government to change NHS policy

Perhaps the single biggest problem that an incoming Secretary of State will inherit is a lack of legal 'levers' to pull to make changes happen. Under the National Health Service Act 2006 all NHS bodies other than GPs and NHS Foundation Trusts were required to follow 'directions' made by the Secretary of State. GPs were excluded because they were independent contractors and NHS Foundation Trusts were excluded from the Secretary of State's direction-making powers in order to give them independence. However the Secretary of State was able to issue directions to all NHS commissioners who could, in turn, use their contractual powers to effect necessary change. The direction-making powers of the Secretary of State have virtually disappeared as a result of the Health and Social Care Act 2012.[18] The Secretary of State does not now even have a clear power to issue directions to the NHS Commissioning Board (also known as NHS England) and in turn NHS England only has very limited direction-making powers in respect of CCGs.

There are ways of influencing the actions of NHS England and, through NHS England, other NHS bodies. The days of instructions coming from Richmond House with the force of law are over. In fact, however, little if anything has changed, and edicts from ministers remain part of the NHS. As political realities emerged, the naivety of a 'Bank of England' style NHS became clear. Ministers have thus reasserted political control and are acting as if they remained in charge. At present, however, they have no legal right to do so. At some point the power of persuasion may not be enough, as NHS bodies assert the legal freedoms they were given under the 2012 Act. At that point, ministers may be gently but firmly told to back off. There is an inherent contradiction between a legal Bank of England style NHS and ministers being politically accountable for an NHS they cannot control. It is an issue that will need to be resolved.

An agenda for reform

So what are the major legal issues that an incoming Secretary of State might wish to consider? I would suggest that they should include the following.

Restoring the Secretary of State's direction-making powers

There are three reasons why an incoming Labour government should rapidly change the law to restore (or create for the first time) the Secretary of State's power to issue directions to NHS England, and in turn to give NHS England the power to issue directions to any public (or private) body delivering NHS services:

1. The Secretary of State is accountable to Parliament for the delivery of NHS services. That accountability is meaningless without giving the Secretary of State the power to intervene if those charged with the day-to-day delivery of the services fail NHS patients.
2. The resumption of NHS direction-making powers will make it clear that the NHS is a *national* health service directable by a single Secretary of State, and not a joined up collection of local health services.
3. NHS direction-making powers will make it clear that the Secretary of State retains a measure of control over all NHS services, and thus will allow the NHS to remain outside of the regime for EU procurement law. It will help bring the NHS back within the *Teckal* exemption (which avoids the need for procurement exercises when services are commissioned from public bodies under a common system of control by the purchaser).[19]

The Secretary of State imposing his will by making directions is, of course, a last resort. The existence of the power usually means that it does not have to be used. However, now that NHS England has been created as a stand-alone board for the NHS, it makes far more sense to channel a direction-making power through NHS England (with the Secretary of State directing NHS England and NHS England then directing individual NHS bodies) rather than have the Secretary of State directing individual NHS bodies.

Making NHS contracts the norm

An incoming Secretary of State should change the law to insist that *all* arrangements between NHS commissioners and providers for the delivery of services to NHS patients must be set up as 'NHS contracts'[20] and not as legally binding contracts. This may appear to be a minor technical change but it will save substantial legal costs and reduce the scope for providers to miss the big picture when delivering NHS services. Partners who work together under an NHS contract are far more likely to work cooperatively to deliver integrated services for patients as opposed to those who are worried about protecting their own position by attempting to assert their legal rights. It will also assist in ensuring that EU procurement law obligations stay out of the NHS to the greatest extent possible.

Creating legal structures that can take binding decisions on NHS acute service reconfigurations against a fixed timetable

The NHS has some of the finest hospitals in the world, and the Labour government from 1997 to 2010 had a proud record of building new hospitals. But the time has come for the NHS to focus care for fewer patients in fewer hospitals and to deliver far more healthcare in the community. That requires NHS hospital reorganisations, but these have been plagued with both political and legal controversy, in part because of a lack of clear structures that define how such decisions should be taken, by whom and against what timetable.

For example, an attempt to reduce the number of centres at which children's heart surgery should be delivered suffered setbacks as a result of two judicial reviews that challenged the lawfulness of the complex process adopted by the NHS to resolve this problem. That process has now been effectively abandoned, even though there was a wide medical professional consensus that reducing the number of centres would save the lives of sick children. That consensus did not, of course, extend to which centres should be removed from the list. The NHS will not be able to deliver more services for an ageing population in the community unless robust action is taken to reduce investment in secondary care, which inevitably means fewer and larger hospitals. Four key points about these issues should be noted:

1. Although politicians are neither qualified nor politically able to take decisions about the downgrading of individual A&E or maternity services, Labour politicians must be wary of supporting every local service in the run-up to the 2015 election. This was the Conservative approach in the period leading up to 2010 – supporting

every local unit under threat of change. This approach resulted in the ludicrously vague and unworkable 'four tests' policy introduced in May 2010. This approach makes it extremely difficult to take lawful decisions to make changes to a local health economy because every set of local GP commissioners effectively has a veto to stop change in local services.[21] The only responsible approach by politicians is to make the case for change and to emphasise that decisions about the most clinically effective arrangements for local health services must, at least in the first instance, be for medical and managerial professionals. It may be too much to ask the public to accept that the NHS should be focused on healthcare services and not institutions, but opposing every NHS reconfiguration is a political cul-de-sac.

2. Decisions about configuration of local NHS services must involve multiple CCG areas in order to be effective. The NHS Act 2006 does not recognise the term 'NHS local economy' but decision making on configuration of local NHS services is rarely effective if confined to a single CCG area. Thus new legal structures needed to take these decisions must treat the local NHS commissioners as participants and consultees, but ultimately cannot give a veto to each individual CCG.

3. Reconfigurations of NHS services are afflicted by timidity, delay and uncertainty. The legal structures an incoming Secretary of State should create for taking these decisions should therefore allow NHS England to initiate the process rather than waiting for the local NHS politics to be sufficiently acute to allow a change programme to be examined, provide for clear timetables, and allow (as now) for expert advice and validation to any change plans, but then require swift implementation.

4. The role of the Secretary of State for Health as the appellate body for the final decision (on referral from the local authority committee) may need to be reconsidered. Is it a proper use of the Secretary of State's time to take a decision about the future of a local A&E unit and/or does it unnecessarily 'politicise' the process? Or is a final appeal to the Secretary of State a feature of his or her political accountability for NHS services? There are fine arguments both ways but there is a compelling argument that any

appellate decision by the Secretary of State or an appellate body should be taken within a short time period (of say three months).

Investing properly in NHS commissioning

Doctors and other medical professionals work with skill and dedication to treat their patients. But without effective commissioners the NHS does not know whether the treatments being provided are either clinically effective or cost-effective, or whether doctors are pursuing a course of treatment which is neither. The only justification for the commissioner/provider divide is that NHS commissioners are able effectively to represent both the patient (but to be more informed than many patients) and the taxpayer to ensure that all NHS care is being delivered in a way that is both clinically effective and cost-effective. But there is precious little evidence that this is happening or has ever happened. The 'world class commissioning' programme aimed to achieve this and was widely welcomed, although it was discontinued by the present government before reaching its potential and, of course, many if not most of those who were part of the programme are no longer working in the NHS. In March 2010 the House of Commons Health Select Committee observed:

> *The key question is whether WCC [world class commissioning] will be enough to address the enduring weakness of commissioning. Although WCC seeks to bring about a 'step change' in the capacity and capability of PCTs to act as effective commissioners, some witnesses thought that the enduring weakness of commissioning was unlikely to be addressed by WCC alone.*[22]

The answer from the Committee to that question was that WCC was not sufficient, of itself, but it was part of the answer in developing an NHS that commissions care in an effective manner. A new Secretary of State should explicitly recognise that effective commissioning is a difficult, technical process that requires attention to detail and the confidence to confront clinicians. The present structures deliver greater clinical involvement in commissioning and it is possible that this will deliver more effective commissioning. But that will only become a reality if both GPs and secondary care consultants recognise and respect the role of commissioners, which in turn needs an enhanced role and status for commissioners. The NHS thus needs politicians who abandon the lazy rhetoric of 'manager bashing'. A key role for the new Secretary of State will be to promote the role of those who speak up on behalf of patients and the taxpayers in the NHS system – namely the commissioners. Either that or to abandon the whole commissioner/provider divide as a waste of time and money.

Tackling postcode prescribing

The NHS has never given patients a legal right to the same level of medical treatment anywhere in the country. Decisions about what medical treatment a patient is entitled to as part of NHS funded healthcare are decisions of local NHS units, with patients being subjected to 'postcode prescribing'. Variation between policies of different NHS commissioners is thus both lawful and inevitable. Thus a patient who is registered with a GP in Stoke can be entitled to a life-saving bariatric surgery operation with a threshold body mass index of 35, whereas patients would lawfully require a BMI of 50 in neighbouring North Staffordshire.[23] The creation of the National Institute for Health and Clinical Excellence (NICE) was designed to inch the NHS in the direction of a national service as a result of directions made in 2003 which required PCTs to fund treatments recommended in NICE Technology Appraisal Guidance. However, only a tiny number of treatments have been taken through the laborious NICE process. Even then, there are legitimate complaints that NICE decisions involve a process of decision making that is focused solely on the individual treatment in question and does not properly ask how that proposed investment fits into a scheme of local or national priority-setting.

There are two interconnected problems when attempting to tackle postcode prescribing. First, the NHS cannot afford to 'level up'. Any expansion of mandatory treatment rights would inevitably result in local NHS commissioners being unable to afford other treatments that they currently fund, which would be presented as 'cuts'. Second, a politician cannot ever be seen directly to take a 'prioritisation' decision because those who are denied any item of care will loudly cry foul in the media. The answer to this age-old problem may be for the Secretary of State to set a much more detailed framework and to influence NHS England (via the Mandate[24] if needed) to impose much greater standardisation of commissioning policies across CCGs, thus reducing the more glaring disparities. However, in the end difficult decisions on which treatments are to be made available to which patient groups face formidable difficulties if they fall to be taken by anyone who directly faces election by the public.

Joining up healthcare and social care

The Shadow Secretary of State for Health, Andy Burnham, is presently discussing the most effective way to join up health and social care so that, particularly for the elderly, it becomes about *care* services and not whether these are health or social care services. There are obviously difficult issues about funding such a service and worries about meeting the cost of the increased demand that such a service change would trigger. However if an incoming Secretary of State was minded to expand the social care services that could be provided free at the point of use, there is an established mechanism that could be used to bring this about without the need for primary legislation. Section 3(1)(e) of the NHS Act 2006 provides that CCGs must provide such 'other services' as part of the NHS as the group considers are 'appropriate as part of the health service'. This is the power that is used by the NHS to fund social care and accommodation costs of patients who are eligible for NHS Continuing Care.[25] The process that CCGs are required to follow to decide whether a person is eligible for social care (as part of NHS funded care therefore free at the point of use) is set out in regulations,[26] which currently require CCGs to follow the National Framework for NHS Continuing Care in making decisions as to where the health/social care boundary lies. This boundary is crucial for patients as it defines the boundary between services that are provided free of charge and those that are provided on a means-tested basis. However, if a future Labour Secretary of State wished to expand the areas of social care that were to be provided without charge, this appears to be the most appropriate mechanism to do so. Adding care services which can be delivered under section 3(1)(e) to include a greater level of social care (and thus making them free at the point of use) would deliver on a joined-up service without major structural reorganisation.

Becoming Secretary of State for Health in a Labour government is both the best and the worst job in government. It is the best because the NHS is so close to the heart of the Labour Party, and is the worst job for the same reason. The above are a series of practical steps that an incoming Labour government could take to regain control over the NHS, restore it as a politically accountable public service and to stop the slide towards the NHS becoming a state-funded healthcare insurance system.

Summary of principal recommendations

- To restore the Secretary of State's power to issue directions to NHS England, and in turn to give NHS England the power to issue directions to any public (or private) body delivering NHS services.
- To change the law so that *all* arrangements between NHS commissioners and providers for the delivery of services to NHS patients are set up as 'NHS contracts' and not as legally binding contracts.
- To create legal structures that can take binding decisions on NHS acute service reconfigurations against a fixed timetable.
- To invest properly in NHS commissioning.
- To tackle postcode prescribing.
- To join up healthcare and social care by, in the first instance, expanding the 'other services' that can be commissioned under s. 3 of the NHS Act.

11

Personal Injury Law

Andrew Dismore LLM, AM

The Conservative–Liberal Democrat coalition government has shown itself unable and unwilling to comprehend the plight of someone injured in an accident, whether at work, in a car, on the street or when visiting someone else's premises. While the fundamental principle of personal injury law still prevails – that compensation is only recoverable if someone else is to blame for the accident (the 'polluter pays' principle that runs throughout the law of tort), the coalition government has undermined this principle with its avowed policy goal of reducing the number of claims overall.

In pursuing this objective, ministers have developed policies that are mutually contradictory, do not take account of the evidence and do not allow one change to settle down before another is introduced. Change is uncoordinated. Meanwhile, the person injured through no fault of their own has everything to prove when taking on a highly resourced insurance company with no commercial interest in paying out compensation unless it is forced to do so.

Obsessed by the so-called 'compensation culture' and 'health and safety red tape', we discuss in this chapter how the coalition government has introduced changes to substantive law, procedure and the financing of claims to make it far harder for anyone with a genuine case to secure fair compensation. The only beneficiaries are insurance companies, who have collected the premiums but do not wish to pay out fairly on good claims. In fact the government loses money on fewer claims because the present system claws back from successful claimants the cost of any social security benefits and some NHS treatment costs, so fewer cases mean less reimbursement to the Treasury.

Every investigation there has been has shown that while there may be a perception of a 'compensation culture', the reality is that this is a myth. Even the government's attack on whiplash victims – a constant series of changes instigated by the insurance industry that have been implemented by the government with no heed to the interests of accident victims or representations on their behalf – is misplaced and misdirected, as the parliamentary Transport Committee report of July 2013 showed.[1] Rather than increasing, the number of road accident claims has been falling, with the insurers in large part to blame for practices that have led to potential fraud (for example third-party capture, where they approach accident victims direct and encourage them to claim without legal advice, or by making offers to settle without medical evidence) – a responsibility the government has half-heartedly only recently acknowledged. Instead of robustly demanding that insurers justify their extravagant claims of a crisis by producing robust data, the government has accepted what they say at face value, to the detriment of injured people.

In the workplace, the changes initiated by Lord Young's tendentious report on health and safety regulation[2] have led to the removal of the right to claim for a breach of statutory duty (so that those injured as a result of a breach of safety regulations could claim compensation without also having to establish negligence) – a right going back to the 1898 case of *Groves v Lord Wimborne*[3] enforcing the rights set out in the early Factories Acts from 1844 onwards – ignoring the fact that such claims made a major contribution to workplace safety.

The cost to society of accidents has been overlooked in the government's policy formulation, as has the prevention of accidents, which is always better than retrospective compensation for injuries. This is not to say that there were no problems with the system as it stood in 2010. Merely turning the clock back is an insufficient answer, though much of the coalition's assault must be repealed.

Reforms to civil justice have to be weighed against the impact they may have on access to justice and on access to quality justice – a balance the coalition has signally failed to achieve. Labour's reforms to put this right must aim to restore confidence in the system and put the individual consumer of legal services – in this case the claimant – first, before the interests of the big insurance companies or the lawyers for either side. Labour's priority must be to restore access to justice to all those who have lost out as a result of the government's attack on the civil justice system.

Liability reform

Victims of accidents at work have suffered from the coalition's ill-considered changes affecting personal injury claims and ideologically rooted reforms.

In his report commissioned by the government, Professor Löfstedt recommended that regulations imposing strict liability (enabling those injured as a result of a breach of safety regulations to claim compensation without also having to establish negligence) should be reviewed, and either qualified with 'reasonably practicable' where strict liability was not absolutely necessary or amended to prevent civil liability from attaching to a breach of those provisions.[4] In s. 69 of the Enterprise and Regulatory Reform Act 2013 the coalition government has gone much further than this, with wholesale abolition of statutory liability for workplace accidents.

Section 69 came into force on 1 October 2013, bringing an end to statutory liability for accidents at work by amending s. 47 of the Health and Safety at Work Act 1974. This had codified the settled case law since 1898, creating a presumption that a breach of health and safety regulations carried civil liability for consequent injuries, unless expressly excluded. The amended Act now requires an express inclusion to be created for each and every regulation: this has not occurred, so statutory civil liability (including strict liability) for such accidents no longer exists.

An example of the effect of this is illustrated by regulation 5(1) of the Provision and Use of Work Equipment Regulations, which provides that 'every employer shall ensure that work equipment is maintained in an efficient state, in efficient working order and in good repair'. Before s. 69, the injured employee would have to prove the equipment was not in accordance with the regulation, but did not have to show the employer was at fault. Now, proving a machine is unguarded, or scaffolding not properly constructed, is not enough. The victim will be forced to establish that the employer was negligent under common law. In today's complex workplace world, this is a major barrier.

Proving negligence is inevitably going to be a more difficult and time-consuming operation, and under the coalition's new court funding rules, the costs of proving a claim may not be proportionate to the seriousness of the claim, so some claims may not even get off the ground. The consequences of s. 69 will also prove to be counter-productive, in that cases that previously would have settled at an early stage will be more likely to be defended all the way. The defendant's insurers don't have anything to prove, they simply have to deny liability and force the injured person to make the running.

There will also be a negative impact on health and safety in the workplace with this removal of civil liability at a time when the Health and Safety Executive (HSE) is itself being cut, because reducing the extent of liability for accidents reduces the cost of breaches of health and safety law and is thus a disincentive to comply fully.

The next Labour government must reverse this change and reintroduce the presumption of civil liability for a breach of health and safety regulations. But that is not enough. It has long been an argument that when implementing EU directives many of the detailed regulations (known as the 'six pack' as there are six main regulations) that should create strict liability do not do so. They are qualified by 'reasonable practicability', creating even under the former law an additional hurdle for the victim to overcome. The 'six pack' and subsequent similar regulations should be amended to implement properly the directives and ensure the strict liability originally intended.

Moreover, cases that are brought under health and safety regulations should face a reversed burden of proof, which would require the employer's insurers to prove the regulations were not broken rather than for the accident victim to prove that they were.

The Health and Safety at Work Act 1974 did not create civil, but only criminal liability. It is time for this anomaly to be changed too, with civil liability for a breach of the 1974 Act introduced so as to provide greater protection to workers and the public through stronger incentives to comply.

Industrial illnesses

Further assistance is needed for victims of industrial diseases where the insurance company cannot be traced – a particular problem where the disease is 'long tail' and not diagnosed until many years after the exposure to the relevant hazard, such as in the case of asbestos-related diseases.

A consultation process set up by the last Labour government in 2010 resulted in a proposal for an Employers' Liability Insurance Bureau (ELIB), an insurance fund of last resort, modelled on the Motor Insurers' Bureau (MIB) which is funded by the insurance industry for those injured by untraced or uninsured motorists. The proposed ELIB would have compensated *all* industrial disease victims where the employer has gone out of business and the employer's insurer is untraced.

The coalition government has not followed this up, and the Mesothelioma Act 2014 is the result of yet another deal between the government and the insurance industry, ignoring the views of claimants, support groups or trade unions. It will be funded by a levy on current employers' liability insurers. The woefully inadequate Act establishes a scheme of last resort for untraced employers' liability insurance claims. The Act compensates only mesothelioma claimants who cannot trace the liable insurer and not claimants suffering other asbestos-related diseases, or indeed other industrial diseases not caused by asbestos but due to exposure to other dangerous chemicals or processes. Furthermore, the scheme limits compensation to 75 per cent of the average value of similar court awards, and also imposes an arbitrary cut-off date of diagnosis of mesothelioma on or after 25 July 2012, meaning many historic cases are unfairly excluded.

These failings need to be corrected, and a full ELIB, funded by the insurance industry, must be created. Like the MIB, it would pay compensation on the same basis as a standard civil claim, and cover all industrial diseases. It must not exclude old cases, but operate under the normal rules of limitation.

Road accidents

The most vulnerable road users are cyclists and pedestrians. When

hit by a motor vehicle, injuries can be serious, and the law consequently expects a higher standard from drivers who have the capacity to cause far more serious harm. If injured in a road accident by
a vehicle, pedestrians and cyclists have a high chance of success,
even if damages are reduced due to their contributory fault. Primary
liability (against the party who is entirely or mainly to blame and
who is almost always the driver of the vehicle involved) is usually
established. Although there is an argument that strict liability should
be introduced for such claimants to reduce legal costs in the light of
the fact that they are more likely to win, at the least the next Labour
government should reverse the burden of proof for pedestrians and
cyclists when injured by a motor vehicle, requiring the insurer of the
driver concerned to show the driver was not negligent in causing the
accident. This will also help to reduce costs and speed up claims.

The next Labour government should also ensure that the Motor
Insurers' Bureau agreement to compensate those who are injured by
uninsured and untraced drivers complies fully with EU directives,
which currently it does not. The only exception to cover should be for
those travelling in a stolen car, knowing it to be stolen.

Defendants' insurers far too often rely on a bald denial of liability. This results in increased costs and protracted litigation,
especially if they later withdraw the denial and admit liability.
Although in theory defendants' insurers are no longer permitted to
rely on a simple denial when defending claims, but are expected
to plead a positive case under the Civil Procedure Rules (CPR),
in practice they do not comply with this. A defence that does not
comply with CPR rule 16.5 should be struck out automatically.

Process reform

The coalition government's changes to process, when linked to their
funding changes, are uncoordinated and counter-productive. The
portal computerised claim processing system, which was designed for
low-value road traffic accident (RTA) claims with no liability issues
and was successful in reducing costs and speeding up simple claims,
has been extended to higher-value RTA claims up to £25,000 and to

employers' and public liability claims to the same value. This has raised the potential for serious under-settlement of these larger claims.

With a very low fixed costs regime in the portal, the work needed to bring higher-value claims worth £25,000 will not be carried out competently and satisfactorily, because the amount of work needed is beyond what the costs limit will provide, with the greater range of heads of damage and calculations that are required. In addition, the coalition government has extended the portal to disease claims, which cannot be presented fairly within the costs straitjacket provided. One of the early consequences has been to show these changes to be counter-productive as a higher proportion of cases now drop out of the portal and enter the litigation system, either because the insurers' offer was too low, or their decision on liability was not made in time.

Other government proposals to extend the small claims limit to £5,000 for road accident cases, in a misguided attempt to reduce alleged fraud, run the risk of destabilising the portal system by removing the lower-value cases from the portal. These claims would now end up in the small claims court. The £5,000 limit proposed is for general damages only, so with special damages on top, the value of a claim in the small claims court could easily be double or even three times the £5,000 limit proposal. Such an increase cannot be justified. While there is an argument that any increase should reflect inflation since the limit was last reviewed, raising it to about £1,500 or so, to raise it beyond that risks injustice.

In the small claims court, especially with a higher limit, unrepresented claimants do not have a clue as to the value of their claim. They are faced by an insurance company represented by an experienced claims assessor or lawyer, resulting in a complete inequality of arms. This can only be bridged by claims management companies filling the gap in return for a cut of the damages, as costs are not recoverable in the small claims court.

As a result of the intervention of the Transport Select Committee amongst others, the government finally decided to defer any increase in the limit due to concerns over the impact on access to justice, but the threat of an increase remains. The next Labour government should commit to not increasing the small claims limit beyond inflation; and to reduce to that level any higher limit which is introduced beyond inflation.

As an early priority, the next Labour government should review the operation of the portal, its fixed costs regime and the small claims court limit simultaneously and together, to ensure that the system is coordinated and operates fairly for claimants, in claims where liability is not disputed. In particular, the review must consider whether the £25,000 limit in the portal is too high, and whether the portal is inappropriate for some types of claim, such as disease cases.

In a recent YouGov poll, only one in four people said they would make a claim if they were injured, which must to some extent reflect their view of the accessibility of the current system. In reforming the claims process, the next Labour government must work in the consumer interest to develop accessible and efficient systems that are user-friendly and help achieve what consumers want and need.

If the policy objective is to reduce costs and speed up claims, then a better solution is to consider a specialist personal injury court or tribunal that could deal with claims up to the fast-track limit, including cases involving disputed liability and alleged fraud. (Cases are allocated by the court to a procedural track depending on their value and complexity: fast track is where the personal injury claim is likely to be worth in total up to £25,000 and the final hearing is likely to take less than one day.) Specialist judges would have the experience and expertise to deal with claims more efficiently than generalist civil courts. Whether a specialist formal court or the informality of a specialist tribunal is preferred, the approach adopted should be inquisitorial rather than adversarial, as this will enable unrepresented claimants to have a fairer hearing. The next Labour government should consult on the benefits and disadvantages of a specialist personal injury court or tribunal.

Insurance industry complaints of fraud ring hollow because, when the evidence is properly analysed, fraudulent claims represent only a tiny proportion of cases, even for whiplash. As the parliamentary Transport Committee report of July 2013 identified,[5] and the coalition government has finally acknowledged, the insurers are themselves in large part responsible for encouraging claims. If an insurer suspects fraud, then they should be required to inform the claimant's representatives of this fact at the earliest opportunity, backed up with the evidence to support the allegation. If a claimant has made multiple claims, his lawyers should be so informed by the insurers.

Third-party capture, by which insurers try to reduce their liability by settling claims direct without the claimant having access to appropriate independent professional advice, and which results in significant under-settlement, must be outlawed. People are tempted into accepting early offers due to being in debt or in hock to payday loan companies. Any direct settlement with insurers should be voidable if made without legal advice. Before such a settlement is finalised, the insurers should be required to pay reasonable and necessary costs for the claimant to get independent legal advice (and that advice should not be from any law firm with a financial or other relationship with the insurance company).

The insurers also attempt to force settlements without medical evidence. Such pre-medical offers should either be banned or treated as representing interim payments only, and to have no other legal effect. In particular, they should not be seen as in full and final settlement. A claimant must be able to come back for more if medical evidence is subsequently obtained that shows the settlement was too low.

The next Labour government must take action to control the sharp practices of the insurance industry. It must require the Financial Conduct Authority to take its responsibilities more seriously in policing the activities of insurance companies in personal injury settlements.

Damages
General damages

General damages for pain, suffering and loss of amenity for personal injury are too low. The Law Commission inquiry into damages in the mid-1990s reported that personal injury damages were even then between a third and a half too low, and required uprating.[6] The later case of *Heil v Rankin* [2000] 3 All ER 138 did not achieve this outcome. Lord Justice Jackson's recommendation[7] of a 10 per cent uplift, as a vehicle to pass costs to the claimant that should properly be met by the defendant or his insurers, led the coalition government to follow the same route by attempting to get the courts to implement it. As this was to compensate for costs bills to be met by the claimant, it cannot be taken into account when considering the correct level of general damages because there is no benefit from the increase to the claimant.

In most cases the practical effect of the increase has been to leave the claimant worse off because it has had little impact on smaller claims. A 10 per cent increase, when translated into cash terms, is within the margin of error of the valuation in negotiations for settlement. The theoretical outcome of an academic statistical uplift has not reflected the reality of the cut and thrust of settlement negotiation in individual cases.

Any uprating should represent a much greater figure to reflect the true extent to which damages have fallen behind, as established by the Law Commission, irrespective of the costs debate. There can be little confidence that this can be achieved through judicial intervention, so the next Labour government should, through legislation, restore general damages to historic levels by an across the board uplift of at least one-third, and should provide for regular statutory uprating in line with inflation.

Fatal accident damages

Nowhere is the law of damages more out of kilter with public expectations than in its failure properly to compensate those who suffer the consequences of a fatal accident.

– Statutory death payment

It is cheaper in some circumstances to kill than to maim. For example, the family of an unmarried man in his twenties with no dependants would receive only the funeral costs in the event of his death due to the fault of another. It cannot be right that death is compensated at a lower figure than serious injury. Many years ago, there was thought to be a case for 'lost years' in such cases, where a claim could be brought for the deceased's future earnings that would now never be received. However, such cases were ruled out by the courts.

A better approach is to reflect that a lost life has a value in itself: for example, in 2009 the Department of Transport estimated the cost to society of a lost life to be in excess of £1.5m. Another way would be to value the lost life on a par with an injury of maximum severity, and to award damages in the form of a new statutory death payment in a sum equivalent to the current valuation for general damages (not including consequent special and future loss damages) for maximum severity, such as severe brain damage or quadriplegia. Currently, this would be about £250,000 to £300,000. Loss of life must be compensated properly in itself.

– Dependency claims: Dependency

The dependent family of a fatal accident victim is entitled to claim for the extent to which they were financially dependent on the victim. However, there are anomalies here too. Those who can claim are set out in a finite statutory list of possible claimants.

In 1999 the Law Commission recommended that dependency claims be extended to include anyone who was being wholly or partly maintained by the deceased immediately before the death, and anyone who would have been so maintained in the future but for the death.[8] In the Civil Law Reform Bill 2009 the last Labour government accepted part of the Commission's proposals, that dependency claims should include those 'wholly or partly maintained by the deceased immediately before the death', but this Bill fell at the election and was dropped by the coalition. Such a formulation would avoid problems of uncompensated dependants, excluded under the current exclusive statutory list.

The calculation of the dependency award is in itself pretty unscientific. It treats the assessment of dependency as a future loss running from the date of death. This flies in the face of reality, as the case may take several years to conclude, thus reducing the potential value of the award. Losses to the date of settlement or trial should be treated as special damages, and a future losses multiplier applied only to the remaining period for which dependency is awarded.

The next Labour government should implement the Law Commission recommendation on the definition of dependency in full, and should correct the anomaly of past dependency being treated as future loss.

– Dependency claims: Bereavement damages

The list of people who can claim the statutory bereavement damages of £12,980 is limited to the wife, husband or civil partner of the deceased, or the parents of a deceased child who was never married or who never had a civil partner. Cohabitees and children of deceased parents are excluded, as are relatives who bring up children in the place of parents, such as aunts, uncles or grandparents. There is only one bereavement award payable, so if there are two or more claimants (for example two parents of a killed child), they share the award between them, the assumption apparently being that if there are two parents they only suffer half as much.

Amendments were included in the last Labour government's Civil Law Reform Bill 2009 to extend eligibility for bereavement damages to those who had been cohabiting with the deceased as husband, wife or civil partner for a period of at least two years ending with the date of the death; and to the deceased's children aged under 18 at the date of the death. The Bill was dropped by the coalition.

Bereavement damages reform proposed by the last Labour government should be reintroduced. The categories of claimants should also include relatives who act as parents, in the event of a deceased child. There should also be an award for each eligible claimant, not a single award shared between them, as well as provision for regular uprating for inflation.

Punitive damages

The criminal law does not provide adequate remedies for accident victims, even after the last Labour government introduced the new offence of corporate manslaughter (under the Corporate Manslaughter and Corporate Homicide Act 2007). The Health and Safety Executive (HSE) and other prosecuting authorities rarely mount criminal prosecutions, and these can be expected to become even rarer as a consequence of the coalition's cuts in HSE budgets and attempts to reduce health and safety protection generally. The penalties imposed by the criminal courts for health and safety regulatory offences are considered by many victims to be woefully inadequate.

The civil law should provide an alternative remedy through

punitive damages in the most blatant cases. It is not suggested that such damages should become widely available, but it should be open to a court to make a punitive award in cases involving the most serious torts committed in the most reckless of circumstances, resulting in serious injury or death. Such a remedy would go a long way to satisfying public concern over the failure of the law to penalise those responsible for the most outrageous acts and omissions. The next Labour government should build on its success in introducing corporate manslaughter by establishing clear criteria for punitive damages awards.

Future financial loss

While actuarial tables are now regularly used in the courts, the rate of return and discount rates used when calculating future loss fail to track the prevailing rates of return and interest on investments. This is in large part because changes to the court rates are made by the Secretary of State through statutory instrument, which inevitably means there is a long lead time before any change takes effect. A more automatic tracking arrangement is needed to allow rate changes to reflect the realities of the investment market, and so to ensure compensation is fairly calculated. The methodology used should also reflect a cautious, low-risk approach to investment generally adopted by claimants, for example by using index-linked government securities.

Recoupment of NHS costs

Some of the costs of ambulance and hospital treatment of accident victims by the NHS are recoverable directly from the compensator, but these are capped at £46,046. However, no such cap applies to the recovery of medical expenses by private medical insurance companies, like BUPA, who expect to recover their full outlays as a subrogated part of any personal injury claim.

It does not seem right that the NHS should be at a disadvantage when compared with private health providers; nor can it be right to expect the taxpayer to pick up the full cost of an accident victim's medical treatment. The next Labour government should ensure full recovery of NHS costs from all tortfeasors.

Access to the law
Funding

It is in the area of funding that the coalition government has caused the greatest disadvantage to claimants, with its abolition of recoverable success fees and after-the-event insurance premiums, and by providing for fixed costs at rates that are uneconomic for lower-value cases and incompatible with competent professional representation.

In pursuing these policies, the coalition accepted the arguments of the insurance companies and ignored those who represent claimants. Purportedly relying on the report of Lord Justice Jackson,[9] they cherry-picked his recommendations, ignoring those that favoured claimants. The coalition took no account of the evidence of the costs of bringing a claim professionally, nor of overheads such as marketing costs, in their drive to eliminate their perceived ill of referral fees.

The introduction in April 2013 of qualified one-way costs shifting (QOCS) is an improvement, but did not go far enough, leaving claimants in a weak negotiating position when faced with formal 'part 36' offers. Under QOCS, if a claimant loses, in normal circumstances they will not be liable for the defendant's costs, only their own. A party, usually the defendant, can protect themselves in costs by making a part 36 formal offer to settle the claim, normally stating how much that party is prepared to pay or settle for. One of the ways QOCS can be disapplied is if the defendant makes a part 36 offer, and the court later makes a damages award in the same or lesser sum. Then the claimant is liable for the defendant's costs from the date of the offer as well as the claimant's own costs. As a part 36 offer thus trumps QOCS, the claimant faces paying the insurance company's costs as well as his or her own costs if the claim goes on but does not beat the offer. This can result in 100 per cent of the damages award being wiped out to pay the defendant's cost bill.

In contrast, when an insurer fails to beat the claimant's part 36 offer to settle, they only have to pay 10 per cent extra damages. This should be increased so as to provide an effective incentive to the insurers to consider a claimant's offer; and the insurer should also be required to meet all of the claimant's liabilities for success fees and other costs if the insurer fails to beat the claimant's part 36 offer.

The loss of recovery of after-the-event (ATE) insurance premiums (which insurance protects the claimant against costs bills, and for which the insurance premium itself was in the past recoverable as part of the costs of the claim if the claim was successful) has also benefited insurers, by increasing pressure on claimants to accept a part 36 offer rather than take the costs risk of rejection. Under the previous system, the ATE policy insured a claimant against adverse costs if he was acting on advice to reject the part 36 offer, but in the end failed to beat it.

Claimants also now face deductions from their damages to meet costs shortfalls, either through contingency fees known as damages-based agreements (DBAs) or through paying the solicitor's success fees. All this has meant a huge windfall for the insurance industry, through lower costs in cases that succeed, fewer cases being pursued as lower-value cases become less economic, and cases settling for less than they are worth, only offset in small part by their new QOCS liabilities.

The funding reductions, carried out in isolation from many of the procedural and substantive law changes, are having a serious impact on access to justice for accident victims.

Representation

The new proportionality rule means that many lower-value claims that are disputed but after proper investigation are found to be meritorious (and would in the past have had a fair chance) are far less likely even to find a lawyer to take them on in the first place. For example, sex abuse claims have a relatively low damages value as against the costs of pursuing them against a wealthy, high-profile defendant. Many industrial diseases will attract comparatively low damages when compared with the costs of proving liability, and the same can apply to clinical negligence claims. The proportionality rule should be abolished, and costs assessed fairly.

Lawyers have been left with little option but to cherry-pick good cases and turn down cases that, although they may have a greater than 50 per cent chance of success, are not 'open and shut'.

While the coalition government sees people taking out 'before the event' legal expenses insurance policies (BTE) as part of the solution

– usually as an untransparent 'bolt-on' to motor or home contents policies – this is not an option for the less well off, who find even basic household insurance unaffordable. The small print of most BTE polices also means that, other than for the most straightforward of claims, they provide very little protection or support for claims. The next Labour government should ensure greater transparency to consumers about the costs of BTE policies and what cover is provided under them.

The failure of the coalition to accept Sir Rupert Jackson's recommendation to abolish the indemnity principle[10] also needs to be addressed. The consequence of this failure is to open up their new costs regime to years of satellite litigation (with court cases being litigated more for the costs liabilities than the real issues in the case) as to its interpretation; and to require lawyers to draft opaque costs agreements with their clients that are far more complex than should be the case, rather than being able to offer simpler to understand 'no win, no fee' deals. The long outdated indemnity principle should be abolished, to make costs more understandable to the public.

Steps to better access

The next Labour government must have a speedy and comprehensive review of the impact of the coalition government's changes on access to justice, and thereafter bring in reforms to ensure better access to justice and equality of arms in litigation.

The brief for such a review must be to ensure that the overall costs regime acts to facilitate claimants' rights to pursue legitimate claims; that there is a level playing field in the standard of representation that a claimant can expect when fighting a multinational insurance company; that the claimant is able to receive any damages in full without deductions for costs shortfalls; and that the claimant is not under unfair pressure to under-settle the claim. Following the 'polluter pays' principle, the outcome should be that an unsuccessfully defended claim brings to the insurer the reasonable costs bill incurred by the successful claimant to pursue it.

This review should not be carried out in isolation, but should be linked to the procedural and substantive law reviews and changes proposed earlier. It should research and take account of the true costs of claims brought at different levels of damages and types of case in the portal, including overheads and the underwriting of disbursement outlays (for example, for expert fees).

The fast-track fixed fee regime needs to be broadened to reflect a wider matrix of costs for different types of claim and stages of process, and also to reflect better the real costs of representation at an appropriate skills level. As an immediate step pending the review, the fixed costs arbitrarily imposed by the coalition government consequent on private meetings with insurers should be replaced with those recommended by Sir Rupert Jackson, uprated for inflation since publication of his report.

Consideration should also be given in the review to a reformed recoverable success fee, perhaps linked to damages, with a backstop cash limited cap. Either separately, or included in this recoverable success fee, the review should consider a recoverable fixed sum contribution towards ATE insurance for residual risks.

The QOCS and part 36 imbalance should be addressed, to ensure that claimants are not unduly pressurised into under-settlement. This could be underwritten by the suggested ATE residual risks policy recoverable premium.

Conclusion

The need for reform of the law of personal injury is urgent in order to redress the worst depredations of the coalition government at the behest of the insurance industry and at the expense of innocent accident victims. But restoring the balance is not enough. The next Labour government needs to effect real reform that will show it is firmly on the side of the small person as against the big multinational insurance industry.

This chapter has set out just some of the changes that need to be made to start the process of levelling the playing field by ensuring access to justice; and when access is achieved, then ensuring that real justice is done.

Summary of principal recommendations

- To reintroduce the presumption of civil liability for a breach of health and safety regulations.
- To create an Employers' Liability Insurance Bureau, funded by the insurance industry, paying compensation on the same basis as a standard civil claim, and covering all industrial diseases.
- The burden of proof should be reversed for pedestrians and cyclists when injured by a motor vehicle.
- The next Labour government should commit to not increasing the small claims limit beyond inflation; and to reduce to that level any higher limit that is introduced beyond inflation.
- To review the operation of the portal, its fixed costs regimes and the small claims court limit, to ensure a coordinated and fair system for claimants where liability is not disputed.
- Consultation on the benefits and disadvantages of a specialist personal injury court or tribunal.
- To control the sharp practices of the insurance industry.
- To restore general damages to historic levels by an across the board uplift of at least one-third; and provide for regular statutory uprating in line with inflation.
- Loss of life must be compensated properly.
- To introduce clear criteria for punitive damages awards.
- A speedy and comprehensive review of how the coalition's changes have affected access to justice; and thereafter bring in reforms to ensure better access to justice and equality of arms in litigation.

12

Planning Law and Housebuilding

John Hobson QC and Reuben Taylor QC

The modern planning system was introduced by the Labour government in 1947 and it has been very successful in regulating the use of and development of land in the public interest. It has enabled urban sprawl to be contained and the countryside to be protected for generations, which is no small feat for a highly populated country.

The planning system was further sharpened in June 1991 when, during parliamentary debate on the Planning and Compensation Bill, s. 54A was added as an amendment promoted by Labour. That provision established that determinations under the planning Acts should be made in accordance with the development plan (which sets out a local authority's policies and proposals for the development and use of land in its area) unless material considerations indicate otherwise. This provision (now to be found in s. 38(6) of the Planning and Compulsory Purchase Act 2004) laid the foundation for what is now known as the plan-led system; a system that enables public participation in plan making and decisions, reflecting the needs of the area as defined in the development plan.

Housing

The most crucial element of need that the planning system has to address now is housing need; more houses are required, for more people on a more affordable basis.

In 2012–13 England, with just 108,190 housing completions, had one of the lowest housebuilding rates since 1923. The lack of affordability has become a crisis, with the average house-price-to-salary ratio almost doubling in the past forty years. The price of the average home purchased is now almost seven times the average annual salary of the buyer and that figure is increasing. First-time buyers are at record lows, with eight out of ten of them requiring financial help from family or friends. The average age of unassisted first-time buyers has soared. Close to a fifth of women and a third of men aged between 20 and 34 are still living at home. Social housing waiting lists have almost doubled in the past 10 years to 1.85 million households, and around 5 million people are waiting for a home. Meanwhile, some 76,000 children live in temporary accommodation and 250,000 families in social housing are in overcrowded accommodation.[1]

There can be no mistaking that there is a serious housing crisis that a future Labour government will need to address. In recent years the planning system has frequently been criticised for obstructing rather than facilitating the provision of necessary new housing but, in our view, much of this criticism is unfounded and unfair.

There are many reasons that account for the decline in housebuilding. Spiralling house prices,[2] particularly in the south-east, have been caused by a number of factors, including:

- Overly easy access to lending.
- The continuing concentration of economic activity in the south-east as opposed to other parts of the country.
- The removal of the right of local authorities to build homes and the curtailment of the publicly funded housebuilding programme.
- The 'right to buy' scheme resulting in the loss of affordable public sector housing.
- Shortage of materials (for example, brick production has been cut back during the recent recession leading to shortages of building materials now).

Recent soaring house prices in London demonstrate that it is not the planning system that is to blame for the property market cycle of boom and bust. Builders in the capital registered 26,230 new flats and houses with the National House-Building Council (NHBC) in 2013.

This was a 60 per cent rise on 2012. Thus, house prices rose significantly during a period of increased supply in 2013 but did not during a period of reduced supply in 2012. That suggests that there must be some different cause of the sudden increase in house prices, other than the supply of housing regulated by the planning system.

We would suggest that the most obvious other cause stems from the 'Help to Buy' scheme, which has enabled first-time buyers to enter the property market when previously they could not. It has resulted in a significant level of demand that did not previously exist. Thus, notwithstanding the material rise in the number of housing completions, demand has suddenly outstripped supply and a large rise in house prices in London has followed (so much so that the government is now considering 'paring back' the Help to Buy scheme).

We believe that it is not the lack of supply of housing that is causing unsustainable and unaffordable house price rises; rather it appears to be directly related to the availability of lending and the amounts that lenders are prepared to offer compared to earnings.

Landbanking

There is often a perception that houses are not coming forward because developers are deliberately sitting on large banks of land in order to restrict supply and increase prices. We believe that this perception is wrong and not supported by the evidence. It certainly runs counter to the nature of the housing industry. Holding on to land represents a massive capital investment for a housing developer, for no return so long as the land is held. As a matter of common sense it is not in developers' interests to tie up capital in land that they have no intention to develop; quite the reverse. So usually developers are keen to get on with construction in order that they can obtain a return on their capital investment.

However, developers need an assured land supply to build homes – land is in essence the crucial raw material to run a development business. It can take many years to acquire land, obtain planning permission, discharge planning conditions, and construct and sell all the homes on a site. Accordingly, a housebuilder has to hold enough land to sustain its business.

In addition, the process of building and selling houses is such that not every plot on a site can be built at the same time. On any site, new homes can be built only at a rate at which they can be sold and, importantly, at a sustainable rate for employment of the many different trades needed to construct each house. Plots within medium and large sites have to be built in sequence due to the phasing of the provision of infrastructure and services. In other words, it is impossible to build a very large site of say 1,000 units in a year, no matter what state the property market is in.

The 2004 Barker Review conducted for the previous Labour government dismissed the view that 'landbanking' was being actively pursued by housebuilders, stating: 'The Review has found little evidence, at least across the country as a whole, to substantiate concerns that option contracts and the practice of landbanking allow housebuilders to erect barriers to entry into the market.'[3]

In 2008 the Office of Fair Trading (OFT) concluded after its review of landbanking within the housebuilding industry:[4]

> We have not found any evidence to support the view that, at the national level, homebuilders are hoarding a large amount of land with implementable planning permission on which they have not started construction. This suggests competition has not been impaired by homebuilders mothballing permissioned land to create a barrier to entry and artificially raise prices even during the long upturn in the market until 2007. Equally, there is little evidence to suggest that homebuilders have been able to systematically obtain market power at a local level by acquiring planning permissions.
>
> In order to maintain an ongoing build programme, homebuilders must ensure they have a development pipeline of land – a 'land bank'. The timescales to build and sell homes, and also the uncertainties in planning outcome and timing, mean that most homebuilders hold a mix of land types at different stages in the planning process. Holding sufficient land for future years serves a practical purpose in acting as a buffer for the time lag from land acquisition through to starting work on site.

A recent survey by the Home Builders Federation (HBF)[5] found that only 4 per cent of house plots with an implementable planning permission were on sites where work had not started; 63 per cent of plots held by housebuilders were on sites where construction work was under way; 31 per cent were on plots with outline planning permission (and thus where further consent is required before construction can commence); and 2 per cent of plots were on sites that were not being developed because it was not economically viable to bring them forward.

While statistics from a housebuilders group might have to be viewed with caution, the previous studies by Barker and by the OFT strongly support the conclusions that the HBF survey statistics point to – that housebuilders are not landbanking in order to manipulate the market. It is also important to recognise that a large amount of land is held by non-developer landowners. The 2008 OFT report concluded:

> *It is possible that other industries, land traders or strategic land funds for example, may landbank permissioned land more extensively than homebuilders. The fragmented nature of land records has made it impossible for this study to consider these industries' practices within the scope of the current study. Notwithstanding this, the evidence suggests that, whatever the practices of non-homebuilder private landowners with their land banks the land bank owned by the public sector is at least as large if not larger.*[6]

This latter point is very important; the publicly owned 'land bank' is very large. Independent estimates suggest the public sector holds up to 40 per cent of developable sites.[7] While the Conservative agenda is to require this land to be sold off to the private sector, we believe that this large amount of potential supply could and should be developed by the public sector itself.

We do not consider, therefore, that landbanking is creating any real problem in relation to the supply of housing and recommend that the next Labour government focuses instead on ensuring that the 'land bank' held by the public sector is brought forward for housing as quickly as possible.

Liberating public sector housebuilding

Although the planning system enables permission to be granted for development to meet needs, there is a limit to which it can achieve that goal. Planning authorities have to wait for private developers to make applications for them to be to able grant planning permission. Even once approved, local planning authorities cannot secure the implementation of developments they have permitted.

Despite the claimed success of the right to buy scheme introduced by the Conservative government in 1980, the restriction on council's being able to use the proceeds of sale to replace lost housing stock has had catastrophic consequences. The reality is that the total number of housing completions between 1990 and 2010 remained relatively static but at levels materially below that which was achieved between 1970 and 1980 when the public sector retained the power to provide housing itself.[8]

An incoming Labour government should immediately liberate local authorities and public sector housebuilding from the shackles it was placed under by the Conservatives. We firmly believe that if a marked increase in housebuilding is to be secured there has to be a significant programme of public sector housebuilding. Just as they built homes to overcome the housing crisis following the Second World War, local authorities need to be given the power to build homes again to address the current housing crisis. This would enable local authorities not just to plan for how needs should be met but also to actively set about providing the development to meet those needs through a significant programme of public sector housebuilding.

A significant public sector programme of housebuilding will not occur without funding and investment in the skills and infrastructure necessary to build. For example, training those who will work in the construction of the new homes and investment in the supply chain for building materials and machinery.

Retail

There has been growing concern that our high streets have become copies of one another, containing nothing but national chain stores with a resulting loss of local identity. In many cases it is very difficult to identify one high street as different from another.

The reason for this is that property within the high street is generally owned by institutional investors who look for a secure return on their investment. They want to have tenants who can give 'good covenant' – i.e. who will not go into administration and who will always be able to pay the rent. The result has been the loss of independent retailers from many high streets as institutional landlords prefer to sign 'safe' lease deals with national multiples.

In recent years, however, the number of independent shops has increased as a result of national chains closing stores in response to the recession. Indeed, there has been an increase in independent retail openings year on year since 2009, although the growth has tapered with each passing year. In 2010 the net opening figure was 4 per cent, but by 2013 it had narrowed to 0.7 per cent as 15,908 openings were offset by 15,182 closures. By comparison, multiple retailers continue to pull out of the high street with their numbers falling 0.6 per cent as they focus on their better-performing retail destinations.[9]

We believe that the planning system already regulates retail issues well and that current policy protects town centres appropriately. However, more needs to be done to support the independent retailer. We believe that a differential system of rates should be considered by the next Labour government; one where independent traders pay less in rates and where chain stores pay more.

It is a fact that many chain stores are owned by companies who have engaged in tax practices that see them pay little by way of corporation tax in the UK. Their physical presence on the high street however means that those companies do pay some tax via the rating system. If higher rates bills were paid by chain stores the resulting income stream could be used by local authorities to help fund their housebuilding programmes. We regard this as a win-win policy that would address the perceived unfairness of major companies avoiding tax and also the need for more homes.

Industry

The industrial sector of the UK economy has, of course, been diminishing for a number of decades. Between 1997 and 2007 the number of factories employing 50 or more staff declined by 33 per cent. Prior to the recession the number of such factories in the UK was falling at an annual rate of 2 per cent.[10]

This trend is of course a result of globalisation – the emergence into the global market-place of a number of countries, but particularly China and India, as major industrial powers with access to comparatively very cheap labour. For example, China's share of world output increased from 2.6 per cent in 1980 to almost 5.5 per cent in 2006. Its hourly manufacturing cost in 2004 was one-twentieth of that of the UK.[11] This has been combined with rapid technological change resulting in strong productivity growth. More can be made, more cheaply and with fewer people.

The UK has found itself unable to compete in many of the traditional industrial activities, and manufacturing's share of total economic output almost halved from around 25 per cent in 1980 to some 13 per cent in 2005.[12] But the service sector meanwhile has expanded significantly. The real estate, renting and business services sector has grown particularly significantly, as has financial services. Indeed, in the past two decades business services have nearly doubled their share of GDP from 7 per cent to 14 per cent and, prior to the recession, accounted for an increase of 1.7 million jobs over the previous decade.[13] So when recession hit the world financial markets, the UK with its highly service-based economy reaped the whirlwind.

There is general agreement that the economy needs to be rebalanced, with a move away from over-reliance on service industries and towards manufacturing. The planning system has a role to play in ensuring that land is available to meet the need for manufacturing floorspace. We believe that the next Labour government should consider requiring local planning authorities to designate land for industrial use on a long-term basis; just as with green belt policy this land should only be removed from such a designation in exceptional circumstances. This would have the effect of depressing the value of such land and would remove, for example, hope value for housing. A reduction in manufacturing land costs can only assist in encouraging manufacturing to come forward.

Further, a new Labour government should consider retaining and utilising centralised planning powers to direct that planning permission should be granted for manufacturing industrial uses in combination with proposals to provide government subsidies for companies investing in industrial development. Where a direction has been made, local planning authorities could only refuse planning permission on an exceptional basis. This power could be used to kick-start major manufacturing investment in a local area by streamlining the planning process and enabling development to come forward quickly.

The local plan framework

The current framework for local plans was introduced in 2004 by the Labour government, requiring councils to set housing targets and identify a rolling five-year supply of developable land. The framework enables needs to be identified and decisions to be made as to how those needs should be met in the way that most accords with the public interest. The most significant problem at a local level is that of delay in the plan-making process. Too many local authorities have not been able to keep their plans up to date.

The issues that have arisen are usually as a result of a number of factors, including lack of resourcing for planning within local authorities, sudden changes in government policy requiring authorities to start their plan-making processes again and the complexity of the issues to be faced (such as how to meet demand for housing in areas heavily constrained by 'green belt' designation).

Where local plan making is falling down is in relation to the difficult decisions that have to be made where needs can only be met through development on environmentally sensitive land such as green belt land. Politicians at a local level are reluctant to promulgate local plans that advocate building on such land because it is highly unpopular locally. The issue is highlighted by the large number of green belt local authorities around the M25 who have yet to promote local plans under the National Planning Policy Framework (NPPF) requirement to demonstrate how needs are to be met.

This reluctance has resulted in some local authorities identifying a reduced level of housing need compared to that which they had previously identified. While this may be politically expedient, we believe that if local authorities are permitted to identify artificially low levels of housing need, this will further exacerbate undersupply and add pressure for an increase in house prices, thereby undermining affordability yet further.

The duty to cooperate is simply not functioning in practice. Councils are not prepared to identify additional land in their local plans to meet housing needs arising within their neighbours' areas. Many authorities have neighbours who are similarly environmentally constrained. Where there are two green belt authorities with need they cannot accommodate, the theory behind the duty to cooperate is that the need will be passed on further to a local authority beyond the green belt that will have to accommodate the overspill. This is not happening in practice. Even if it did it would result in housing being provided in the wrong location to meet needs.

It follows that, if need is to be met where it arises, difficult decisions have to be taken. If they are not be taken at a local level, they will have to be taken at a national level. We recommend that the next Labour government examines the possibility of introducing a mechanism whereby the level of housing need to be addressed in a local plan is approved by central government at an early stage in the plan-formulation process, with the government retaining the ability to impose a need requirement where a local authority's need assessment is flawed.

In essence, the current bottom-up approach to meeting need is not working in some parts of the country. In these locations the government should retain the ability to impose a top-down approach where required.

National policy

Although plan making and policy formulation at a local level is generally working well,[14] the situation at a national level is far from satisfactory. The present government has been desperate to reduce the volume of national policy that had built up over many years providing advice and guidance on a broad range of subject areas, from tree protection to waste and energy incineration. The policy and guidance produced in its place has the virtue of brevity, although, as Sir David Keene said in the Court of Appeal in a recent case,[15] 'the process of simplification has led to a diminution in clarity'.

Also, the policy focus upon the promulgation of sustainable development within the National Planning Policy Framework appears to be a laudable goal until one has to decide what 'sustainable development' actually means in practice. For planning practitioners, the advice on what constitutes sustainable development is uncertain and ambiguous.

The focus of the present government on providing more concise advice has been at the expense of clarity, but clarity in policy is what the planning system needs if its users are to know where they stand. Ambiguity in policy leads to unpredictability, unpredictability leads to risk and risk deters development. It is crucial that policy is clear so that the users of the planning system know where they stand and developers can make their investment decisions on a firm footing.

We would recommend a reversion to the preceding system: a clear and concise statement of policy and guidance for each of the significant subject areas that the planning system touches upon.

Compulsory purchase

The compulsory purchase system has become complicated and convoluted because of the sheer number of statutory provisions that have accumulated over the years. We support the call made by the Compulsory Purchase Association for a consolidation of the legislation to make it more streamlined and easier to understand and use.

Some have suggested that including 'hope value' within the compensation payable by local authorities is preventing redevelopment schemes from coming forward. We disagree. In our experience most compulsory purchase order (CPO) led schemes involve a local authority working in partnership with a commercial developer. Indeed, to obtain a CPO it has to be demonstrated that the necessary funding is in place to bring the scheme forward and this usually necessitates a local authority entering into partnership with a developer wherein the developer underwrites the costs of the scheme. Where this is the case, the land acquisition cost is passed on to the developer as part of the transaction. We are unaware of any evidence that hope value is preventing CPO-based schemes from coming forward.

To remove hope value from within the compensation payable would be to fundamentally alter the basis on which compensation has been paid for centuries – i.e. market value. It would result in less than market value being paid. In other words, the landowner the subject of the CPO would in effect subsidise the state's acquisition of the land. While this might not infringe upon human rights, we do not think it is necessary or fair.

Step-in rights to allow local authority completion of housing

We believe that a future Labour government should consider providing local authorities with a power to require the owner of land that satisfies three conditions – (a) it has the benefit of planning permission which has been implemented more than five years ago, (b) but it is not developed out and (c) it is included in the authority's five-year housing land supply – to complete the development or to allow the local planning authority to step in and complete the development.

Such a power would need to provide compensation in the event of step-in. However, this compensation should be valued on a basis that excludes the 'scheme' – i.e. on a basis that ignores the value of the land for the housing development. This approach would be entirely consistent with established and current compensation principles.[16]

Summary of principal recommendations

- To focus on ensuring that the 'land bank' held by the public sector is brought forward for housing as quickly as possible.
- To promote a significant programme of public sector housebuilding.
- To consider introducing a differential system of retail rates under which independent traders pay less in rates while chain stores pay more.
- To retain and utilise centralised planning powers to direct that land should be allocated on a long-term basis for manufacturing industrial uses.
- To provide government subsidies and planning permission granted by central government for companies investing in industrial development.
- To consider introducing central government prior approval mechanisms for levels of housing need in local plans, with central government reserving the power to impose a need requirement where appropriate.
- To introduce a system of clear and concise statements of national policy and guidance for each of the significant subject areas within planning.
- To consolidate the compulsory purchase legislation to make it more streamlined and easier to understand and use.
- To consider providing local authorities with a power (on payment of compensation) to require the owner of land satisfying certain conditions to complete stalled housing development, or to allow the local planning authority to step in and complete the development.

13

Policing Reform

Vera Baird QC

Whether it is 'neighbourhood policing', 'community policing' or even 'bobbies on the beat', policing reform always returns to 'the Peelian principles', describing the philosophy developed by Sir Robert Peel (twice British prime minister and creator of the Metropolitan Police) to define an ethical police force.[1] The principles offer vision, coherence and a democratic view of the policing role involving the communities that officers serve. Lord Stevens, a former Commissioner of the Metropolitan Police, echoes the founder's beliefs in his recent Independent Police Commission report, *Policing for a Better Britain*,[2] when he states that, with some updating, Peelian principles work just as well today as they did in the 1800s.

This chapter looks at how the principles can be reasserted to help underpin public trust and confidence in the police, to further develop highly successful neighbourhood policing, and whether at least the direct democracy element of the new style of police governance can help build and improve the reputation of policing in England and Wales.

The relationship between police and public

Peelian principle number seven (the most well-known) clearly states the police should maintain relationships with the public, yet Her Majesty's Chief Inspector of Constabulary, Tom Winsor says in his annual assessment of policing in England and Wales, 'It is very much to

The Peelian principles

1. The basic mission for which the police exist is to prevent crime and disorder.

2. The ability of the police to perform their duties is dependent upon public approval of police actions.

3. Police must secure the willing cooperation of the public in voluntary observance of the law to be able to secure and maintain the respect of the public.

4. The degree of cooperation of the public that can be secured diminishes in proportion to the necessity to use physical force.

5. Police seek and preserve public favour not by catering to public opinion but by constantly demonstrating absolute impartial service to the law.

6. Police use physical force to the extent necessary to secure observance of the law or to restore order only when the exercise of persuasion, advice and warning is found to be insufficient.

7. Police, at all times, should maintain a relationship with the public that gives reality to the historic tradition that the police are the public and the public are the police; the police being only members of the public who are paid to give full-time attention to duties which are incumbent on every citizen in the interests of community welfare and existence.

8. Police should always direct their action strictly towards their functions and never appear to usurp the powers of the judiciary.

9. The test of police efficiency is the absence of crime and disorder, not the visible evidence of police action in dealing with it.

be regretted that the confidence of the public in their ability to trust the police has been so severely shaken by controversies which have recently achieved public prominence and ones which have been the subject of public concern and criticism for many years.'[3]

Meanwhile, research for Lord Stevens's Commission[4] shows that only 65 per cent of people currently trust the police to tell the truth, a lower percentage than for scientists, teachers and doctors. The local community has a role to play in policing: if the public do not identify themselves as being on the same side as police this causes problems, conflict arises and we have seen the consequences of such a break-down. To get neighbourhood policing right, it needs to be delivered in a positive manner from the top of every force in the country.

The police establishment is often seen as an over-powerful and out of touch group – what a Police and Crime Commissioner colleague calls 'the old silverbacks in the Association of Chief Police Officers'. At the root of much of the breakdown of public trust in the police is the need for this core to cease acting as a vested interest and to develop more trust in the public. If police leadership is questioned they should be able to stand up and defend their decisions, but often the phrase 'in the public interest' is used, which at times has been questionable, with the 'old silverbacks' refusing to acknowledge being wrong because they feel it undermines their reputation or that of the force.

Since the introduction of Police and Crime Commissioners (PCCs), chief officers are open to much more scrutiny. I have no doubt that ACPO officers have similar endearing terms for PCCs, although the fact is that that the latter's democratic role is to work with the local community to ensure their policing needs are met, and that the police work for the people that they serve. Those officers who have come through the ranks of neighbourhood policing know the value that this brings; these officers trust the public and develop a two-way partnership. Some of the older guard struggle with this concept but, if the police do not believe in the public they serve, their rights will be undermined as we saw at Hillsborough (the football stadium disaster in 1989 resulting in the deaths of 96 people and injuries to 766 others). The terrible events on that day were followed by cover-ups and changing of statements. If such action is allowed to go unchallenged, what happens to more minor cases? A review of the outcomes for police complaints made to Professional Standards Departments shows that they similarly reflect the gulf between two sides.

The former Metropolitan Police Commissioner, Paul Condon described an aspect of this lack of trust when he acknowledged what he called 'noble cause corruption' in his force.[5] That is where detectives 'fit-up' defendants they believe are guilty because they think it is in the public interest to do so and, by implication, do not expect the public on a jury to see the 'truth'. A string of similar events old and new seem to have happened through a mixture of distrust and contempt, including attempts to undermine those who question the police, and what ACPO would probably term 'responding in an attempt to preserve confidence' but others might judge were examples of lying to save face.

For instance, another former Commissioner of the Metropolitan Police, who had not caught up with the omnipresence of mobile phone cameras, foolishly chose to deny any contact with Ian Tomlinson who died at the G20 protests in 2009, instead of admitting that he had been pushed by what the public could have understood was a rogue officer. Similarly, Sir Bernard Hogan-Howe lauded the universal integrity of his officers against Andrew Mitchell MP, only to find at least one of them had lied.

Senior officers published misleading propaganda, apparently seeking to imply wrongdoing by Jean Charles de Menezes, who in 2005 officers wrongly shot as a terrorist, by assuring the public that he vaulted over barriers at Stockwell tube station wearing a heavy jacket on a summer's day. The same was done in respect of the killing of Mark Duggan when it was suggested that the officer who shot him had a lucky escape from a bullet that lodged in his radio, and by implication therefore was only returning fire, when, in fact, it was a police bullet lodged in the radio.

It is hard to know whether these were deliberate lies or just the police leaping to defend themselves before they had properly investigated what happened. However, there can be no such doubt about senior police conduct in the Orgreave riot trial, arising from the confrontation between police and picketing miners during the miners' strike in 1984. There detectives were told to dictate 'scene-setting' statements to arresting officers, listing incidents of disorder that in many cases the officers had not seen and yet were expected to give evidence about. It was an attempt to implicate every picket arrested in serious disorder so as to lead to convictions for riot, which at that time carried a life sentence.

There is strong concern too about the behaviour of police officers who sought to alter witness statements about the Hillsborough disaster by excluding criticism of police and emphasising the few available references to drunkenness and violence from fans. This seems likely to have been an attempt to deflect any allegations of culpability for the tragic deaths of the 96 fans. There is also little doubt of the contempt for the public shown by the Special Demonstration Squad infiltrating environmental protesters for many years, carefully garnering evidence and, at times when it showed they were innocent of crime, equally carefully hiding it again.

Perhaps worse was the willingness of covert officers, some of them married, to improve their cover by lying their way into sexual relationships with women protesters, who would never knowingly have slept with police.

Abysmal too are the never-ending twists and turns to the saga of the investigation into the murder of Stephen Lawrence, most recently the disclosure that the Metropolitan Police bugged the victim's family while pretending to investigate his killers. Some of these stories are old but many of them occurred within the career spans of current ACPO officers.

Governance and complaints

Since the governance changes to policing set down in legislation in the Police Reform and Social Responsibility Act 2011, the situation has changed and it is harder for there to be cover-ups. It is the essence of the PCC to challenge and probe on behalf of the public in ensuring the police do their job properly, and when they get it wrong that the truth comes out and they don't try to blame innocent parties or muddy the waters. The PCC in turn is scrutinised about strategic issues, integrity and performance by a Police and Crime Panel made up of seconded councillors with some 'independent' members – perhaps an imperfect double-tier structure but nonetheless a structure with teeth.

In the past, although there has been some questioning of decisions taken by the police, nobody locally had the power to compel a thorough response, nor to call for and scrutinise internal papers, to require statements from officers and to pin down responsibility. Now that has changed and Chief Constables know that they must take a stand for or against the decisions of their officers and must have rational explanations for what their force is doing. If they don't then PCCs can take up the case and ultimately publish their findings and recommendations.

There is little doubt that most police officers are disturbed by issues of police integrity such as those highlighted earlier. As Tom Winsor says in his annual assessment of policing, 'Honest professional police officers are disgusted and distressed at instances of police corruption … the police today are far more honest and honourable than they were 30 and 40 years ago.'[6] He is right on both counts, but the problem is that what Paul Condon characterised as the 'noble cause' – broadly put as advancing/protecting the reputation of the police – has become almost institutionalised so that similar conduct is likely to recur.

In Northumbria policing has generally been popular and public confidence is consistently high. Nevertheless, there was a recent case when a convicted murderer escaped from a secure hospital and was not recaptured speedily enough to avoid public worry. If the Chief Constable had not taken action I would have ordered an inquiry into this failure and would have been able to call for all of the evidence – phone print-outs, call-taker and car radio tapes, internal correspondence and authorisations – and, if I chose, to publish my report to the public. As it was, the Chief Constable ordered her own inquiry and I merely reviewed it and published an outline, confining detail to an internal report. The public were reassured that the Chief Constable and I put changes in place to minimise the chances of this happening again.

Had Northumbria Police tried to take the justification route, the drawbridge would have been pulled up, blame would have been allocated as far away as possible from the command structure and those in charge would have waited for media attention to die down before resuming business as usual. That would have been much harder to accomplish now that there is close democratic scrutiny and Northumbria has acknowledged that although they will be criticised from time to time, by working with the community through the PCC, positive change can be achieved and a trusting relationship encouraged to the long-term benefit of both sides.

National failings such as those touched upon earlier have lesser counterparts in individual forces when Professional Standards Departments, who deal with complaints against local officers, do their work in a dismissive way. For instance, such departments will often take the tack that a complaint is not a complaint, but what they term an issue of 'direction and control' or a 'miscellaneous matter'. This means that a complainant will get a letter in response telling them that their issue falls within one or other of those categories and thus, contrary to their intention, they have not made a complaint. The police doctrine of what is a matter of 'direction and control' was in truth so rarely applicable (yet so frequently used to fob people off) that the Independent Police Complaints Commission (IPCC) has now recategorised direction and control matters as within the complaints system so as to nullify this technique.

Other cases are labelled 'locally resolved' through a process by which local police inspectors try to get agreement. However, 'local resolutions' are frequently appealed. It is a strange kind of agreement that leads to an appeal and it seems that a 'local resolution' is sometimes chalked up when an officer has simply spoken to the complainant and perhaps told them that there is nothing to be done.

Investigations into misconduct allegations can sometimes focus on vindicating the officer or on finding a way out. PSDs across the country seem to have a particularly entrenched defensiveness, but if complaints are sent out to local stations they seem to deal with them just as dismissively. It is extraordinary to see that happen when the same local police would deal professionally and attentively with all reports of crime.

None of this is to suggest that there are not well-investigated complaints, but as with bigger national conduct issues, when the police are distrustful and defensive that makes the public rightly distrustful of them.

Equally incompatible with Peel's principles is the casual way in which senior police announce new shifts in strategic direction without consulting the public. Although the Crime and Disorder Act 1998 imposed an obligation on the police regularly to survey the public's wishes, there are few indications that the police have felt obliged to carry those wishes out. So Metropolitan Police Commissioner, Sir Bernard Hogan-Howe, on appointment said that 'his' officers were there to wage 'total war on crime',[7] while many Londoners may be unhappy with the notion of cops as storm troopers, worried about how virtuous this righteous army would be and might ask exactly who would be defining the enemy. Under the new governance arrangements this problem should be overcome because it is the role of the PCC, not the police themselves, to set strategic direction through a five-year 'Police and Crime Plan' drawn up after consulting the public.

The power of the police establishment to put its own vested interest ahead of its public duty is now more limited, so that there is hope of building at all levels the positive joint working and relationships of trust that characterise neighbourhood policing in many communities across England and Wales.

It is puzzling how that partnership approach has been able to evolve at the grassroots of a hierarchical police force run by a defensive officer corps. What is clear is that, in terms both of performance and of generating public confidence, neighbourhood policing is successful, impressing even senior officers schooled long before the advent of public partnerships and community policing. It is the most successful area of policing, which demands from its officers the opposite of the lack of trust discussed here.

Local officers know what the community priorities are and they work with the public in delivering against the Police and Crime Plan. Sir Robert Peel would approve as it is in accord with his seventh principle. Neighbourhood/community policing should be further developed as both an excellent model in itself and because it has brought the fresh air of public involvement into policing.

Neighbourhood policing

It was the previous Labour government that created neighbourhood policing almost a decade ago. The model involves local police and what were then newly created civilian Police Community Support Officers, with lower level powers being assigned long term to a specific community, where they build ties and work with agencies such as local authorities and housing providers. They prevent problems developing and tackle crime and anti-social behaviour so as to keep the community safe and to develop confidence. The Crime Survey for England and Wales shows that confidence grows from people's sense of community cohesion and their belief that things are under control, and not solely or even mainly as a result of changes in levels of crime.

Neighbourhood policing requires a wide range of personal communications and problem-solving skills from officers, in addition to formal police training in law, evidence and process. As Peter Neyroud QPM told the Stevens Commission, 'the critical quality is to apply the powers of the law with a careful discretion with regard to the community's needs'.[8]

Neighbourhood police teams play a number of leading roles in their community. Understanding how other authorities work, they have the status and skill to facilitate local change and to recruit others to help people to get what they are entitled to. The police represent the values of the law-abiding majority. For victims of crime, who may blame themselves and feel demeaned by the disregard implicit in being used for the offender's purpose, a sympathetic police response can provide reassurance that they are valued citizens nonetheless – a reassurance said by victims' charities to be as important to the process of recovery as hearing that the culprit has been caught.

Lord Stevens and Her Majesty's Inspectorate of Constabulary (HMIC) both regard neighbourhood policing as at the heart of British policing, central to the consent and cooperation of the community and of significance from the street to the strategic level. In the latter context, neighbourhood police are a fruitful source of both community intelligence and local reassurance. Only recently, the North East Regional Special Operations Unit took part in dawn raids to investigate drug and money laundering offences. The successful operation was founded upon local intelligence provided by neighbourhood officers and, after the event, it was the neighbourhood teams who were patrolling in the affected areas to provide reassurance to local residents.

It has been claimed that only 20 per cent of officers' time is spent on crime, but HMIC has recently found that if dealing with situations in which there is a risk of crime is also included, at least 80 per cent of police time is spent 'on crime' including such activities as investigating reports of suspicious conduct and dealing with missing persons.[9] Thus it is clear that officers at work in the community are fighting crime in the broadest sense, and there is every reason to value their role as key to the whole policing function. It is exactly the mechanism where the police become the public as Peel's seventh principle expects, and it facilitates too the supportive engagement of other agencies in crime prevention.

Good examples of effective partnership of this kind abound. There is a pilot of a joint neighbourhood management scheme in Sulgrave, a part of Washington New Town in Northumbria. Representatives of the Safer Sunderland Partnership, Sunderland City Council, anti-social behaviour staff, probation officers, the housing provider Gentoo, domestic abuse, drug and alcohol services and the police are all co-located in a property in the centre of the community. There is close liaison too with private landlords to help deter criminal behaviour and improve local housing standards. People only need to make contact with any one of these organisations, or simply to drop into the shared premises, for all the services to be made available to tackle their problem. By working in partnership the scheme is showing the local community that prevention of crime is better than catching criminals. The police role is to identify and help to solve problems that might otherwise degenerate into discord and ultimately perhaps into crime or disorder. This approach saves money and protects victims, there is no costly investigation, the courts' time isn't taken up and the opportunist criminal knows that there is a strong likelihood that the police are aware of what they are up to and will be on hand to tackle it.

Although it is too early for evaluative evidence, the new scheme in Sulgrave is clearly contributing to better quality of life. This kind of police work is part of the social fabric, is responding to public expectations, and is building and sustaining confidence. Lord Stevens calls this the 'social justice model of neighbourhood policing'[10] and suggests that it needs to be tightly focused. The community should be asked to describe the crime and disorder issues they face, enabling the police to undertake an analysis of that information and bring proposals back to the community so that targeted interventions can be prioritised. Stevens recommends that the social purpose of policing should be set out in statute in order to banish the argument that working in this way in communities is not core policing. He suggests a similar form to the policing principles set out in the Police and Fire Reform (Scotland) Act 2012, which are (s. 32):

a) that the main purpose of policing is to improve the safety and wellbeing of persons, localities and communities in Scotland and,
b) that the police service working in collaboration with others where appropriate should seek to achieve that main purpose by policing in a way which:
    i.   is accessible to and engaged with local communities and
    ii. promotes measures to prevent crime, harm and disorder.

Another example of how core policing has been improved by partnership concerns a brilliantly simple scheme initiated by the Sunderland domestic violence refuge, Wearside Women in Need (WWIN). An outreach worker accompanies police on every call relating to domestic abuse. The officer tackles the policing issues and the outreach worker talks to the victim and tells her what help and support is available.

An initial evaluation shows that workers and police cope well together in crisis situations, both targeting a long-term joint preventive approach as well as the immediate policing response. The refuge team regards the pilot as a resounding success with the potential to transform domestic violence policing nationwide. Police are clear that the outreach workers' experience greatly improves risk assessment and, most importantly, support has been provided to many women who had not accessed help before – 55 per cent of victims given the outreach helpline number by the worker during the pilot used it later, whereas before the pilot when police were offering that number, only 1 per cent of victims were responding.

Sir Kenneth Newman, when Commissioner of the Metropolitan Police, thought that involvement of the community, like this, was crucial to tackling crime: 'Crime is a problem for society as a whole ... too important to be left to the police'.[11] This kind of integrated working is encouraged by the new police governance model, which requires that the elected representative carries out independent consultation of the public as to what is wanted, works cooperatively with Community Safety Partnerships and has some resource with which to lever in support from the voluntary and community sector, all helping to build relationships that both add value and bring an extra element of local police accountability.

Promoting integrity

This relentless work on the ground to build relationships so as to better understand the needs of local people and to get closer to the pulse of neighbourhoods can only be done effectively where integrity is promoted at every step and within every level of the police organisation. To achieve this, the belief that it is in the public interest for the police always to win and never to admit mistakes has to be rooted out at all levels.

In 2012 Northumbria Police had of any force the highest number of successful appeals to the IPCC against how it dealt with complaints about itself. I held an inquiry which disclosed the characteristic defensiveness of a deeply embedded Professional Standards Department and, further, that the police were gratuitously making enemies.

To combat this, a pilot scheme for low-level complaints has been introduced. Police staff trusted by officers and located in the PCC's office, outwith the defensive culture, act as first responders to all complaints and adopt a customer relations approach. They pass directly on to the PSD any serious issues. So far, monitoring shows that about 30 per cent of complaints are being resolved by a pleasant conversation, providing an explanation or giving an apology. An open dialogue is beginning in this small way between the public and police representatives. The public feels it is being listened to, the local branch of the Police Federation is supportive of this flexible approach and the Home Secretary approves of it, in particular as it does not require any change to the formal complaints process.

In addition, there is a newly established volunteer scrutiny panel, which looks at complaints that have been appealed from Northumbria Police to the IPCC, and advises the PCC on how these failures can be used to encourage positive change.

Both the pilot process and the scrutiny panel are small beer in the context of Hillsborough-scale misbehaviour, but they are further examples of police working with the public as valuable stakeholders, by analogy with Lord Stevens's advocacy of his consultative model of social purpose policing. If police can be encouraged to admit when they are wrong, at this level, and can see that the public nonetheless retains confidence in them, confidence and integrity should be strengthened.

All of these aspects of public involvement are helping make the police operationally more in tune with the public's wishes and democratic governance. The question is what policing changes should be introduced to further this by the next Labour government.

Reform agenda for an incoming Labour government

Police governance is evolving, searching for that model that brings the public closest to the police. It started with David Blunkett and later Jacqui Smith, both of whom when Home Secretary sought to introduce direct elections either for whole Police Authorities or for their chairpersons, as a means of democratising governance and sharpening and professionalising scrutiny which was not being offered by the Police Authorities. As Home Secretary Theresa May put it in opening the House of Commons Second Reading debate on the Police Reform and Social Responsibility Bill in 2011:

> ... although giving strategic direction and obtaining value for money are their two main functions, Police Authorities have neither the democratic mandate to set police priorities nor the capability to scrutinise police performance nor are they properly accountable themselves.[12]

Two-thirds of the public, both in Jacqui Smith's time and in 2012, wanted more influence on how the police serve them. Only 7 per cent of people had ever heard of Police Authorities at the date of their abolition. In his recommendation that policing governance should be returned to a committee of local authority leaders, Stevens is out of step with what the public want and his recommended alternatives are more compatible. They are that PCC-type figures are directly elected to chair a governance board of local authority leaders, or to elect the whole board.

Local authorities currently have an important role to play in preventing and tackling crime, in particular through Community Safety Partnerships (CSPs). However, CSPs are likely in future to have less success in delivering for specific local authority areas and, particularly with ever decreasing resources, they are likely to work more closely with other local authorities in developing initiatives. Domestic abuse or drug-related crime for instance can and should be tackled similarly whether the victim lives in the area of Council A or nearby Council B. Opportunities to jointly commission could bring both economies and improve best practice. In addition, few police basic command units will continue to be co-terminous with local authority boundaries. Financial pressures are leading to mergers – in Northumbria, for example, six area commands (one for each local authority) are being cut to three.

In addition, Home Office funding to the CSPs was removed in 2013 and has been rolled into the Police Main Grant to support the implementation of the Police and Crime Plan. There is a statutory duty on CSPs and PCCs to have regard to each other's priorities but the Police and Crime Plan will shape policing and drive related activities to prevent crime and to divert those at risk. Many crime prevention initiatives are delivered by the voluntary and community sector across the whole force area. In Northumbria the new Community Rehabilitation Company will be co-terminous with the force, while the Crown Prosecution Service and Her Majesty's Courts and Tribunal Service are regional in structure. Thus the picture for much of the crime and justice sector is one of larger units and cross-border delivery, which suggests that CSPs will need either to work coherently together in joint pursuit of the Police and Crime Plan aims or even merge so as to match police force boundaries. Very local delivery will continue as it is currently, shared between councillors and neighbourhood police at ward level, with opportunities to bid for funding both from the councils and the new but small community funds that are typically being set up by PCCs.

There is everything to be said for a new force-level model of Community Safety Partnership. CSPs currently get funding direct from local authorities and, in some cases from the health sector to support, as in Sunderland, work-streams such as drugs intervention. Health service providers ought to be increasingly involved in community safety, in particular as we improve our understanding of the links between vulnerability and victimisation, and of the profound impact on well-being of hate crime, domestic and sexual abuse and culture-related crimes. Many people with mental health issues or alcohol and drug addiction get involved in crime yet need a health-based solution. There are sufficient overlaps to form a strong argument for broadening the category of responsible authorities who are required by statute to participate in CSPs to include NHS Direct, Public Health England, Hospital and Mental Health Trusts and representation from the Clinical Commissioning Groups.

The question may then become whether those new CSPs may be a close match for Lord Stevens's second preference model for police governance boards. They would represent the responsible authorities and could be led by a directly elected executive leader, similar to PCCs.

PCCs also have a statutory duty to work with the membership of Local Criminal Justice Boards to produce an effective and efficient criminal justice service – essentially a force-wide responsibility. There is no financial leverage from the PCC to further this and some of the member agencies, such as the Crown Prosecution Service, are perceived to need to be independent. However, there is work to be done to introduce public engagement and public scrutiny into these agencies similar to that brought to policing by the introduction of democratic governance, although, of course, the judiciary will always be independent.

Lord Stevens recommends that local authorities should keep part of the police precept raised within their own boundaries, and not give it directly to the police. That would enable them to buy in specific police services as and when necessary to meet local need. This is a recipe for fragmentation. How would the holistic integrity of the force-wide Police and Crime Plan be secured amidst the patchwork of spending priorities that would emerge as local politicians served their local interests? Funding would in effect be annexed from the main police grant and redirected, leaving the Chief Constable without overall operational control.

Local residents already have a say in how the policing budget is both raised and allocated through the process that underpins the Police and Crime Plan. The Chief Constable and the PCC invest money in those priorities and there is no need for mini manifestos in every local authority, undermining strategic direction.

Currently under the PCC model, policing is one of the few public services that at a local level has a directly elected and visible quasi-executive head, accountable for the budget, the setting of priorities and delivery of the strategic plan: if it goes wrong, there is one person the public can blame and that person can be removed from office. The jury is out on whether that model is exactly the right model for police governance. From a Labour perspective they were not supported as a concept, although, of course, the elections were contested (successfully in 13 cases) and there are currently Labour Commissioners driving change and implementing Labour policy in all the major metropolitan forces except London. Through that experience the PCCs are capable of significant input into the development of party policy on policing and crime issues. Some of those individuals are champions now of the role of PCC and see it expanding to take democratic control over the courts service, probation, local prisons and arguably the Crown Prosecution Service.

Although police must retain coercive powers over individuals in order to fulfil their functions, strategic power, including budgetary control, has moved through the advent of democratic Commissioners away from the institution into the hands of the public it serves. Enhanced scrutiny is improving transparency; the police will begin trusting the public when they have nowhere to hide. They will find that the public wants to trust them. Trust in working relationships has grown neighbourhood policing into the powerhouse it is, and can bring innovative solutions at all levels and all points of policing. Whatever governance structures are adopted going forward, public engagement with policing, reflecting Peel's seventh principle, has grown in the past 18 months through the introduction of democratic governance and it cannot easily be turned back.

Summary of principal recommendations

- To involve the public as partners in keeping their own communities safe, in a practical way through further developing neighbourhood policing and by retaining democratic police governance of some kind so as to preserve the consultative channels that have already brought better accountability.
- Following Lord Stevens's recommendations, to define the 'social justice model of policing' in legislation.
- To reshape management of community safety by legislating to join health agencies as responsible authorities into CSPs made co-terminous with police force areas.
- To preserve the democratic principle in policing governance as a proxy for Peel's principle that the police are the public and the public are the police, to drive transparency and to build better public trust.

14

Public Procurement

Samuel Townend and Simon Taylor

One of the major and traditionally undervalued economic tools that government has available to it is the way that it spends public money. UK public procurement expenditure accounts for about £227bn a year, of which about £45bn is by government departments (the remainder being mainly health and local authorities). It affects roughly 20 per cent of UK gross domestic product.

This purchasing power can be used to maximise value for money for taxpayers. It can also be used to promote industrial policy aims, such as stimulating underperforming parts of the economy and establishing sustainable markets, but also social aims such as improving labour practices and encouraging small and medium-sized enterprises (SMEs). The use of this power is guided and constrained by the public procurement rules, which are based on European Union (EU) law.

This chapter takes stock of how the UK is doing at public procurement, looks at the causes for any shortcomings, proposes a reassessment of priorities in line with Labour values and makes some suggestions as to how best to use this valuable resource in a period of austerity. It concludes that a government procurement strategy is urgently needed to restore an efficient balance of economic purchasing, social progress and business growth.

Is Europe to blame?

Public procurement is fundamental to cross-border trade and

investment. It is therefore regulated at EU level through a series of procurement directives including 2004/18/EC and 2004/17/EC.[1] These set out detailed requirements as to the way in which contracts above certain thresholds are to be tendered by public bodies and certain utilities with monopoly rights. They include the manner of advertising (in the *Official Journal of the European Union* (OJEU)), the procedures to be followed, the basis on which bidders may be eliminated and evaluated, and rules on due process such as the debriefing of unsuccessful bidders and effective remedies.[2] The EU rules are primarily aimed at ensuring the free movement of persons, goods, services and capital within the EU by outlawing discrimination between companies on grounds of nationality. They also use fair competition to drive value for money and transparency to prevent corruption.

The pursuit of other policy aims, including the environmental and social agenda, is also sanctioned by the procurement rules, provided this does not conflict with the primary aim of EU free movement. Indeed, the EU Treaty (Treaty on the Functioning of the European Union (TFEU)) enshrines in its preamble the pursuit of social as well as economic progress as a fundamental objective,[3] and much of the worker protection legislation in the UK is based on EU law. But there is tension between these various aims which has given rise to case law.[4]

EU procurement law is much maligned, often with apocryphal tales of Eurocrats determined to make life difficult for British business, while foreign governments cheat the system and favour their own national champions, which in turn steal British contracts and jobs. The truth is that British businesses do reasonably well out of European public procurement. Research prepared for the European Commission in 2011 showed that UK business won 17 per cent of foreign contracts awarded across the EU (second only to Germany at 26 per cent, with France at only 5 per cent). That isn't bad when you consider that foreign tenders are likely to be conducted in a foreign language and the British are not famed for their linguistic adaptability. In relation to UK procurement, only 3 per cent by value of UK public contracts were awarded to firms based in other member states (below the EU average of 3.5 per cent, though higher than France at 1.5 per cent and Germany at 1.7 per cent).[5] In any event, our membership of the EU is conditional on the procurement and other free movement rules.

Furthermore, if we didn't have the procurement rules we would need to invent them. This is because, if done properly, regulated public procurement safeguards public value for money through competition for contracts and ensures public sector accountability through transparent procedures. EU procurement regulation also enables British companies to access tender opportunities in a range of major trading nations under the General Procurement Agreement umbrella (including the United States, Canada, Hong Kong, Japan and Singapore).

The EU rules are not perfect and a recently adopted directive[6] introduces reforms that will, to a degree, create more streamlined and flexible procurement (for instance, more scope for negotiation, electronic documents and more practical rules on dynamic purchasing systems). They will also confirm that procurement can be used strategically to advance social aims and help smaller companies (Art. 46 on lots, Art. 67 on award criteria and Art. 70 on contract conditions), that authorities can exclude companies from tenders for a wide range of misconduct (including persistent deficient performance, collusion and fraud, Art. 57), take bidder past performance into account at selection stage (Art. 58) and that pre-tender engagement is permitted (Art. 40). In these and many other respects, the new provisions codify and (on the whole) clarify EU law. These are positive developments for which the UK negotiators at the Cabinet Office can take some credit.

Taking stock of how the UK is doing at public procurement

The real problem is not the EU procurement rules but the way in which public procurement is carried out in Britain. This was the view of the House of Commons Public Administration Select Committee (PASC) in their July 2013 report on government procurement.[7] Having heard extensive oral evidence and studied written reports from a wide range of sources, the Committee concluded that:[8]

- UK procurement is risk-averse, process-driven and inefficient: 'It is intolerable that UK public procurement still takes 50 per cent longer than it does in France and Germany: the Cabinet Office does not seem to know why this is the case'.[9]

- There is a failure to ensure proper consideration of social and economic objectives in procurement exercises.
- There is no coherent procurement strategy: 'The government has failed to set out a clear strategy for public procurement. There remains a lack of clarity about the government's longer term policy for the consolidation of government and wider public sector procurement.'
- There is a skills gap in government as to both procurement capability and the commercial nous needed to manage contracts with contractors.
- Aspirations to support SMEs are commended, but procurement favours large companies and SMEs do not win a fair proportion of public contracts.
- There is insufficient leadership even to drive change in Whitehall, never mind the wider public sector. The Cabinet Office is commended for its reform initiatives but lacks the authority to make things happen. The UK Cabinet Office Minister, Francis Maude, acknowledges in his evidence the dispersed civil service reporting structures and its system of 'siloes'.

The inefficiency and lack of capability and vision in government and the wider public sector mean that the fundamental aim of ensuring value for money in procurement spend is not being met. The PASC found that despite an overseas perception that Britain has a reputation for good procurement practice, the overriding impression was one of poor execution of the procurement rules.

What goes wrong in practice?

A significant cause of the problem, which is evident from the cases that find their way into the UK courts, is the failure by public bodies to plan tenders properly. Too often procurement project plans begin with the publication of an OJEU notice and only then proceed to the consideration and preparation of the other tender documents (first the Pre-Qualification Questionnaire (PQQ), then the Invitation to Tender

(ITT), and so forth). This is often driven by political urgency but is the wrong way round and stores up all sorts of risks, delays and inefficiencies for later on in the process.

Key decisions should be taken in advance of advertising the tender. These include:

- The strategic aim of the tender (best value only, innovation, social or environmental aims, regeneration, market-making, etc.).
- What is to be procured (the specification, duration, whether a framework, whether divided into smaller lots, how much risk transfer, etc.).
- How it is to be procured (the process – e.g. e-auction or restricted procedure, timelines, e-portal technicalities and so on).
- What types of bidders should qualify to bid (the pre-qualification of eligible and capable bidders with sufficient financial robustness to take on the risk transferred under the contract).
- How the winner will be chosen (the objective, fit for purpose award criteria – what good looks like and how to assess it).

All these decisions are interrelated and once you have started the process it is risky to change tack because that may unfairly prejudice certain bidders (e.g. those who have already been eliminated or did not respond to the advert). But that is what often happens. The greatest flexibility for public bodies is at the planning stage and it is generally a good idea to engage with potential suppliers in the market at this stage in order to assess, for example, what they are capable of delivering. Procurement officers have traditionally shied away from doing this out of a concern that it may breach the rules. This concern is misplaced provided things are done fairly and openly.

Poor execution is often the result of poor planning. Court proceedings typically begin because the debrief provided to unsuccessful bidders reveals errors or concerns over fair play. Sometimes the scores have not been added up properly or there are obvious inconsistencies. The court disclosure process then typically makes the claim stronger by revealing, for example, that controversial evaluation or exclusion decisions are not supported by an adequate paper trail or that undisclosed methodologies were used. A costly settlement or lengthy proceedings then follow.

The West Coast fiasco

There are many high-profile examples where poor planning and poor execution have led to procurement disasters, many of which end up in the courts. When the Department for Transport's tender for the 15-year contract to run the West Coast Main Line franchise agreement hit the buffers in 2012 following a procurement challenge brought by the incumbent Virgin Rail, the cost to the public purse was conservatively estimated at £40m by the government. The Laidlaw report found fundamental flaws in the evaluation of bids, a lack of transparency, inadequate planning and insufficient governance.[10] The government dodged ministerial responsibility by a swift Cabinet reshuffle and blamed human error by civil servants, but the problems ran deeper. They included a government franchising policy predicated on conferring a 15-year monopoly on the successful bidder, the failure to design a robust tender process to deal fairly with the complex variables (such as passenger growth projections and the capital needed to cover franchisee insolvency) that such a long-term contract entailed, insufficient resourcing due to government austerity cuts and inadequate oversight by senior civil servants and government ministers.

Does government use procurement strategically?

As for policy aims, some, such as the SME agenda, are now being pursued albeit belatedly. However, in spite of the fact that 6 out of 10 private sector jobs are created by SMEs, direct spend by government to SMEs is only about 10 per cent (in years 2011–12).[11] The government correctly recognises that SMEs provide the engine for economic growth and innovation, as demonstrated by Germany's economic success. It has therefore declared the 'aspiration' that 25 per cent by value of all government contracts are to be won by SMEs by 2015. Yet the PASC was rightly sceptical of the government's ability to deliver on this target. In December 2013 the government announced various initiatives to encourage public bodies to make it easier for SMEs to bid for public contracts.[12] The PASC also collected evidence of positive initiatives, such as the 'G-Cloud Framework', on which around 75 per cent of suppliers are SMEs.[13] However, it seems doubtful that the public sector will come close to achieving the stated objective without a more fundamental government-led approach, which changes the way that procurements are devised and conducted throughout the public sector. A paradigm shift is needed, not tinkering at the edges.

As for social policy, the Minister for the Cabinet Office made it clear in his evidence to PASC that he doesn't think initiatives such as that pursued by the Department for Work and Pensions (DWP) to encourage contractors to take on apprentices (which have led to 2,000 new apprentices being hired) should interfere with the pursuit of value for money.[14] That is despite the savings to the welfare budget that would result from the ensuing reduction in youth unemployment.[15] In our view, a more positive approach is required (and one that clearly won't be made by the present government).

Does government manage its suppliers well?

The oral evidence on outcomes and supplier relationships provided to the Committee also makes for grim reading. The Chief Procurement Officer points to the fact that about half of central government spend is with a very small number of suppliers (between 50 and 100) – suppliers for whom government is likely to be their biggest customer. Yet their performance is typically worse than you might expect for their least-valued customer. One case was cited of a supplier with government contracts worth over £500m per annum that was charging government a supernormal profit well above that set out in its published accounts.[16]

It is fair to acknowledge efforts are now being made by the Cabinet Office towards management and supervision of the biggest contracts. A review led by the Chief Procurement Officer at the Cabinet Office investigated contracts worth £5.9bn held by Serco and G4S and found that Serco had been overcharging on its electronic monitoring contracts. On 19 December 2013, it was announced that Serco will repay £68.5m to the Ministry of Justice. The matter has also been referred to the Serious Fraud Office for investigation.[17]

We agree that these steps are well taken. But such contracts need to be properly managed and supervised as a matter of course, rather than exception, and more needs to be done to ensure that fraudulent companies are not given public contracts in the first place. The new EU directive makes it clear that the tools are available under EU law to exclude errant bidders. A coherent procurement strategy is required and it needs to carry sufficient weight to be effective, not only in central government but also in the wider public sector.

Our proposals for reform

Above all, a realistic but ambitious *strategy* is needed. Given the scale of the issues and the potential gains in getting this right, it is government that needs to act, and the current government is not doing enough. In their report to the PASC, Future Purchasing Inc. and the Henley Business School estimated that the positive initiatives of the Cabinet Office and the Government Procurement Service (recently renamed the Crown Commercial Service) currently touch only about 5 per cent of overall public procurement spend. They estimate that procurement-led efficiency savings could amount to £75bn over the whole public sector, which could be used to cut the deficit either directly or, as they advocate, be reinvested in growth initiatives through service delivery and infrastructure projects.[18] As the TUC advocates in its written evidence,[19] that strategy should also support the quantity and quality of employment, assist economic inclusion and underpin a modern industrial strategy – all objectives which are consistent with EU law and have been for some time, but are largely neglected by this government.

We consider that the pillars of that procurement strategy would include:

- investment in skills and capability
- structural change and leadership
- joined-up public sector procurement
- the pursuit of social and industrial aims, as well as value for money
- a stronger SME agenda
- increased focus on ensuring that fraudulent and underperforming companies do not win public tenders.

Investment in skills and capability

The strategy must involve investment aimed at establishing a new generation of extremely able procurement leaders throughout the public sector with responsibility for the planning and execution of tenders, as well as contract management. This will help ensure that 'corporate knowledge' within the civil service and wider public sector is retained by motivating and retaining a highly skilled workforce, reducing dependence on expensive short-term external consultants and recognising the value and significance of procurement as a public service function. The strategy would mark a departure from attempts to outsource responsibility for commissioning and procurement to private providers – such as the recent failed tender for a Ministry of Defence 'government-owned, contractor-operated' (GoCo)[20] – and a move towards nurturing the necessary skills within the public sector.

Structural change

Urgent consideration of options is required. These could include establishing a 'Crown Procurement Service' with the remit and capability of addressing all (or the vast majority of) public sector procurement.[21] Alternatively, it could comprise a less monolithic but no less powerful structure with top-down support from a Minister for Procurement and each procurement leader's deliverables reviewable by a Public Procurement Reform Board.[22]

The responsible procurement body should then show *leadership*, not only in guiding the public sector towards better procurement but also in interpreting the rules and negotiating with Brussels. By way of example, leadership is needed to take certain 'public sector' bodies such as higher educational bodies, registered providers of social housing and NHS foundation trusts that operate in regulated but increasingly competitive markets outside the scope of the procurement rules. Another example would be support for public sector alternatives or comparators to be used when assessing the value of private bids on major tenders.[23]

Joined-up public sector procurement

Much of the more radical and progressive procurement comes from local authorities in areas such as shared service provision and joint buying. The strategy must embrace local authorities, NHS bodies, educational bodies and other public bodies subject to the rules. Localism in this context has been used by the government to dodge responsibility. Under the Localism Act 2011, local authorities are required to share the financial burden of any penalties for poor procurement imposed on the government by Brussels. Yet after years of austerity and with their budgets cut, local authorities often do not have the expertise or resources to procure properly. Government can't completely devolve its responsibility for efficient and lawful procurement – it is too difficult and too important to the economy. It needs to step in and help.

As for the NHS, the government has restructured the sector and introduced binding sector-specific procurement rules,[24] which add to the burden under general procurement law, and it expects clinical commissioning groups (CCGs) of GPs to make decisions as to when they are obliged to go out to tender and how to do it. It is not practical or efficient for the Department of Health to cut CCGs loose, as the increasing number of disputes and challenges in the sector demonstrates. The same point applies to free schools or small housing associations. How can they be expected to run tenders without close support and guidance from government? The wider public sector is fending for itself over procurement in a variety of ways with differing degrees of success, but it is taxpayers' money that is being spent and the government's responsibility to ensure a coherent approach.

A successful strategy must require the restructured government procurement function to be far more proactive in providing training, templates, guides, advice and set procedures, as well as resources to support procuring bodies in relation to all stages of the procurement process and contract management. This need not all be centralised. There could be regional and sectoral centres of procurement excellence, but a full programme of help and support is required and it needs to be coordinated.

Social measures

There is considerable scope for a future Labour government to use public procurement to promote social ends. EU Directive 2004/18/EC makes it clear at Recital 33 that contract performance conditions 'may in particular be intended to favour on-site vocational training, the employment of people experiencing particular difficulty in achieving integration, the fight against unemployment or the protection of the environment.' It is lawful to impose on contractors a contractual condition that they must employ apprentices or the long-term unemployed provided it does not involve any direct or indirect discrimination against foreign nationals or otherwise make it more difficult for non-national tenderers to compete.[25] Although the award criteria used to select the winning tender must be contract-related, the case law also indicates that appropriate social criteria can be used.[26] The ability to use social criteria is now confirmed by the new public procurement directive (Art. 67(2)).

In spite of the ability to use procurement for social ends, public bodies too often shy away from doing so, either because they (like the cabinet minister) do not want anything to get in the way of best value in its narrowest sense or because they have taken an overly cautious view on their flexibility under EU law. There are notable exceptions to this. The DWP programme for introducing apprenticeships has been referred to earlier. Glasgow Housing Association (GHA) has also adopted a suite of contract and tender documents for a construction framework that introduces contractual conditions (KPIs) based on meeting training, recruitment and apprenticeship targets. The GHA applies selection and award criteria designed to evaluate contractors' ability to meet and perform such conditions.[27] In our view, other public bodies should follow the lead set by bodies such as GHA and plan tenders in a way that can achieve economic as well as social aims to the benefit of the recipients or users of the services or works procured as well as the wider community. A Labour government should endorse and promote strategic procurement of this kind.

One positive result of such social measures in procurement is that they are likely to have local benefits. It is no coincidence that countries with a more progressive social policy agenda, such as France and Germany, award more public contracts to national companies who are no doubt better able to meet social conditions in tenders than their foreign competitors. This is not cheating the system, but simply cleverer application of the rules.

The other means of using procurement to promote industrial development is to plan and specify tenders in a more strategic way. It is not difficult to see how this can be arranged. If, taking another example in the rail industry, there were a choice between a disaggregated programme of smaller train rolling stock contracts (possibly tendered together as separate lots or in a framework, or tendered sequentially) and one very large one-off contract which would meet government needs for the foreseeable future, the two options may present different risks for a UK-based train design and manufacturing base and UK jobs. The small contract option may give rise to a more diverse, sustainable production market. The large contract option may (or may not) give rise to a short-term cost advantage, but limit the future market to fewer suppliers and result in a 'winner takes all' tender. The loser may need to close its factory gates (unless, that is, it can mount a successful procurement challenge).

Sadly, such strategic considerations seem to have been absent when, in June 2013, the government awarded a £1.6bn contract to Siemens to build 1,140 carriages for the Thameslink rail line, leading Bombardier to shed about half its UK workers.[28] The ensuing public outcry has, according to press reports, led the Department for Transport to incorporate socio-economic conditions in their £1bn tender for Crossrail rolling stock.[29]

So government and other public bodies can and should think through at the procurement planning stage how social ends can lawfully be protected or encouraged. It is fair to acknowledge that the Public Services (Social Value) Act 2012 now requires public bodies, prior to commencing a procurement, to consider how what is to be procured might improve the economic, social and environmental well-being of the relevant area. There is little evidence, however, that the Act has made any substantive difference.

We think that a future Labour government needs to act strategically to ensure that the opportunities in procurement to drive favourable socio-economic outcomes are not missed. We propose:

- Positive and active help from government encouraging the incorporation of legitimate social aims and advice on how to do this lawfully and effectively.
- The systematic inclusion of contract performance conditions requiring contractors to introduce apprenticeships and address other socio-economic concerns, with social criteria being introduced where appropriate and contract-related.

Promoting SMEs

SMEs are the engine of innovation, growth and job creation, and strong economies are built on a strong SME sector. In our view, government can and must do more to secure greater participation by SMEs in public contracts.

The way in which tenders and selection criteria are structured will have a direct impact on the ability of SMEs to qualify for and win public contracts. SMEs are having a difficult time with the banks unwilling to lend and the tendency of the public sector to procure ever larger contracts. We think that public bodies can do a great deal to foster local business by simply making it easier for SMEs to compete for public contracts. We noted earlier that the government is now taking steps to smooth the procurement processes for low-value contracts. However, nothing in the proposed measures encourages authorities themselves to procure with smaller contracts to effect real change.[30] If contracts can be broken down into more accessible lots this will attract SMEs and no doubt result in a more diverse and innovative tender competition. If training days and other help and guidance are offered to SMEs to help them put their best foot forward, as well as simplifying the process, this will both encourage participation and improve their performance. Mechanisms such as frameworks and dynamic purchasing systems (which are to be made more flexible under the new directive) must be used to make procurement more nimble and responsive to the SME market. We therefore propose that a concerted public sector effort takes place to increase SME participation in public tenders, with effective leadership from government.

Eligibility issues – excluding fraudulent companies

Most public procurement involves two distinct stages – pre-qualification and award. The pre-qualification stage is when the contracting authority determines whether the potential bidder is eligible and suitable. The authority may reject bidders who lack the financial robustness or technical capability to perform the contract. The authority *must* reject bidders where it has actual knowledge that the company, or its director(s), or other person with 'powers of representation, decision or control', has been convicted of a number of serious listed offences including bribery, fraud, conspiracy to defraud, cheating HMRC, theft, fraudulent trading, money laundering and drug trafficking. The UK practice is to 'box tick' and accept self-certification. The government should be able to demonstrate how it ensures that companies found guilty of fraud, companies whose directors have been found guilty of fraud and unrepentant companies with a demonstrable record of grave misconduct do not win public contracts.

We think that a future Labour government should put in place more robust measures to ensure that self-certifications provided by bidders in public tenders are collected centrally, substantiated by evidence and regularly verified so as to ensure that they are correct. Similar steps are provided for in the new EU directive .

There is a second tier of elimination factors that *may* be treated by a public authority as rendering a company ineligible. These include bankruptcy, a failure to pay taxes and where the company has committed an act of 'grave misconduct' in the course of its business or profession. Under the new directive the list has been extended to encompass a number of examples of unacceptable behaviour, including anti-competitive conduct and serious misrepresentation to the tendering authority.

The ongoing investigations of Serco and G4S illustrate the consequences if the integrity of government suppliers is not tested. We think the government ought to provide a strategic lead in rooting out contractors who are guilty of fraud or other unacceptable misconduct, using available legal tools to ensure that they are excluded from tenders where appropriate.

The Welsh government has introduced a policy on blacklisting in the construction industry, which is a good example of how government intervention can help give effect to these rules. Blacklisting is the specific activity by which construction companies draw up lists of active trade unionists or whistleblowers on health and safety issues and use the list to block their employment opportunities. This is an unlawful practice. The practice was investigated by the Information Commissioner in 2009, who identified over 40 construction companies that had used the lists. The issue arose whether the blacklisting amounted to grave misconduct and whether public bodies could or should exclude the companies involved from public tenders.

The Welsh government issued a Policy Advice Note in September 2013 confirming that blacklisting could amount to grave misconduct but that exclusion from tenders must be proportionate and considered on a case-by-case basis. Exclusion must be justified by evidence and should not be used as a punishment, but rather as a means of putting right past misconduct. By way of example, companies should not be excluded if they can show that they have taken steps to 'self-clean' through clarification of their actions, repair of the damage caused (for instance, compensation of victims) and personnel and structural measures to avoid recurrence.[31]

At selection stage, there is scope to vet contractor capability against prior performance on similar contracts. Measures to encourage this practice in Whitehall have been introduced by the Office of Government Commerce[32] but a public sector wide approach is needed.

We propose that:

- Government act to provide leadership to ensure that grave misconduct is investigated and taken into account at the pre-qualification stage on government contracts. This would act as a real deterrent to unacceptable corporate activity and ensure that public money is directed towards companies with better governance.
- Government should provide guidance as to how public procurers are to assess companies that are under investigation for fraudulent activity or other grave misconduct. Some form of suspension pending the outcome of investigations may be appropriate.
- There should be an effective, coherent and transparent approach to the enforcement by public bodies of the eligibility rules.

- Contractor past performance should be fully assessed by all public sector bodies at selection stage.

Conclusion

British public procurement is in need of improvement. That much is clear from the PASC findings if it wasn't evident before that. We can't blame Brussels, and the government must take responsibility. The potential gains in terms of cost efficiency and socio-economic benefits far outweigh the investment of time and money needed to sort out the problems. It will require a shift in thinking from short to medium term, greater confidence from public procurers and, above all, strategic leadership from policy makers. If this government won't act, the next Labour government should embrace the task.

Summary of principal recommendations

- To invest in and nurture a new generation of able procurement leaders within and throughout the public sector and reduce the dependency on expensive, short-term, external consultants.
- To provide top-down leadership and support for all public sector procurement instead of leaving local public sector bodies to fend for themselves.
- To foster strategic public procurement, including the use of contract performance conditions and award criteria designed to meet social needs.
- To promote SMEs by facilitating access to public contracts, including breaking down contracts into more accessible lots and the use of dynamic purchasing and other flexible procurement.
- To strengthen the ability of public procurers to exclude fraudulent suppliers from public tenders and ensure that past performance is fully assessed by all public sector bodies.

15

Responsible Capitalism: What it Means in Practice[1]

Stephen Hockman QC

The financial crisis in 2008 exposed some basic weaknesses in our capitalist system, but it was not until Ed Miliband's speech at the 2011 Labour Party Conference that there was an explicit recognition of the need for a more responsible form of capitalism, not only as an end in itself but as a means to achieving a more successful economy.

Since then, the concept of 'responsible capitalism' has been the subject of widespread discussion.[2] This chapter examines what the concept could mean in practice – in other words, in what way could the structure and practice of capitalism be made more responsible and what means are available to achieve this.

The existing capitalist system

Ever since the eighteenth century, business under the capitalist system has been carried on for the most part through the limited company. The essence of this system is that the company has a corporate legal personality of its own and is distinct from both its shareholders and its directors. The shareholders are the owners of the company (sometimes called its members), but that does not mean that they automatically control the way the company is run. Their powers are usually defined (in a quite limited way) in the company's articles of association, while the actual management and day-to-day control of the company is in the hands of the directors. Although directors have a range of legal responsibilities, some created by the general law and some created by the articles of association, they owe their duties to the company itself, not to the shareholders or to the customers of the company, let alone to the public at large.

In the Companies Act 2006 the last Labour government introduced a provision, in s. 172, whereby directors must act in the way they consider most likely to promote the success of the company for the benefit of its members, and in doing so they must have regard to various factors, including the impact of the company's operations on the community and the environment. Moreover, under s. 417 of the Act the directors' report contained in the company's annual report must, in the case of a quoted company, include information about the impact of the company's business on the environment and about social and community issues. This has now been replaced by a new requirement, under ss. 414A–D of the Companies Act 2006, for companies to prepare a strategic report. The purpose of the strategic report is to help members of the company assess how the directors have performed their duty under s. 172, and it must contain a fair review of the company's business, and a description of the principal risks and uncertainties facing the company.

It would, however, be a mistake to assume that these Companies Act 2006 provisions change the basic legal position of individual companies or of their directors. The duties mentioned in s. 172 continue to be duties owed to the company itself, which it would be for the company (generally controlled by the directors) to enforce. The requirement in s. 417 for information in the directors' report – an obligation imposed on the company – was not readily enforceable by any third party. The same would appear to be true in the case of the new requirement for a strategic report, save that there is a criminal sanction for complete non-compliance.

Defra has recently made regulations requiring a directors' report to disclose relevant information about emissions of greenhouse gases arising from certain companies' activities. These regulations were made under the Companies Act 2006 s. 416.

Non-statutory rules and codes

There are also non-statutory rules relating to corporate governance, in the form of The UK Corporate Governance Code, published by the Financial Reporting Council (FRC).[3] The Code is said to consist of principles rather than a rigid set of rules. By way of example, it contains a section entitled 'Accountability', but the main principle under this heading goes no further than to state that the board of directors should present a balanced and understandable assessment of the company's position and prospects. Under the heading 'Remuneration', the main principle is that levels of remuneration should be sufficient to attract, retain and motivate directors of the quality required to run the company successfully, but a company should avoid paying more than is necessary for this purpose.

In a schedule to the Code it is suggested that long-term incentive schemes should be approved by shareholders. Under the heading 'Relations with shareholders', the main principle is that there should be a dialogue with shareholders based on the mutual understanding of objectives. The Code contains an important section headed 'Comply or Explain' which makes it clear that there is always the option, as an alternative to following a provision in the Code, of explaining to shareholders why the provision is not being followed and why it is said that good governance could be achieved by other means.

In addition to the Corporate Governance Code there is the UK Stewardship Code, also issued by the FRC, which is addressed primarily to firms who manage assets on behalf of institutional shareholders. Again, the 'Explain' option is provided. The Stewardship Code, as its name implies, embodies (but does not define) the concept of 'stewardship'. It contains, for instance, a principle that institutional investors should publicly disclose their policy on how they will discharge their stewardship responsibilities, but, especially in the absence of a definition, it cannot be assumed that the stewardship role is intended to protect anyone other than the particular beneficiaries of the fund for which those investors have responsibility. The 2010 Labour Party election manifesto suggested that the UK Stewardship Code for institutional shareholders should be strengthened, and indicated that Labour would require institutional shareholders 'to declare how they vote'. However, as Professor Brian Cheffins has pointed out,[4] there has been a marked shift in share ownership patterns in favour of foreign investors and hedge funds. The fact that the Code is directed towards UK-based asset managers and domestic institutional investors, who own less than one-third of the shares in UK quoted companies, means that it is unlikely to have a transformative effect on corporate governance.

In general, these codes seem to be somewhat imprecise and to contain virtually no reference to sanctions for non-compliance. The Listing Rules do require a company that has a premium listing of equity shares to include in its annual report and accounts details of compliance with the Corporate Governance Code, and the Financial Conduct Authority Handbook requires investment managers to disclose on their website the nature of their commitment, if any, to the Stewardship Code. However, the codes appear to have had minimal impact upon the course of events leading to the financial crisis. Indeed, as Professor Cheffins points out,[5] institutional shareholders have arguably been part of the problem rather than the solution, as they were relaxed about banks using leverage to pursue high returns on equity, tended to deride cautious management, and applied pressure for high dividends and share buy-backs that depleted capital.

Public procurement

An important player (i.e. buyer of goods and services) in the modern capitalist system is of course government itself at all levels, and government procurement arrangements are made subject to a complex and detailed legal regime. However, for present purposes, the rules governing the wider responsibilities of government in procuring goods and/or services are extremely limited in scope. The Public Contract and Utilities Contract Regulations 2006 prohibit a public authority from awarding a contract to a company if it knows that the company has been convicted of serious listed offences, including bribery and fraud. The Social Value Act 2012 requires a public body to consider, in its discretion, how the procurement process might improve 'the economic, social and environmental well-being' of the relevant area. There is no other general provision mandating the way in which, or the purposes for which, procurement powers ought to be exercised. There is moreover a tension between the EU procurement rules (and the EU principle of non-discrimination which is enshrined in the EU Treaty) and any government procurement that overtly seeks, for example, to protect UK jobs.

In general, companies and those who run them are bound by the general law, both criminal and civil, not to act so as to cause harm to others, but proof of intentional wrongdoing may raise significant evidential problems. As noted in an interesting article by Iris Chiu, Reader in Law at UCL,[6] the post-crisis reviews into the failed UK banks conducted by the Financial Services Authority resulted in blame being attributed to only one individual, although the verdict of the Parliamentary Commission on Banking Standards has been more wide-ranging.

The current investigation into alleged Libor-rigging will be an interesting litmus test as to the capacity of the law to constrain this kind of errant behaviour, but even in this case it has taken many years and a major regulatory investigation to bring the issues to light. In general, in all such situations it is necessary to prove that there was deliberate dishonesty.

A little-known body, Companies Investigation, is part of the regulatory arm of the Insolvency Service and can carry out investigations where fraud or corporate misconduct are suspected.[7] Such an investigation can lead to an application to the High Court for a winding-up order under s. 124A of the Insolvency Act 1986. This may also lead to the directors being disqualified. Information obtained by Companies Investigation may be passed to the police or other investigatory agencies.

Foreign government controls

In Australia there is much more explicit statutory control affecting the conduct of business. Section 20 of the Australian Consumer Law provides that a person must not, in trade or commerce, engage in conduct that is unconscionable within the meaning of the 'unwritten law' from time to time, though this does not in itself apply in relation to financial services for which there is another provision. However, it has been said that there can be no finding of unconscionable conduct in this context where the parties are experienced operators accustomed to making commercial judgements and are acutely aware of their own interests and how to advance them. A distinction exists between parties who adopt an opportunist approach to strike a hard bargain and those who act unconscionably.

In 2010 the US Congress enacted the Dodd-Frank Act. A formidable tome of over 1,500 pages of closely printed text, the Act targets a number of issues related to the financial crisis. These include setting up an agency to protect consumers against abusive lending practices, and regulation of credit rating agencies, trade in derivatives and hedge funds.

The Dodd-Frank Act also extends to corporate governance. The areas selected for reform are shareholder nomination of candidates for director positions and a non-binding shareholder vote on executive compensation, or 'say on pay'. The Securities Exchange Commission (SEC) has framed Rule 14a-11 to implement the directive under the Dodd-Frank Act to provide access to shareholders in nominating directorial candidates. The rule came under legal challenge by the US Chamber of Commerce and the Business Roundtable, which filed an action in the US Court of Appeals for the DC Circuit. These business groups attacked the rule on the ground that it does not consider the effects on 'efficiency, competition, and capital formation'. So far, at least, the challenge has been unsuccessful.

Recent reform proposals

While Ed Miliband was the first to highlight the general question of making capitalism more responsible, various bodies have been working on particular aspects of the problem.

In June 2010 the EU Commission produced a green paper on corporate governance in financial institutions,[8] and in April 2011 another on corporate governance generally. More specific recommendations were made at the instigation of the Commission by the so-called Reflection Group on the future of EU company law.[9] For example, the group supported the provisions in the UK Stewardship Code whilst noting that its provisions were often not complied with. The group said that the Commission should be neutral as between member states' systems that have a regime for worker participation at board level and those that do not.

In May 2011 the High Pay Commission reported its findings on high pay and boardroom pay across the UK public and private sectors.[10] It made a dozen or so recommendations, including the following:

- Radically simplifying executive pay.
- Putting employees on remuneration committees.
- Publishing the top ten executive pay packages outside the boardroom.
- Forcing companies to publish a pay ratio between the highest paid executive and the company median.
- Making companies reveal total pay earned by executives.
- Establishing a new national body to monitor high pay.

In October 2011 the Relationships Foundation produced an interesting report entitled *Transforming Capitalism From Within*, arguing in favour of the 'relational company' that would pay greater regard to all its stakeholders' interests.[11]

Later, in a speech in January 2012, the Business Secretary, Vince Cable MP announced various proposals on executive pay, including for more transparent remuneration reports, for binding shareholder votes on future pay policy for the board as a whole, and for companies to report on their boardroom diversity policy. In June 2012 he told Parliament that these changes would be enacted through amendments to the Enterprise Bill, and some of the issues (in particular votes on pay policy) are now dealt with in the Enterprise and Regulatory Reform Act 2013.

Owners and fiduciary duties

In March 2012 a report was published by the Ownership Commission, an independent commission set up by the Cabinet Office with the initial brief of looking at employee and cooperative forms of ownership that might be applied in the public sector.[12] Chaired by the political economist Will Hutton, the Commission's recommendations included the need for more plurality of forms of ownership, which would involve 'new mechanisms and tax concessions to support the build up of equity capital in the medium sized family business sector'. They also favour the employee-owned company receiving greater support including via the tax system. They consider that shareholders and directors should have the definition of their fiduciary obligations widened to include better stewardship (a matter now being considered by the Law Commission), and for this to be enforced by closer links between the ultimate owners of the company and its managers. They suggest that government should consult as to the extent to which fiduciary duties are too narrowly defined, and should offer a redefinition to include a 'duty of stewardship'. They say that institutional investors should be required to comply with the Stewardship Code.

In April 2012 the House of Commons Treasury Select Committee set up a new inquiry into corporate governance in systemically important financial institutions, which is still ongoing.

In July 2012 the Kay review into UK equity markets and long-term decision making, set up by the Business Secretary in 2011, produced its final report.[13] This report recognises that lack of accountability of a company to its shareholders is far from being the only or even a central weakness in our present capitalist system, since many bad corporate decisions in recent years have been supported or even encouraged by a majority of the shareholders. Rather, the report opines, the effectiveness of modern equity markets depends almost entirely on their effectiveness in promoting goals such as better stewardship and governance. The report includes 'Good Practice Statements' for asset managers, asset holders and company directors, though these are once again very general, and the concept of stewardship is used in a very loose way. The report suggests that the law as to the fiduciary duty of asset holders to beneficiaries is ill-defined (although I would argue that this view may be based on a confusion between the law itself and the way it has sometimes been applied).

The Law Commission has now been asked to consider how the law of fiduciary duties applies to investment intermediaries, and in October 2013 the Commission issued a cautious consultation paper.[14] There is at present no indication of any significant strengthening of the scope or application of the concept of fiduciary duty, nor does it seem likely that there will be any further clarification of the concept of 'stewardship'. As matters stand, it seems likely that many key features of the present market will remain unaffected, including the fact that there is usually a long chain of intermediaries between the original investor and the investee company or companies, and the fact that in practice these intermediaries, and their ability to raise charges based on a not insignificant percentage of the sums invested, will remain relatively uncontrolled.

In his interim report,[15] Professor Kay pointed out that the long-term public goal for equity markets is in securing the public purposes of high-performing companies, and strong returns to savers through an effective asset management industry, and in ensuring that the profits earned by companies are as far as possible translated into returns to beneficiaries by minimising the costs of intermediation. Public policy, it was stated, towards equity markets should be judged by its contribution to these goals.

The final report[16] recommends that asset management firms should better align managers' interests with those of their clients, so as to provide a long-term performance incentive in the form of an interest in the relevant fund – either directly or via the firm – to be held at least until the manager ceases to be responsible for that fund. The report also confirms that, in general, long-term performance incentives should be provided only in the form of company shares to be held at least until the executive retires from the business.

The report also recommends that institutions should hold more concentrated portfolios comprising shares in fewer companies, in order to form deeper and long-term relationships with their investees.

There are perhaps at least two areas where more radical thinking may be required, namely the continuing potential for conflicts of interest on the part of investment managers, which they currently have to 'manage' rather than avoid, and the continuing potential for the unnecessary incurring of intermediation costs through pointless repetitive trading.

In April 2013, pursuant to the Financial Services Act 2012, a new regulatory regime for financial services came into effect, with the demise of the Financial Services Authority and the creation of the Prudential Regulation Authority (PRA) and the Financial Conduct Authority (FCA).

EU initiatives

Also in April 2013 the European Commission adopted a proposal for a directive enhancing the transparency of certain large companies on social and environmental matters. This directive would amend the Fourth and Seventh Directives on Annual and Consolidated Accounts, 78/660/EEC and 83/349/EEC, respectively. The objective is to increase EU companies' transparency and performance on environmental and social matters, and, therefore, to contribute effectively to long-term economic growth and employment.

In June 2013 the legislative package known as the Capital Requirements Directive IV (CRD IV)[17] was published in the *Official Journal of the European Union*, following the approval of its text by the European Parliament in April. CRD IV was supplemented by the Capital Requirements Regulation (CRR)[18] published on the same day. CRD IV includes various provisions in relation to the financial services sector, most notably new rules requiring affected institutions to limit the ratio of fixed to variable remuneration of certain staff. Colloquially, this has become known as the 'bonus cap' because the measures are largely a response to perceived excessive bonuses in the banking industry.

The entities impacted by CRD IV are, broadly speaking, credit institutions and investment firms within the Markets in Financial Instruments Directive, which includes all retail and investment banks, but also other forms of investment firm such as hedge funds. The bonus cap provisions apply in respect of work done from January 2014 onwards. Those affected are described as 'senior management, risk-takers, staff engaged in control functions' and certain similarly compensated senior personnel. The starting point of the bonus cap is that an affected individual's variable remuneration must be no greater than 100 percent of his or her fixed remuneration. In other words, the ratio of fixed to variable remuneration must be 1:1 or higher. However, the variable remuneration element can be increased to 200 percent of the fixed pay, namely a ratio of 1:2, if the firm's shareholders agree. This requires a 66 per cent majority of shareholders representing a quorum of at least 50 per cent of the voting shares. If that quorum is not achieved, then a 75 per cent majority is required. If shareholders are asked to approve a change to the ratio, they must be provided with a detailed recommendation containing certain specifics such as the number of employees affected. Any such affected employees who are also shareholders are not allowed to vote.

Up to 25 per cent of the variable remuneration may be awarded in the form of discounted long-term instruments. These are instruments that are deferred for at least five years and which may be valued for the purposes of the ratio on a discounted basis. At least 50 per cent of the variable remuneration must consist of shares or equivalent instruments or other instruments that can be readily converted to equity in adverse circumstances. At least 40 per cent of the variable remuneration must be deferred. In the case of high amounts of deferred remuneration (£500,000 or more in the UK), at least 60 per cent must be deferred.

In July 2013 the Secretary of State for Business, Innovation and Skills issued a consultation paper, entitled *Transparency and Trust*, containing proposals for achieving greater transparency as to the identity of the owners of a company, and for widening the powers of the courts in relation to directors' disqualification.

Potential policy objectives

In reviewing the efficacy of existing arrangements, and of current reform proposals, it is necessary to be clear as to one's policy objectives. There is a range of potential policy aims that proposals for more responsible capitalism might seek to achieve.

One group of aims relates to the structuring of companies and, adopting this approach, it is assumed that if appropriate requirements are imposed as to the way in which a company is structured then the company is more likely to behave in a socially responsible way. Under this heading will be included proposals for spreading ownership more widely and for increasing the powers of owners/shareholders.

Another group of policies would bear upon the way in which a company is run by those who manage its affairs. Here policy might involve regulating the identity of board members as well as their behaviour, as for instance by requiring the inclusion of employees as board members. In general, policy aims in this area have focused upon the need for greater long termism as regards the aims of the company itself, although (as discussed later) there are wider potential aims.

A specific issue arising in the context of the management of the company's affairs concerns executive pay, the extent to which executives should be rewarded by percentage-based remuneration and/or by share options, and the extent to which aggregate remuneration should be subject to control, whether in absolute terms or at least by comparison with the earnings of others within the company.

More generally, there is a group of aims which would seek to impose on companies and/or their owners and/or directors explicit obligations towards the wider community. Among the relevant policy aims here one could include such matters as increasing diversity, protecting the environment, reviving manufacturing industry and maintaining a sound financial system.

Policy proposals: The way forward

The difficulty in achieving a more responsible capitalism lies partly in the inherent nature of the capitalist system itself. The main purpose of establishing a limited company with its own separate corporate identity is to limit the liability of the individuals involved, whether as shareholders, directors or otherwise. The system rests on the assumption that even if those involved in the ownership and management of companies act for their own selfish ends, nonetheless the net result will be for the benefit of the community as a whole. It is this assumption that the events of recent years have once again called into question, and that Keynes himself showed to be fallacious.

It seems clear, however, that the way forward cannot be to return to the pre-industrial era, when those involved in business remained personally responsible throughout. The way forward must be to develop mechanisms (if necessary imposed by legislation, or at least by non-statutory codes of guidance) that will prevent the harmful consequences of unrestrained business activity, while at the same time allowing such activity to continue to benefit the community through the production and distribution of goods, services, jobs, etc.

How companies are structured

It seems logical to start by discussing mechanisms relating to the way in which companies are structured. On this, the work of the Ownership Commission seems of greatest interest and relevance. However, greater clarity is required as to the mechanisms/tax incentives that might achieve its objectives. A call for a duty of stewardship means little until this concept is defined and enforced, a topic to which I return later.

The powers and responsibilities of shareholders need to be considered as a separate topic. In some respects there can be little doubt that the powers of shareholders need to be increased, so as to enable them to control more effectively the composition and remuneration of the board of directors. However, by itself a measure conferring greater control on shareholders is likely to be insufficient because shareholders, particularly those who have invested in more substantial and profitable companies, are themselves likely to be motivated primarily by the profitability of their own investment, and will not necessarily promote the long-term success of the company, let alone the benefit of the community generally.

In his recent review for the Labour Party entitled *Overcoming Short-Termism*, Sir George Cox, Vice Chancellor of the University of Nottingham, recommends annual tapering of capital gains tax on shares and of income tax on dividends in order to encourage long-term investment.[19]

There are two particular aspects of corporate ownership where better regulation is clearly needed. The first is in relation to takeovers and mergers where, in a recent Policy Network paper,[20] a new public interest test is suggested, to be applied through a new independent body. The second is graphically outlined by Mariana Mazzucato in her book *The Entrepreneurial State*[21] where, under the heading 'financialisation', she observes:

> *whilst causality may be hard to prove, it cannot be denied that at the same time that private pharma companies have been reducing the R of R&D, they have been increasing the amount of funds used to repurchase their own shares – a strategy used to boost their stock price, which affects the price of stock options and executive pay linked to such options.*[22]

The problem here is that funds are in this way being drawn out of the company for the benefit of particular individuals rather than being invested in future growth. Study is required as to the best fiscal or other disincentives to such socially adverse behaviour.

Directors' responsibilities

As regards the general responsibilities of directors, some measures were introduced by Labour in the Companies Act 2006, but there must be scope for greater progress in this area. It may be that the most promising approach for the foreseeable future will be to work on the development of codes of conduct like the Corporate Governance Code. Ed Miliband has suggested that those in business, particularly in banking, ought to be bound by similar codes of conduct to those who work in teaching, medicine and the law. As he pointed out, 'those professions have clear rules, codes of conduct which lay down what is expected. We need the same for banking; anyone who breaks the rules should be struck off.'[23]

Also worthy of note is the suggestion by Ferdinand Mount that all companies above a certain size should have a 'supervisory' board,[24] though one might question why non-executive directors do not always fulfil such a supervisory role. Rod Dowler of the Industry Forum has suggested that non-executives should be required to provide a separate report to stakeholders containing positive assurances as to the management of the company (and see now the Companies Act 2006, s. 414Aff discussed earlier), while Russell Wallman proposes a requirement for a certain component of the board to be appointed as 'public interest directors' required to comply with defined 'public interest' criteria.[25] All these ideas are worthy of consideration by a Standing Commission on Responsible Capitalism (see below).

The TUC has recently published two important reports on corporate governance reform. *Workers on Board* argues that reform is necessary if we are to significantly challenge short-termism, and the report[26] makes three proposals: that directors' duties should be reformed so that directors are required to promote the long-term success of their company, rather than prioritising shareholder interests as at present; that shareholders' corporate governance rights should be dependent on a minimum period of shareholding of two years; and that the UK should establish a mandatory system for the representation of workers on company boards.

The TUC's *Workers' Voice in Corporate Governance: A European Perspective*,[27] shows that workers have the right to be represented on company boards in 19 European countries, including many of Europe's most successful economies such as Germany, the Netherlands, Sweden and Austria. Significantly, workers are represented on company boards in countries where companies have a single 'unitary' board of directors such as Sweden and Ireland, as well as countries like Germany that have a two-tier or supervisory board system.

Executive pay

Decision making on executive pay has historically been in the hands of the directors themselves. It now seems to be widely accepted that there should be greater involvement by the company's owners/shareholders and by its employees, not least because they have an obvious financial stake in the way in which the company's available resources are applied.

Steps to ensure greater transparency in relation to remuneration arrangements are already in hand. However, the time has surely come for society to take a more active role in relation to systems of payment. Ferdinand Mount[28] proposes that the normal ratio of chief executive salary to average shop floor salary should not exceed 20 to 1 in a medium-sized company and 40 to 1 in a large one, that no cash bonus should exceed 20 per cent of salary, and that any bonus paid in shares should be barred from being cashed in for 3 years. In addition, performance-based remuneration should as far as possible be retained pending longer-term review of performance, perhaps for several years or even until retirement.

The Cox Review[29] suggests that under the Corporate Governance Code, 30 per cent of executive directors' remuneration might be deferred subject to long-term (five-year) results, while 50 per cent of non-executive directors' remuneration might be paid in the form of shares not vesting for five years or until any earlier departure from the board. These ideas echo those already to be implemented in the banking sector under EU regulations discussed earlier.

The central point is that performance-based remuneration should not generally be based on the paper value of transactions without any attempt to correlate that paper value with the true underlying value of the transaction to the company concerned.

More generally on executive pay, it has been pointed out by David Coats[30] that:

> ... as the International Monetary Fund (among others) has argued, the relative decline in the bargaining power of workers on median earnings and below was one of the causes of the crisis, especially in the United States. High levels of ultimately unsustainable household debt were used to compensate for the stagnation of wages. If we want a better capitalism then there needs to be less income inequality for reasons both of social justice and of economic stability; and wage growth needs to be reconnected with productivity growth.

Accordingly, says Coats:

> ... there can be no doubt that rebuilding workplace institutions influencing the initial distribution of incomes (before the tax and benefits system intervenes) is an essential element in the policy mix. A shift in bargaining power might impose some constraints on executive pay too, not least because there will be a strong workers' voice demanding that the same principles apply to pay across the organisation.

A clearer definition of stewardship

The Stewardship Code was designed (though there have been some misinterpretations) to address the role of those acting as 'stewards' of funds on behalf of others. Hence we are here talking about bodies such as pension funds who have a trusteeship role, and their appointed asset managers whose role is generally defined by their contract. I pointed out earlier that the Code fails adequately to define the concept of stewardship, and does not make it at all clear to whom it is really directed.

Therefore, what is required is for the Code to be amended to make it clear that institutional investors like pension funds, and then subsequently their appointed managers, all have stewardship duties towards the ultimate beneficiaries of the funds. In particular, it should be made clear (which astonishingly at present it seems that it is not) that these beneficiaries are likely to require those acting on their behalf to have primary regard to the long-term success and share value of the investee company. Fair Pensions, the campaigning organisation of responsible investment, has proposed that this be achieved by a new piece of legislation for a fiduciary investor, equivalent to the Companies Act 2006 s. 172, whereby in the performance of investment functions a fiduciary may have regard to much wider and longer-term factors.

A recent example of the apparently successful deployment of relevant regulatory powers concerned a proposal by Barclays to comply with new leverage requirements by reducing business lending. This was the subject of rapid PRA intervention and the agreed outcome was that Barclays decided instead on a substantial share issue to raise the necessary capital.[31]

Public procurement decisions

Another obvious area for action arises in relation to procurement decisions, and as an example of what is achievable Labour has said that it would make it a condition that firms winning large government contracts should offer apprenticeships. Other options might include requiring vacancies to be advertised locally, insisting on improved subcontract payment terms, dividing contracts up into lots to make the process easier for SMEs, and awarding points for local knowledge or resources. This issue is now the subject of detailed consideration by a joint working group of the Society of Labour Lawyers and the Labour Finance and Industry Group.

David Coats has observed that another obvious step would be to ratify the International Labour Organisation's convention on labour clauses in public contracts, which requires the government only to do business with those who observe either the wages and conditions negotiated with trade unions or the prevailing wage in a sector.[32]

No one would suggest that issues relating to the conduct of business should be subject to frequent direct legal or judicial intervention, but there are nonetheless legal improvements that can be made on both the criminal and civil sides. For example, there seems to be scope for the creation of additional criminal offences, not necessarily involving proof of deliberate dishonesty. Thus the Parliamentary Commission on Banking Standards has recommended the creation of an offence of reckless misconduct in managing a bank. The need for a tighter approach to prosecution in relation to financial crime has also been emphasised by the Treasury Select Committee in its initial report on Libor.

On the civil side the biggest problem remains the funding of litigation, and there is considerable concern that the reforms introduced by the Legal Aid Sentencing and Punishment of Offenders Act 2012 (based on the recommendations of Jackson LJ[33]), by diminishing the profitability of the conditional fee agreement, will make it very much harder for claimants to pursue civil claims, especially in group litigation.

Another area for greater focus is tax policy. Tax incentives for particular kinds of economic or investment decisions are an obvious example. Some form of tax credit for child care would be likely to have a positive impact on the diversity of the workforce. It has been suggested that all tax proposals should be subject to a 'sustainability audit'.

The most difficult but also the most important area to address concerns the wider policy aims mentioned earlier – namely, seeking to impose on companies and/or their owners and/or directors explicit obligations towards the wider community. What mechanisms might be available to guarantee that business activity in general works for the benefit of the community, and not to its disadvantage? There is no doubt that greater transparency is a first step in this respect, and measures such as those requiring that directors' reports provide environmental information are to be applauded. However, what is lacking is any coordinated monitoring (let alone regulation) of the extent to which this kind of disclosure is made, or as to the longer-term results.

Conclusion

It is increasingly clear that a 'Standing Commission on Responsible Capitalism', which could carry forward such proposals and build on the work of the various temporary inquiries referred to earlier, is what we now urgently need. As Keynes observed, a system that works for the collective benefit also tends to maximise individual profit, but (as we have all observed much more recently) a system that *fails* to work for the collective benefit risks destroying individual profitability, and thereby destroying the system itself.

Summary of principal recommendations

- Reforming the ownership and structure of limited companies so as to achieve more varied forms of ownership.
- Adjusting the powers and responsibilities of shareholders so that more power may be vested in them compared with the board of the directors.
- Addressing executive remuneration so that more influence can be exerted by and for the benefit of the community at large.
- Amending corporate governance and stewardship so that the above changes can be implemented and enforced.
- Reforming public procurement, which should be deployed more proactively to promote responsible practice.
- Ensuring fiscal policy can also be used more proactively to help achieve wider social objectives.
- Focusing criminal justice policy in ways that deter irresponsible financial methods.
- Improving litigation funding, without which the courts will be powerless to support all these developments.

Notes

1 Child Abuse

1. House of Commons Home Affairs Committee, *Child Sexual Exploitation and the Response to Localised Grooming*, Second Report of Session 2013–14, June 2013, p. 40 (available at: http://www. publications.parliament.uk/pa/cm201314/cmselect/cmhaff/68/68i.pdf).
2. Jonathan West, 'It Took Four Years', *Confessions of a Skeptic Blog*, 17 October 2013 (available at: http://scepticalthoughts.blogspot.co.uk/).
3. See Press Association, 'Failures to Intervene Pinpointed in Case of Murdered Four-Year-Old Daniel Pelka', *The Guardian*, 5 February 2014.
4. NSPCC Strategy Unit, *Mandatory Reporting: A Consideration of the Evidence*, NSPCC Strategy Unit Briefing Paper, January 2014, p. 4 (available at: http://www.nspcc.org.uk/Inform/policyandpublicaffairs/ england/briefings/mandatory-reporting_wdf97356.pdf).
5. Keir Starmer, 'Britain's Justice System Fails the Vulnerable: We Need a Victims' Law', *The Guardian*, 3 February 2014.
6. Judge Pigot, *Report of the Advisory Group on Video-Recorded Evidence*, Home Office, London, December 1989 (available at: http:// www.law.cam.ac.uk/faculty-resources/download/pigot-report/8979/pdf).
7. Toulmin Lecture in Law and Psychiatry, *Half a Century of Change: The Evidence of Child Victims*, The Right Honourable the Lord Judge, Lord Chief Justice of England and Wales, 20 March 2013 (available at: http:// www.judiciary.gov.uk/wp-content/uploads/JCO/Documents/Speeches/ lcj-speech-law-and-psychiatry.pdf).
8. House of Commons Home Affairs Committee, op. cit.
9. Andrew Norfolk, 'Humiliation in Court: How the Law Treated Abuse Victims', *The Times*, 23 May 2013.

2   *Civil Legal Aid*
1. See the LSC Technology Innovation Grants website (http://tig.lsc.gov/resources/summit-report/components-integrated).

3   *Constitutional Rights*
1. See the BBC News (2001) review of his career, 'Lord Hailsham: The Passionate Peer' (http://news.bbc.co.uk/1/hi/uk_politics/319002.stm).
2. Vernon Bogdanor, 'An Era of Constitutional Reform', *The Political Quarterly*, vol. 81, Supplement s1, September 2010, pp. S53–S64.
3. Lord Neuberger, 'Judges and Policy: A Delicate Balance', speech delivered to the Institute for Government, 18 June 2013.
4. Martin Howe QC, 'A UK Bill of Rights', in Commission on a Bill of Rights, *A UK Bill of Rights? The Choice Before Us, Volume 1*, Commission on a Bill of Rights, December 2012, pp. 192–216.
5. Timothy Garton Ash, *The Polish Revolution: Solidarity 1980–82*, London, Jonathan Cape, 1983.

4   *Employment Law*
1. Section 230(1) (http://www.legislation.gov.uk/ukpga/1996/18/section/230).
2. In s. 230(3).
3. [2011] UKSC 41.
4. Mark R. Freedland, *The Personal Employment Contract*, Oxford, Oxford University Press, 2003, p. 28. The explanatory fuller formulation of the concept that Dr Freedland puts forward is 'in the course of a process or practice of production of goods including intellectual goods or provision of services of which process or practice the contractor is the primary and substantially autonomous organiser'.
5. 93/13/EEC, implemented by the Unfair Terms in Consumer Contracts Regulations 1999, SI 1999/2083.
6. The Law Commission, *Unfair Terms in Contracts* (Law Com No. 292, 2005), Clause 12 of the draft Unfair Contract Terms Bill, at p. 154.
7. See Joellen Riley, 'Regulating for Fair Dealing in Work Contracts: A New South Wales Approach', *Industrial Law Journal*, vol. 36, issue 1, 2007, pp. 19–34, in which the author considered the jurisdiction available between 1959 and 2006. This jurisdiction was first provided for after the insertion of s. 88F into the Industrial Arbitration Act 1940 (NSW), which conferred a power to vary contracts where employers sought to avoid industry-wide awards fixing wages and conditions.

8. Industrial Relations Act 1996 (NSW) s. 105.

9. The Industrial Relations Commission of New South Wales in Court Session, which was previously the Industrial Court.

10. Industrial Relations Act 1996 (NSW) s. 106.

11. See Young Legal Aid Lawyers, *Social Mobility and Diversity in the Legal Aid Sector: One Step Forward, Two Steps Back*, October 2013 (available at: http://www.younglegalaidlawyers.org/sites/default/files/One%20step%20forward%20two%20steps%20back.pdf).

12. The Chartered Institute of Personnel and Development (which surveys employers) estimates that 24 per cent of public sector employers and 34 per cent of third sector employers now use ZHCs, compared with 17 per cent in the private sector. According to the government's 2011 *Workplace Employment Relations Study*, the proportion of employers (in all sectors) using ZHCs between 2004 and 2011 doubled to 8 per cent. In workplaces of 100 employees or more the rate of use was 23 per cent.

13. Alexander Ehmann, 'Zero-hours Contracts: Are They Bad for Workers?', *The Guardian Five-minute Video Debate*, 12 August 2013 (available at: http://www.theguardian.com/commentisfree/video/2013/aug/12/zero-hours-contracts-five-minute-debate-video).

14. *Royal Commission on Trade Unions and Employers' Associations 1965–1968: Report*, 1968 (Cmnd 3623).

15. SI No. 3319.

16. HL Debates, 8 July 2013, Column 81.

17. L. Adams, A. Moore, K. Gore and J. Browne, *Research Into Enforcement of Employment Tribunal Awards in England and Wales*, Ministry of Justice, 2009, Research Series 9/09.

18. Department of Business Innovation & Skills, *Payment of Tribunal Awards: 2013 Study*, IFF Research (available at: https://www.gov.uk/government/uploads/system/uploads/attachment_data/file/253558/bis-13–1270-enforcement-of-tribunal-awards.pdf).

5   *Energy Law and Policy*

1. The Labour Party, *Powering Britain: One Nation Labour's Plans to Reset the Energy Market*, November 2013 (available at: http://www.yourbritain.org.uk/agenda-2015/policy-review/policy-review/energy-green-paper-2?download=true).

2. Passenger Focus, *National Rail Passenger Survey: Autumn 2013 Main Report* (available at: http://www.passengerfocus.org.uk/research/publications/national-rail-passenger-survey-autumn-2013-main-report).

3. The European Parliament and Council, *Regulation (EC) No. 1370/2007 on Public Passenger Transport Services by Rail and by Road*, 23 October 2007 (available at: http://eur-lex.europa.eu/LexUriServ/LexUriServ.do?uri=OJ:L:2007:315:0001:0013:EN:PDF).

4. C-105/12, 22 October 2013.

6 Equalities Law and Tackling Inequality

1. The author would like to acknowledge the helpful comments made by Kate Green MP during the preparation of this chapter.

2. Sarah Dransfield, *The Tale of Two Britains: Inequality in the UK*, Oxfam GB, 2014 (available at: http://policy-practice.oxfam.org.uk/publications/a-tale-of-two-britains-inequality-in-the-uk-314152).

3. Tony Judt, *Ill Fares the Land*, Penguin Books, 2011.

4. Benjamin Disraeli, *Sybil*, book 2, chapter 5, Henry Colburn, 1845.

5. Richard G. Wilkinson and Kate Pickett, *The Spirit Level: Why More Equal Societies Almost Always Do Better*, Allen Lane, 2009. (Second edition published in 2010 by Penguin Books with the subtitle, *Why Equality is Better for Everyone*.)

6. Thomas Piketty, *Capital in the Twenty-First Century*, Harvard University Press, 2014.

7. A comment first made to a US industrialist in California in 1998.

8. James Plunkett, 'The Rising Tide Economy: Lessons From the Squeezed Middle for Progressive Economic Policy', *The Political Quarterly*, vol. 83, no. 3, 1 July 2012, pp. 502–511.

9. Ibid.

10. National Equality Panel, *An Anatomy of Economic Inequality in the UK*, Government Equalities Office, 2010 (available at: http://sticerd.lse.ac.uk/dps/case/cr/CASEreport60_summary.pdf).

11. R. Wilkinson and K. Pickett, 'Is Society Stronger?', *Fabian Review*, Summer 2013, p. 12.

12. National Equality Panel, op. cit.

13. Ibid.

14. For example, *R. (on the application of Luton BC) v Secretary of State for Education* [2011] Eq. L.R. 481 (a challenge to cuts to the Building Schools for the Future programme); *R (W) v Birmingham City Council* [2011] EWHC 1147 and *JM and NT v Isle of Wight* [2011] EWHC 2911

(PSED in the context of care budgets); and *Kaur and Shah v London Borough of Ealing* [2008] EWHC 2062 (Admin) (a challenge to funding cuts to Southall Black Sisters).

15. *R (Fawcett Society) v Chancellor of the Exchequer & Others* [2010] EWHC 3522 (Admin).

16. HM Treasury, *The Green Book: Appraisal and Evaluation in Central Government* (available at: https://www.gov.uk/government/publications/the-green-book-appraisal-and-evaluation-in-central-governent).

17. The 2011 survey by Manifest and MM&K, reported in Brian Groom, David Oakley and Jim Pickard, 'Bosses Failing to Tighten Their Belts', *Financial Times*, 11 June 2012. See also *High Pay Centre Briefing: The Effect of Executive Pay Reforms*, High Pay Centre, 2 June 2014 (available at: http://highpaycentre.org/pubs/high-pay-centre-briefing-the-effect-of-executive-pay-reforms).

18. Richard Henry Tawney, *Equality*, originally published London, Unwin Books, 1931; fifth edition, 1964, at p. 57.

7 Family Law

1. Section 2(2) (a) and (b) and s. 4 Children Act 1989.

2. The Law Commission, *Cohabitation: The Financial Consequences of Relationship Breakdown*, No. 307, July 2007 (available at: http://lawcommission.justice.gov.uk/publications/723.htm).

3. Section 1A SAA 1985.

4. Section 33 HFEA 2008.

5. Section 54 HFEA 2008.

6. For example, where say only an intended female parent's gametes are used, or the surrogate mother is married, in which case neither intended parent is treated as a parent of the child under English law.

7. Section 51 Adoption and Children Act 2002.

8. This assumes the surrogate mother is not married or in a civil partnership.

9. *A and A v P, P and B* [2011] EWHC 1738 (Fam).

10. Section 41 HFEA 2008.

11. Department of Health & Social Security, *Report of the Committee of Inquiry Into Human Fertilisation and Embryology*, July 1984, Cmnd. 9314 (available at: http://www.hfea.gov.uk/docs/Warnock_Report_of_the_Committee_of_Inquiry_into_Human_Fertilisation_and_Embryology_1984.pdf).

12. Margaret Brazier, Alastair Campbell and Susan Golombok, *Surrogacy: Review For Health Ministers of Current Arrangements for Payments and Regulation*, October 1998, Cmnd. 4068 (available at: http://webarchive. nationalarchives.gov.uk/20130107105354/http://www.dh.gov.uk/prod_ consum_dh/groups/dh_digitalassets/@dh/@en/documents/digitalasset/ dh_4014373.pdf).

13. Section 54(6) HFEA 2008.

14. Section 54(7) HFEA 2008.

8 Serious Fraud and White Collar Crime

1. To date, only one senior banker has faced jail for their conduct during the financial crisis: this was in the US in January 2014, not the UK. See Jesse Eisinger, 'Why Only One Top Banker Went to Jail for the Financial Crisis', *The New York Times*, 30 April 2014 (available at: http://www.nytimes.com/2014/05/04/magazine/only-one-top-banker-jail-financial-crisis.html).

2. European Commission Press Release, 'Antitrust: Commission Confirms Unannounced Inspections in Oil and Biofuels Sectors', *Memo/13/435*, 14 May 2013 (available at: http://europa.eu/rapid/press-release_MEMO-13–435_en.htm?locale=en).

3. Alan Travis, 'Labour Will Introduce New Laws Against Dishonest Bankers, Cooper to Say', *The Guardian*, 2 October 2012 (available at: http://www.theguardian.com/business/2012/oct/02/cooper-banking-reform-conference-speech).

4. In November 2012 I met with prosecutors at the US Federal Attorney's Office for the Southern District of New York and the US Federal Attorney's Office for Washington DC. I thank them for their help and hospitality.

5. *Tesco Supermarkets Ltd v Nattrass* [1972] AC 153, at p. 171.

6. HC Debates, 18 June 2013, Column 603W. (http://www.publications. parliament.uk/pa/cm201314/cmhansrd/cm130618/text/130618w0001. htm#130618w0001.htm_spmin10).

7. Caroline Binham, 'Call to Make Companies Liable for Failure to Prevent Fraud', *Financial Times*, 5 June 2013 (available at: http://www.ft.com/cms/s/0/4900db34-cdf4–11e2-a13e-00144feab7de. html#axzz30e171CWp).

8. The Law Commission, *Criminal Liability In Regulatory Contexts: A Consultation Paper*, Consultation Paper No. 195, p. 96, para 5.47

(available at: http://lawcommission.justice.gov.uk/docs/cp195_
Criminal_Liability_consultation.pdf).

9. David Ormerod (ed), *Smith and Hogan's Criminal Law*, twelfth edition, 2008, p. 249.

10. See *El Ajou v Dollar Land Holdings plc* [1994] BCC 143; *Director General of Fair Trading v Pioneer Concrete (UK) Ltd* [1995] 1 AC 456; and *Meridian Global Funds Management Asia Ltd v Securities Commission* [1995] 2 AC 500.

11. The Law Commission, op. cit., p. 106.

12. The OECD Convention on Combating Bribery of Foreign Public Officials in International Business Transactions. See 'OECD Group Demands Rapid UK Action to Enact Adequate Anti-bribery Laws', *OECD Press Release*, 16 October 2008 (available at: http://www.oecd.org/daf/briberyininternationalbusiness/anti-briberyconvention/oecdgroupdemandsrapidukactiontoenactadequateanti-briberylaws.htm). Deficiencies in the UK's laws on corporate criminal liability are discussed from p. 19 in the Working Group's report (available at: http://www.oecd.org/daf/briberyininternationalbusiness/anti-briberyconvention/41515077.pdf).

13. Labour.org.uk (available at: http://www.yourbritain.org.uk/agenda-2015/policy-review/tackling-serious-fraud).

14. For useful summaries, see Clifford Chance, *Corporate Liability in Europe*, January 2012 (available at: http://www.cliffordchance.com/content/dam/cliffordchance/PDFs/Corporate_Liability_in_Europe.pdf).

15. Caroline Binham, 'SFO Notes Rise in Companies Admitting Guilt', *Financial Times*, 14 January 2013 (available at: http://www.ft.com/cms/s/0/a390b1f2-5c1e-11e2-bef7-00144feab49a.html#axzz30wFnry3N).

16. Ibid.

17. Innospec, fined in 2009.

18. Severn Trent Water in 2008.

19. See Freshfields Bruckhaus Deringer, *Bribery and Corruption: Recent Enforcement Activity in the UK and US*, London, Freshfields Bruckhaus Deringer LLP, October 2012, for a table reviewing corporate bribery fines in the UK and US over recent years (available at: http://www.freshfields.com/uploadedFiles/SiteWide/Knowledge/BAR3_A%20log%20of%20recent%20UK%20bribery%20and%20corruption%20related%20enforcement%20activity.pdf).

20. EU cartel statistics (available at: http://ec.europa.eu/competition/cartels/statistics/statistics.pdf).

21. See 'EU Imposes Record $1.92bn Fine on Phillips, Five Others', *Reuters US Edition*, 5 December 2012 (available at: http://www.reuters.com/article/2012/12/05/us-eu-cartel-crt-idUSBRE8B40EK20121205).

22. Office of the Sentencing Council, *Fraud, Bribery and Money Laundering Offences Guideline: Consultation*, 2013, Chapter 9, p. 65 (available at: http://sentencingcouncil.judiciary.gov.uk/docs/Fraud_Consultation_-_web.pdf).

23. Ibid. p. 67.

24. *R v Innospec Ltd* [2010] Lloyd's Rep. F.C. 462; [2010] Crim. L.R. 665, para 32.

25. See Chapter 8, Part B, *US Sentencing Guidelines Manual, 2012*, p. 393.

26. Frances Gibb and James Dean, 'Fraud Office Gets £19m Bailout After Misleading Taxman', *The Times*, 1 March 2014 (available at: http://www.thetimes.co.uk/tto/news/uk/article4019911.ece).

27. Alistair Osborne, 'BAE Documents Lost by SFO Found at Cannabis Farm', *The Telegraph*, 13 September 2013 (available at: http://www.telegraph.co.uk/finance/financial-crime/10307238/BAE-documents-lost-by-SFO-found-at-cannabis-farm.html).

28. *SFO Annual Report, 2012–13* and *2010–11*.

29. James Moore, 'MPs Savage Former Serious Fraud Office Chief as "Sloppy and Slovenly"', *The Independent*, 8 March 2013 (available at: http://www.independent.co.uk/news/business/news/mps-savage-former-serious-fraud-office-chief-as-sloppy-and-slovenly-8525622.html).

30. Gerri Peev, 'Fraud Chief Claimed £100,000 in Expenses for Commuting to London From the Lake District', *Mail Online*, 17 July 2013 (http://www.dailymail.co.uk/news/article-2366358/Phillippa-Williamson-claimed-100–000-expenses-commuting-London-Lake-District.html).

31. Alex Spence, 'Grieve Under Fire Over SFO "Breaches"', *The Times*, 27 July 2013 (available at: http://www.thetimes.co.uk/tto/news/politics/article3826996.ece).

32. Caroline Binham, 'SFO Opted Against Probe Into Libor', *Financial Times*, 29 January 2012 (available at: http://www.ft.com/cms/s/0/b8900f3e-c1d8-11e1-8e7c-00144feabdc0.html#axzz2bOQotIK1).

33. Oliver Wright, 'Revealed: George Osborne's Secret Veto on Fraud Inquiries', *The Independent*, 23 April 2013 (available at: http://www.independent.co.uk/news/uk/politics/revealed-george-osbornes-secret-veto-on-fraud-inquiries-8585215.html).

34. FT Alphaville, 'Whistleblowing Incentives Just Got International,
21 September 2012 (http://ftalphaville.ft.com/2012/09/21/1170551/
whistleblowing-incentives-just-got-international/).
35. Parliamentary answer from the Solicitor General: HC Debates, 4 March
2013, Column 776W.
36. Asa Bennett, 'Serious Fraud Office Whistleblowing Calls Spark
No Investigations', *The Huffington Post*, 26 July 2013 (available
at: http://www.huffingtonpost.co.uk/2013/07/26/SFO-tipoffs-
investigations_n_3657577.html).
37. This argument is made in 'Whistleblowing Incentives Just Got
International', see footnote 34.
38. Caroline Binham, 'Home Office Looks at "Bounty" Plan for Corporate
Whistleblowers', *Financial Times*, 9 October 2013 (available at: http://
www.ft.com/cms/s/0/2a999a90–30d3–11e3-b991–00144feab7de.
html#axzz2iNRH2CZo).

9 Human Rights: Reflections on the 1998 Act

1. In *X v Y* [1988] 2 All ER 648 a health authority sought an injunction
to stop a tabloid publishing the names of doctors who had HIV. The
judge granted the injunction saying that: 'In the long run, preservation
of confidentiality is the only way of securing public health … future
individual patients will not come forward if doctors are going to squeal
on them. Consequently, confidentiality is vital to secure public as well
as private health, for unless those infected come forward they cannot be
counselled….'
2. Paul Seighart, *AIDS and Human Rights: A UK Perspective*, London,
British Medical Association Foundation for AIDS, 1989.
3. *R v Parole Board ex parte Bradley* [1991] 1 WLR 134. See also, more
generally, *Hussain v UK & Prem Singh v UK* (1996) 22 EHRR 1. See
also Nicola Padfield, *Beyond the Tariff*, Willan, 2002.
4. *R v Ministry of Defence, ex parte Smith* [1996] QB 517.
5. *Stafford v UK* (2002) 35 EHRR 32.
6. See footnote 4.
7. *Lustig Prean & Becket v UK* (2000) 29 ECHR 548; *Smith & Grady v
UK* (1999) 29 EHRR 493.
8. In 1993 John Smith made this commitment in his leader's speech at the
Brighton Conference (available at: http://www.britishpoliticalspeech.
org/speech-archive.htm?speech=199).

9. Liberty's policy in the late 1980s and early 1990s was for a Bill of Rights based on international human rights standards. Liberty's *A People's Charter*, published in 1991, was a draft UK Bill of Rights based on international human rights standards that go beyond the ECHR. Andrew Puddephatt was Liberty's General Secretary at the time, and John Wadham, Madeleine Colvin (both lawyers at Liberty) and Francesca Klug (Director of the Civil Liberties Trust) worked on *A People's Charter* together. John Wadham went on to become Liberty's Director.

10. Francesca Klug, Keir Starmer and Stuart Weir, *The Three Pillars of Liberty: Political Rights and Freedoms in the United Kingdom (Democratic Audit of the United Kingdom)*, London, Routledge, 1996.

11. David Kinley, *The European Convention on Human Rights: Compliance Without Incorporation*, Aldershot, Dartmouth Publishing Co Ltd, 1993.

12. *S v Makwanyane* 1995(3) SA 391 (CC); 1995(6) BCLR 665 (CC) Paragraph 88.

13. Derived from *Associated Provincial Picture Houses Ltd v Wednesbury Corporation* [1948] 1 KB 223, which set out the standard of unreasonableness of public body decisions that would make them liable to be quashed on judicial review.

14. HL Debates, 3 November 1997, Column 1228.

15. At this stage Francesca Klug was Senior Research Fellow on the Human Rights Incorporation Project (directed by Professor Robert Blackburn) at King's College Law School.

16. Plus, of course, the wealth of Lord Lester of Herne Hill QC's advice, wisdom and experience proved invaluable.

17. Incorporation of the ECHR was considered to be the least controversial way forward. As further evidence of the conservative nature of what was to become the Human Rights Act, there was a consensus around the substantive rights in the ECHR and the government was already bound by them. There was also concern that consultation on additional rights could take years and might delay, if not stymie, the process of introducing a Bill of Rights. Basing a Bill of Rights on the ECHR was seen as far less controversial, especially with the Conservatives.

18. Jack Straw and Paul Boateng, *Bringing Rights Home: Labour's Plans to Incorporate the European Convention on Human Rights into UK Law*, Labour Party, 1997.

19. Secretary of State for the Home Department, *Rights Brought Home: The Human Rights Bill*, Cmnd. 3782, October 1997 (available at: https://

www.gov.uk/government/uploads/system/uploads/attachment_data/
file/263526/rights.pdf).

20. Section 13, Human Rights Act 1998.

21. Ibid. s. 12.

22. For example, social work records of an allegedly abused woman should
    be disclosed in child proceedings where her alleged abuser is the
    father (*A (A Child)* [2012] UKSC 60); procedural rights for children
    in decisions affecting family life (*Mabon v Mabon* [2005] EWCA
    Civ 634); considering the child's best interests includes hearing their
    own views (*ZH (Tanzania) v Secretary of State for Home Department*
    [2011] UKSC 4); keeping a mother and child together (*EM (Lebanon)
    v Secretary of State for the Home Department* [2008] UKHL 64); no
    corporal punishment in schools (*R (Williamson) v Secretary of State for
    Education and Employment* [2005] UKHL 15); child witnesses giving
    evidence via video link is compatible with the right to a fair trial (*R v
    Camberwell Green Youth Court* [2005] UKHL 4); unnecessary physical
    restraint of young people in custody is a breach (*R (C) v Secretary of
    State for Justice* [2008] EWCA 882).

23. See Keir Starmer QC, 'Human Rights and Victims: The Untold Story of
    the Human Rights Act', *European Human Rights Law Review*, No. 3,
    2014, pp. 215–221.

24. See, for example, *Osborn v Parole Board* [2013] UKSC 61, an appeal
    from three prisoners concerning their right to an oral hearing before the
    Parole Board. The Parole Board refused to grant them an oral hearing
    when deciding whether to recommend their release or transfer to open
    conditions. The court held that the common law duty to act fairly is
    influenced by the requirements of Art. 5.4 ECHR, and if a procedure
    satisfies the former it should satisfy the latter. However, it is a mistake
    to see common law rights and ECHR rights as somehow distinct: human
    rights have long permeated English law, and a consideration of any
    human rights question will not begin and end with Strasbourg case law
    (paragraphs 54–63, 101–113).

25. [2014] UKSC 20.

26. For a detailed analysis of the case, see K. O'Byrne, 'Kennedy v
    Charity Commission: Freedom of Information Under Article 10 and the
    Common Law', *European Human Rights Law Review*, No. 3, 2014.

27. He had set out his stall in an earlier case, *R (Guardian News and Media
    Ltd) v City of Westminster Magistrates' Court* [2013] QB 618. In turn,

that decision was based on the 1913 case of *Scott v Scott* [1913] AC 417.

28. *Kennedy v Charity Commission* [2014] UKSC 20 at [133].

29. A number of House of Lords and Supreme Court cases have been decided on the basis of common law principles in a manner consistent with, but not reliant on, Convention rights: *R (Daly) v Secretary of State for the Home Department* [2001] 2 AC 532; *A v Secretary of State for the Home Department (No 2)* [2006] 2 AC 221; *R (Osborn) v Parole Board* [2013] 3 WLR 1020. See also those common law claims for breaches of human rights which were denied: *Smith v Chief Constable of Sussex Police* [2009] 1 AC 225; *Campbell v MGN Ltd* [2004] 2 AC 457.

30. Section 11, HRA: Safeguard for existing human rights:
    A person's reliance on a Convention right does not restrict –
    (a) any other right or freedom conferred on him by or under any law having effect in any part of the United Kingdom; or
    (b) his right to make any claim or bring any proceedings which he could make or bring apart from sections 7 to 9.

31. Section 2, HRA: Interpretation of Convention rights.
    (1) A court or tribunal determining a question which has arisen in connection with a Convention right must take into account any –
    (a) judgment, decision, declaration or advisory opinion of the European Court of Human Rights, ...

32. [2004] 2 AC 323 at [20].

33. *A.F. v Secretary of State for the Home Department* [2009] UKHL 28, per Lord Rodger at paragraph 98.

34. See Nicholas Bratza, 'The Relationship Between the UK Courts and Strasbourg', *European Human Rights Law Review*, No. 5, 2011, pp. 505–512.

35. *R v Horncastle and others* [2009] UKSC 14 re *Al-Khawaja and Tahery v the United Kingdom* (App. Nos. 26766/05 and 22228/06), judgment of 20 January 2009.

36. *R (Limbuela) v Secretary of State for the Home Department* [2005] UKHL 66; *G (Adoption: Unmarried Couple)* [2008] 3 WLR 76; *E.M. (Lebanon) v Secretary of State for the Home Department* [2008] UKHL 64.

37. [2012] 2 AC 72.

38. [2004] 2 AC 323 at [20].

39. [2012] 1 AC 531.

40. Ibid. at [68].
41. Ibid.
42. Joint Committee on Human Rights: *The Human Rights Act: The DCA and Home Office Reviews* (HC 2005–06, 1694).
43. *The Governance of Britain,* July 2007, Cmnd. 7170.
44. The findings of the Commission have been subject to much criticism. See for example Mark Elliott, 'A Damp Squib in the Long Grass: The Report of the Commission on a Bill of Rights', *European Human Rights Law Review*, No. 2, 2013, pp. 137–151.
45. Section 3, Human Rights Act 1998.
46. Section 28 of the Local Government Act 1988 banned local authorities from promoting homosexuality.
47. 1996 (23 EHRR 413).

10 NHS and Social Care Law

1. The NHS imposes charges on people who are not exempt under regulations for items such as prescriptions and eye tests. Most secondary care ought to be paid for by persons who are not ordinarily resident in the UK.
2. NHS bodies have a range of other duties under other Acts such as the Mental Health Act 1983.
3. The Law Commission, *Adult Social Care*, May 2011, HC 941 (available at: http://lawcommission.justice.gov.uk/docs/lc326_adult_social_care.pdf).
4. The author was the former MP for Wyre Forest who lost his seat over an issue at Kidderminster Hospital in 2001.
5. Even if it was completely different to the NHS plans in the Coalition Agreement.
6. See section 1(3) of the NHS Act 2006 as introduced by section 1 of the 2012 Act.
7. *The Independent*, 13 October 2011.
8. Simon Stephens, 'NHS Reform is a Risk Worth Taking', *Financial Times*, 15 July 2010 (available at: http://www.ft.com/cms/s/0/2932b84e-904a-11df-ad26-00144feab49a.html#axzz349hkxFQY).
9. Royal College of Physicians, *Hospitals on the Edge? The Time for Action*, September 2012 (available at: http://www.rcplondon.ac.uk/sites/default/files/documents/hospitals-on-the-edge-report.pdf).

10. Select Committee on Public Service and Demographic Change, *Ready for Ageing?*, 2012 (available at: http://www.publications.parliament.uk/pa/ld201213/ldselect/ldpublic/140/14003.htm).

11. Quoted by Bean J (as it happens, a former Chair of the Society of Labour Lawyers) in *AC v Berkshire West Primary Care Trust* [2010] EWHC 1162 (Admin).

12. As Nicholas Timmins describes it in his excellent account of the passage of the Health and Social Care Act 2012, *Never Again: The Story of the Health and Social Care Act 2012*, King's Fund and the Institute for Government, 2012 (available at: http://www.kingsfund.org.uk/sites/files/kf/field/field_publication_file/never-again-story-health-social-care-nicholas-timmins-ju112.pdf).

13. House of Commons Health Committee, *Commissioning: Fourth Report of Session 2009–10*, 30 March 2010 (available at: http://www.publications.parliament.uk/pa/cm200910/cmselect/cmhealth/268/268i.pdf).

14. Ibid. p. 3.

15. The attempt to reduce the costs of NHS management by £20bn over four years, commenced under a Labour Secretary of State.

16. The King's Fund and Nuffield Trust, *Clinical Commissioning Groups: Supporting Improvement in General Practice*, 2013 (available at: http://www.kingsfund.org.uk/sites/files/kf/field/field_publication_file/clinical-commissioning-groups-report-kings-fund-nuffield-ju113.pdf).

17. Ibid. p. 40.

18. NHS trusts are still subject to direction because that part of the 2012 Act has not been implemented, but CCGs are not subject to direction by the Secretary of State or NHS England.

19. An excellent explanation of the *Teckal* exemption is contained within the judgments in *Brent London Borough Council and others v Risk Management Partners Ltd* [2011] UKSC 7 (available at: http://www.bailii.org/uk/cases/UKSC/2011/7.html).

20. See s. 9 of the National Health Service Act 2006.

21. Which was part of the reason why in 2013 the Secretary of State for Health lost the case over the reconfiguration of services across south-east London, which primarily affected Lewisham Hospital.

22. House of Commons Health Committee, *Commissioning: Fourth Report of Session 2009–10*, 30 March 2010, at p. 48 (available at: http://www.publications.parliament.uk/pa/cm200910/cmselect/cmhealth/268/268i.pdf).

23. See *R (On the Application Of Condliff) v North Staffordshire Primary Care Trust* [2011] EWCA Civ 910 (available at: http://www.bailii.org/ew/cases/EWCA/Civ/2011/910.html).

24. The Secretary of State is required under the Health and Social Care Act 2012 to prove a 'Mandate' annually to NHS England to set the priorities for the NHS in the coming year. This is an extension of the annual NHS plan previously published by the Department of Health.

25. See *St Helens Borough Council v Manchester Primary Care Trust and Another* [2008] EWCA Civ 931 (available at: http://www.bailii.org/ew/cases/EWCA/Civ/2008/931.html).

26. See the National Health Service Commissioning Board and Clinical Commissioning Groups (Responsibilities and Standing Rules) Regulations 2012 (available at: http://www.legislation.gov.uk/uksi/2012/2996/regulation/1/made).

11 Personal Injury Law

1. House of Commons Transport Committee, *Cost of Motor Insurance: Whiplash*, Fourth Report of Session 2013–14, July 2013 (available at: http://www.publications.parliament.uk/pa/cm201314/cmselect/cmtran/117/117.pdf).

2. Lord Young of Graffham, *Common Sense: Common Safety*, HM Government, October 2010 (available at: https://www.gov.uk/government/uploads/system/uploads/attachment_data/file/60905/402906_CommonSense_acc.pdf).

3. *Groves v Lord Wimborne* [1898] 2 QB 402.

4. Professor Ragnar E. Löfstedt, *Reclaiming Health and Safety For All: An Independent Review of Health and Safety Legislation*, Department of Work and Pensions, November 2011, Cmnd. 8219 (available at: https://www.gov.uk/government/uploads/system/uploads/attachment_data/file/66790/lofstedt-report.pdf).

5. House of Commons Transport Committee, op. cit.

6. The Law Commission, *Damages for Personal Injury: Non-pecuniary Loss*, Law Commission No. 257 (available at: http://lawcommission.justice.gov.uk/docs/lc257_damages_for_personal_injury_non_pecuniary_loss.pdf).

7. Rupert Jackson, *Review of Civil Litigation Costs: Final Report*, The Stationery Office, December 2009 (available at: http://www.judiciary.gov.uk/wp-content/uploads/JCO/Documents/Reports/jackson-final-report-140110.pdf)

8. The Law Commission, *Claims for Wrongful Death*, Law Commission No. 263, November 1999 (available at: http://lawcommission.justice. gov.uk/publications/claims-for-wrongful-death.htm).

9. Rupert Jackson, op. cit.

10. Rupert Jackson, op. cit.

12 Planning Law and Housebuilding

1. Home Builders Federation (http://www.hbf.co.uk/media-centre/ facts-statistics/).

2. Rising prices might be thought to make housebuilding more attractive to developers, but the market will not construct housing if developers and potential purchasers do not have access to funding. Developers will not build houses if purchasers cannot secure funds to buy them.

3. Kate Barker, *Review of Housing Supply: Delivering Stability – Securing our Future Housing Needs*, HMSO, March 2004 (available at: http:// webarchive.nationalarchives.gov.uk/+/http:/www.hm-treasury.gov.uk/ barker_review_of_housing_supply_recommendations.htm).

4. Office of Fair Trading, *Homebuilding in the UK: A Market Study*, OFT, September 2008.

5. Home Builders Federation, *Permissions To Land: Debunking The Land Banking Myth*, HBF, May 2014 (available at: http://www.hbf.co.uk/media-centre/news/view/ permissions-to-land-debunking-the-land-banking-myth/).

6. Office of Fair Trading, op. cit.

7. HM Treasury, *Investing in Britain's Future*, Cmnd. 8669, June 2013 (available at: https://www.gov.uk/government/uploads/system/uploads/ attachment_data/file/209279/PU1524_IUK_new_template.pdf).

8. See Alastair Parvin, David Saxby, Cristina Cerulli and Tatjana Schneider, *A Right to Build: The Next Mass-Housebuilding Industry*, University of Sheffield and Architecture 00, 2012 (available at: http:// www.architecture00.net/news/2755).

9. According to research by BIRA and the Local Data Company (LDC) (http://www.bira.co.uk/news/storm-warning).

10. Department for Business, Enterprise and Regulatory Reform, *Globalisation and the Changing UK Economy*, BERR, February 2008 (available at: http://www.berr.gov.uk/files/file44332.pdf).

11. Ibid., p. 4.

12. Ibid., p. 9, Figure 1.6.

13. Ibid., p. 14.

14. Subject to the matters already set out above.
15. *Hunston Properties Limited v SSCLG* [2014] JPL 240.
16. *Pointe Gourde Quarrying & Transport Co v Sub-Intendent of Crown Lands* [1947] AC 565.

13 Policing Reform

1. This philosophy is commonly known in the UK as 'policing by consent'.
2. Lord John Stevens, *Policing for a Better Britain*, Independent Police Commission, 2013 (available at: http://independentpolicecommission.org.uk/uploads/37d80308-be23–9684–054d-e4958bb9d518.pdf).
3. Tom Winsor, *State of Policing: The Annual Assessment of Policing in England and Wales 2012–13*, Her Majesty's Inspectorate of Constabulary, 2014, p. 59 (available at: http://www.hmic.gov.uk/wp-content/uploads/2014/03/state-of-policing-12–13.pdf).
4. Ipsos MORI, *Level of Public Trust In Professions and Occupations*, 2013.
5. Paul Condon, *Panorama*, BBC, 1993.
6. Tom Winsor, *State of Policing: The Annual Assessment of Policing in England and Wales 2012–13*, Her Majesty's Inspectorate of Constabulary, 2014, p. 63 (available at: http://www.hmic.gov.uk/wp-content/uploads/2014/03/state-of-policing-12–13.pdf).
7. Hannah Godfrey, 'New Met Police Chief Bernard Hogan-Howe Promises "War on Crime"', *The Guardian*, 14 September 2011.
8. Lord John Stevens, *Policing for a Better Britain*, Independent Police Commission, 2013, p. 37 (available at: http://independentpolicecommission.org.uk/uploads/37d80308-be23–9684–054d-e4958bb9d518.pdf).
9. Her Majesty's Inspectorate of Constabulary, *Taking Time For Crime: A Study of How Police Officers Prevent Crime in The Field*, 2012, p. 3 (available at: http://www.hmic.gov.uk/media/taking-time-for-crime.pdf).
10. Lord John Stevens, op. cit., p. 14.
11. Sir Kenneth Newman QPM, *Annual Report of the Commissioner of the Police of the Metropolis*, London, 1986.
12. HC Debates, 13 December 2010, Column 708.

14 Public Procurement

1. Implemented in the UK by the Public Contracts Regulations 2006 as amended in 2009 and 2011, and the Utilities Contracts Regulations 2006 as amended.

2. Unlawful procurement can be challenged before the national courts by economic operators who have suffered as a result of procurement infringements. The European Commission can launch infringement proceedings against member states if the directives are not properly implemented or followed by public bodies.

3. Article 9 TFEU further states: 'In defining and implementing its policies and activities, the Union shall take into account requirements linked to the promotion of a high level of employment, the guarantee of adequate social protection, the fight against social exclusion, and a high level of education, training and protection of human health.'

4. See, for example, *Commission v Netherlands*, Case C-368/10, judgment of 10 May 2012, which confirms that there is considerable scope under EU law for pursuing social and environmental aims in procurement, provided that these do not discriminate against non-national bidders.

5. European Commission, DG Internal Market and Services, *Final Report: Cross-Border Procurement Above EU Thresholds*, March 2011, Tables 19 and 23 (available at: http://ec.europa. eu/internal_market/publicprocurement/docs/modernising_rules/ cross-border-procurement_en.pdf).

6. Directive 2014/24/EU of the European Parliament and of the Council of 26 February 2014 on Public Procurement, and repealing Directive 2004/18/EC.

7. PASC, *Government Procurement: Sixth Report of Session 2013–14: Volume 1 Report and Annex*, July 2013 (available at: http://www. publications.parliament.uk/pa/cm201314/cmselect/cmpubadm/123/123. pdf).

8. Ibid., 'Conclusions and recommendations', p. 44.

9. The source for this is the evidence of Jim Bligh, the CBI Head of Public Service Reform (Q. 67). It is unclear whether this is anecdotal or based on a robust survey of members, but the over-lengthy nature of UK procurement was a common theme in the evidence to PASC.

10. Department for Transport, *Report of the Laidlaw Inquiry: Inquiry Into the Lessons Learned for the Department for Transport From the InterCity West Coast Competition*, December 2012 (available at: https:// www.gov.uk/government/publications/report-of-the-laidlaw-inquiry).

11. Cabinet Office written evidence to PASC, January 2013 (PASC, *Government Procurement: Sixth Report of Session 2013–14: Volume 2 Written Evidence*, Ev 76 at paragraph 10).

12. See HM Government, *Small Business: GREAT Ambition*, 7 December 2013 (available at: https://www.gov.uk/government/uploads/system/uploads/attachment_data/file/266212/bis-13-1313-small-business-great-ambition-FINAL.pdf). The government intends to abolish Pre-Qualification Questionnaires (PQQs) for low-value contracts; mandate the use of a standard core PQQ for high-value contracts and ensure small business needs are taken into account in the design of procurement processes; make contract opportunities accessible on a single online portal; and make sure small firms are treated fairly by mandating prompt payment terms down the supply chain.

13. PASC, *Government Procurement: Sixth Report of Session 2013–14: Volume 1*, p. 14 and Ev 80.

14. Ibid., Ev 88–89.

15. Ibid., *Volume 2*: Evidence of Robert Halfon MP (Proc. 38).

16. Ibid., Ev 77.

17. Cabinet Office and Ministry of Justice press release, *Taxpayer Compensated for Over-Charging as Cross-Government Contract Review Concludes*, 19 December 2013 (available at: https://www.gov.uk/government/news/taxpayer-compensated-for-overcharging-as-cross-government-contracts-review-concludes).

18. See *Government Procurement: Time to Invest in Capacity, Capability and Competence* (Proc. 11).

19. Ibid., Proc. 7.

20. See BBC News, *Defence Procurement Privatisation Plan Axed*, 10 December 2013 (available at: http://www.bbc.co.uk/news/uk-politics-25321111).

21. See Reports (Proc. 22 and 27) and Colin Cram's evidence to PASC.

22. See Proc. 11.

23. See *Montpelier Estates Ltd v Leeds City Council* [2013] EWHC 166 as a recent example of a case where the court has endorsed the transparent use of a public sector comparator.

24. The NHS (Procurement, Patient Choice and Competition) (No. 2) Regulations 2013, 2013 No. 500.

25. *Gebroeders Beentjes BV v State of the Netherlands*, Case C-31/87.

26. *Commission v Netherlands*, Case C-368/10, where the Court held that an award criterion related to whether coffee was of 'fair-trade' origin

was linked to the contract even though it did not relate to the intrinsic characteristics or uses of the product.

27. See The Scottish Government, *Community Benefits in Public Procurement Guidance Note*, 2008 (available at: http://www.scotland. gov.uk/Resource/Doc/212259/0056492.pdf).

28. In this case we recognise that the tender requirements were published back in 2008 under the last Labour government.

29. Jim Pickard and Mark Odell, 'Crossrail Tender Favours UK', *Financial Times*, 27 February 2012 (available at: http://www.ft.com/cms/ s/0/4dac90bc-6174-11e1-8a8e-00144feabdc0.html#axzz32G1StuyE).

30. Though it is noted that the Deputy Chief Procurement Officer said in her evidence to PASC: '*We absolutely need to change from large, monolithic contracts to chunking contracts up*'.

31. See Art. 57(6) of Directive 2014/24/EU which introduces specific provisions on 'self-cleansing'.

32. Cabinet Office and Efficiency and Reform Group, *Procurement Policy Note: Taking Account of Bidders' Past Performance, Action Note 09/12*, 8 November 2012 (available at: https://www.gov.uk/government/ publications/procurement-policy-note-09-12-taking-account-of-bidders-past-performance).

15 Responsible Capitalism: What it Means in Practice

1. This chapter is based on the author's paper, *Legislating For Responsible Capitalism: What it Means in Practice*, published in 2012 by Policy Network (http://www.policy-network.net/).

2. Lord David Sainsbury has recently published a book entitled *Progressive Capitalism*, in which he advocates the need for a new political economy under that description. (David Sainsbury, *Progressive Capitalism: How To Achieve Economic Growth, Liberty and Social Justice*, Biteback Publishing, 2013.)

3. The most recent edition of the Code was published in 2012.

4. Brian Cheffins, 'The Stewardship Code's Achilles Heel', *Modern Law Review*, 2010, p. 1004–1025.

5. Ibid.

6. Iris Chiu, 'Turning Institutional Investors Into Stewards: Exploring the Meaning and Objectives of Stewardship', *Current Legal Problems*, 2013 (available at: http://clp.oxfordjournals.org/content/early/2013/05/10/clp. cuto05.abstract).

7. See the Companies Act 1985 Part XIV.

8. European Commission, *Green Paper: Corporate Governance in Financial Institutions and Remuneration Policies*, June 2010 (available at: http://ec.europa.eu/internal_market/company/docs/modern/com2010_284_en.pdf).

9. The Modern Reflection Group, *Report of the Reflection Group on the Future of EU Company Law*, European Commission, April 2011 (available at: http://ec.europa.eu/internal_market/company/docs/modern/reflectiongroup_report_en.pdf).

10. The High Pay Commission, *Cheques With Balances: Why Tackling High Pay is in the National Interest*, May 2011 (available at: http://highpaycentre.org/img/High_Pay_Commission_More_for_Less.pdf).

11. Jonathan Rushworth and Michael Schluter, *Transforming Capitalism From Within: A Relational Approach to the Purpose, Performance, and Assessment of Companies*, Relationships Global, October 2011 (available at: http://www.relationshipsglobal.net/Web/OnlineStore/Product.aspx?ID=59&RedirectUrl=%7E%2fWeb%2fOnlineStore%2fPr oducts.aspx%3fCatID%3d11%26Page%3d2).

12. The Ownership Commission, *Plurality, Stewardship and Engagement*, March 2012 (available at: http://ownershipcomm.org/files/ownership_commission_2012.pdf).

13. John Kay, *The Kay Review of UK Equity Markets and Long-Term Decision Making*, July 2012 (available at: http://www.bis.gov.uk/assets/biscore/business-law/docs/k/12–917-kay-review-of-equity-markets-final-report.pdf).

14. The Law Commission, *Fiduciary Duties of Investment Intermediaries*, Consultation Paper No. 215 (available at: http://lawcommission.justice.gov.uk/docs/cp215_fiduciary_duties.pdf).

15. February 2012 (available at: https://www.gov.uk/government/uploads/system/uploads/attachment_data/file/31544/12-631-kay-review-of-equity-markets-interim-report.pdf).

16. John Kay, op. cit.

17. http://eur-lex.europa.eu/LexUriServ/LexUriServ.do?uri=OJ:L:2013:176:0338:0436:EN:PDF

18. http://eur-lex.europa.eu/LexUriServ/LexUriServ.do?uri=OJ:L:2013:176:0001:0337:EN:PDF

19. Sir George Cox, *Overcoming Short-Termism Within British Business: The Key to Sustained Economic Growth*, commissioned by the Labour Party, 2013 (available at: http://www.yourbritain.org.uk/uploads/editor/files/Overcoming_Short-termism.pdf).

20. Aeron Davis, David Offenbach, Richard Stevens and Nick
    Grant, *Takeovers and the Public Interest*, Policy Network, 2013
    (available at: http://www.policy-network.net/publications/4435/
    Takeovers-and-the-public-interest).
21. Mariana Mazzucato, *The Entrepreneurial State: Debunking Public vs.
    Private Sector Myths*, Anthem Press, 2013.
22. Ibid., p. 25.
23. BBC News, *Ed Miliband: Bad Bankers Must Be Struck Off*, 9 July 2012
    (available at: http://www.bbc.co.uk/news/uk-politics-18766624).
24. Ferdinand Mount, *The New Few: Or a Very British Oligarchy*, Simon &
    Schuster, 2012.
25. Source: personal discussions.
26. The Trades Union Congress, *Workers on Board: The Case For
    Workers' Voice in Corporate Governance*, 2012 (available at:
    http://www.tuc.org.uk/economic-issues/corporate-governance/
    workers-board-case-workers%E2%80%99-voice-corporate-governance).
27. The Trades Union Congress, *Workers' Voice in Corporate Governance:
    A European Perspective*, 2013 (available at: http://www.tuc.org.uk/
    economic-issues/corporate-governance/workers%E2%80%99-voice-
    corporate-governance-european-perspective).
28. Ferdinand Mount, op. cit.
29. Sir George Cox, op. cit.
30. David Coats, 'The Art of the Possible', *Fabian Review*, Winter 2011–12,
    pp. 16–17.
31. Reported in *The Sunday Times*, 4 August 2013.
32. David Coats, op cit.
33. Lord Justice Jackson (2009) *Review of Civil Litigation Costs: Final
    Report*, Judiciary of England and Wales, December 2009 (available
    at: http://www.judiciary.gov.uk/wp-content/uploads/JCO/Documents/
    Reports/jackson-final-report-140110.pdf).

Index